FAITH ON THE AVENUE

FAITH ON THE AVENUE

Religion on a City Street

Katie Day

Photographs by Edd Conboy

OXFORD
UNIVERSITY PRESS

OXFORD
UNIVERSITY PRESS

Oxford University Press is a department of the University of Oxford.
It furthers the University's objective of excellence in research, scholarship,
and education by publishing worldwide.

Oxford   New York
Auckland   Cape Town   Dar es Salaam   Hong Kong   Karachi
Kuala Lumpur   Madrid   Melbourne   Mexico City   Nairobi
New Delhi   Shanghai   Taipei   Toronto

With offices in
Argentina   Austria   Brazil   Chile   Czech Republic   France   Greece
Guatemala   Hungary   Italy   Japan   Poland   Portugal   Singapore
South Korea   Switzerland   Thailand   Turkey   Ukraine   Vietnam

Oxford is a registered trademark of Oxford University Press
in the UK and certain other countries.

Published in the United States of America by
Oxford University Press
198 Madison Avenue, New York, NY 10016

CIP Data is on file at the Library of Congress

ISBN: 978-0-19-986002-9

9 8 7 6 5 4 3 2 1
Printed in the United States of America
on acid-free paper

For my father, Donald C. Day,
who did not get to see the completion of this project
but believed in its author.

CONTENTS

MAP OF CONGREGATIONS

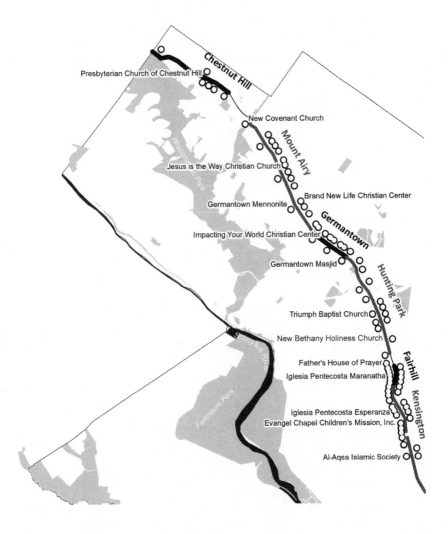

Presbyterian Church of Chestnut Hill

Chestnut Hill

New Covenant Church

Mount Airy

Jesus is the Way Christian Church

Brand New Life Christian Center

Germantown Mennonite

Germantown

Impacting Your World Christian Center

Germantown Masjid

Hunting Park

Triumph Baptist Church

New Bethany Holiness Church

Father's House of Prayer
Iglesia Pentecosta Maranatha

Fairhill

Kensington

Iglesia Pentecosta Esperanza
Evangel Chapel Children's Mission, Inc.

Al-Aqsa Islamic Society

All congregations along Germantown Avenue that were surveyed for the study.
Those featured within the book are identified.

PREFACE

In the fall of 2004, I prepared to welcome a fresh crop of students to the Lutheran Theological Seminary at Philadelphia. My field is "Church and Society," which is the study of social contexts through the social science methodology, as well as theological and ethical traditions, with a view toward helping emerging faith leaders to develop a public theological framework for engaging the complexities of human society. My goal that year was to introduce students to the context in which they would be studying to become religious leaders—Germantown Avenue. Many were coming from outside the region and I wanted them to be aware that *place matters*. Sitting in class they might hear sirens screaming up and down the Avenue and encounter people asking for change while going to Wawa across the street for coffee: all part of their graduate education. Their educational experience would be profoundly different from what it would be at a seminary in Iowa, or South Carolina, or even Chicago. Place matters, and even in the graduate school bubble, the context of education is significant.

To help with the orientation, I assigned Elijah Anderson's *Code of the Street* to the incoming students. To supplement their reading of the book, which includes a rich ethnographic look at street cultures on Germantown Avenue, I developed a slide show focusing on the many communities of faith along "the Avenue." I talked my friend Edd Conboy, a therapist as well as a gifted photographer, into coming along and shooting some pictures. Although I had lived, worked, and conducted research on and around Germantown Avenue for 25 years, seeing the images gave me a different perspective on the familiar streetscape. I noticed for the first time the rich layers of history and culture in sites I had passed thousands of times. There was a beauty to the diversity of people, structures, businesses, and establishments of all kinds. The array of religious spaces, practices, and traditions was far more interesting than I had appreciated. And it was alive—Germantown Avenue was a living, moving, changing ecology. That complexity drew me in. For the last eight years, studying Germantown Avenue has been something between a project and an obsession. Edd is still taking pictures and the photo archive now holds thousands of images. Germantown Avenue has to be one of the most thoroughly documented religious ecologies on the planet.

As the project developed and I became more immersed in research, a number of students and research assistants went "into the field" with me. With curiosity and respect they helped to conduct a survey and interviewed clergy, religious practitioners, and a variety of residents of the community. I am grateful for the good work of Jade King Bass, Nancy Beckwith, Joe Carlsmith, Ann Colley, Becca Ehrlich, Margaret Herz-Lane, David Hoxter, JoAnna Novak, Rozella Poston, Kate Proctor, Rabbi George Stern, Gabrielle Wanamaker, and Willie Walker.

I am especially indebted to two other research assistants who were talented ethnographers of four storefront churches described in these pages and who became true collaborators in field research, final analysis, and writing. Some of their field notes were worthy of publication and their insights into the dynamics of these overlooked yet complex congregations deepened the overall analysis of the Germantown Avenue faithscape. Leila Ortiz was embedded in two Latino churches which are described in Chapter 5. She drew on her experience, insights, and critical capacity to understand the nuanced experience of Pentecostal believers from Puerto Rico, who were establishing themselves in Philadelphia. Beth Stroud conducted participant observation at Father's House of Prayer and New Bethany Holiness Church, and her work is reflected in Chapter 4, "Pound for Pound." Beth had always reflected an uncommon courage as a clergywoman, prior to launching a promising academic career. As this book went to press, that courage was being challenged by a serious health condition. Her contribution to this book was invaluable, and as she continues to write, future readers will be all the wiser for her insights.

I am especially grateful to the quantitative geniuses who compensated for the limitations of this primarily qualitative researcher: Amy Hillier (Cartographic Modeling Lab, University of Pennsylvania), Jason Martin (Temple University), and Reverend Fred Becker (Lutheran Theological Seminary at Philadelphia). Technological help was always available through John Kahler and Bob Hensil. Many others provided information as well as wise insights and feedback on the drafts. Thank you so much to Dave Bartelt (Temple University, Department of Geography and Urban Studies), Bob Jaegar (Partners for Sacred Places), Susan Teegan-Case (Artwell),

Jean Warrington and Gerry Fischer (Historic Fair Hill), Timothy Nelson (Harvard University), Elfriede Wedam (Loyola University, Chicago) and Ken Weinstein (real estate developer, restaurateur and Renaissance man who knows Germantown Avenue like the back of his hand). As I began my research, Ram Cnaan (University of Pennsylvania) was generous in providing data from his research, which was invaluable as I shaped my questions and methodology. I'm sure I sound like a flustered Oscar recipient, as I apologize if I have left anyone out.

Any major research project needs institutional support. I am especially indebted to the Louisville Institute. Its former executive director, Jim Lewis, believed in this project early on. Not only did the Institute provide generous support, but Jim encouraged me to tell the stories of faith communities that are too often unknown and unappreciated. My own institution, the Lutheran Theological Seminary at Philadelphia, has been enormously supportive in ways too numerous to detail. The gift of a sabbatical came at a critical time, as I was conducting research in 2009. My students and colleagues might be tired of hearing me talk about Germantown Avenue, but, to their credit, they never communicated that.

Of course, a critical partner in any publication is the editor. Theo Calderara at Oxford has been enthusiastic and curious about the project from our first conversation. His artful editing and prodding questions have strengthened this text enormously. Thank you, Theo. Charlotte Steinhardt at Oxford patiently worked with me in the more tedious tasks of preparing the manuscript, and I am grateful for her good work.

I am especially grateful to the many congregations on the Avenue that graciously welcomed us into their spaces and into their communities. They extended trusting openness as we listened, asked endless questions, took pictures even as they prayed, and waded through their records and documents. The diversity of faith on the Avenue, the depth of true belief, and engagement with the local ecology was continuously inspiring. Much care has been given to accurately representing the communities of faith in this text. When appropriate, names and identities have been changed (although most informants wanted their real names used). If anyone feels that we "didn't get it right" here, I take full responsibility.

My family and friends have been an ongoing source of strength and patient support in the long process of writing. My son Julian, a poet, reminded me that a poem is never really finished, even though it might be published. My daughter Molly, training to be a teacher, reflected back to me her passion for education and its capacity for transformation. Each has helped me to put this project in a larger frame. My wonderful husband, Jim, has simply made this book possible. He is a terrific editor, asks really smart questions, and gave me the moral and logistical support to complete this marathon. But the study is never really finished.

FAITH ON THE AVENUE

1 MAPPING FAITH ON THE AVENUE

I know no religion that destroys courtesy, civility, and kindness.

— WILLIAM PENN

One street in one city. Eight and a half miles of cobblestone and trolley tracks, the newly paved and the seriously pot-holed, creating one thoroughfare that cuts through Philadelphia from its north-west boundary almost to the Delaware River. Germantown Avenue is older than the city itself, layered upon an ancient trail created by the Lenni Lenape tribes. It bears the history of generations of immigrants who settled, fought, struggled, prospered, and died along its worn Belgian blocks.

A Revolutionary battle was fought on this street. Stone buildings where British troops were billeted still stand. Some still bear the scars of the patriots' bitter loss, and headstones on their grounds mark the soldiers' graves. Other headstones mark the final resting places of victims of the Yellow Fever Epidemic of 1793. George Washington and Thomas Jefferson escaped the epidemic by moving out of Center City into stately homes that still grace the avenue. Over a century before, in 1688, the first remonstrance against slavery was lodged by members of the Germantown Avenue Mennonite-Quaker congregation. The table on which it was signed still stands in the original meeting-house. Slavery and the abolitionist movement would continue to weave their way through the history of a street that was home to both wealthy slaveholders and a stop on the Underground Railroad. Prominent abolitionists such as Lucretia Mott were buried at Fair Hill Burial Ground, one of several old cemeteries on the Avenue.

The five major commercial strips along the Avenue have been hard hit by waves of economic booms and busts. During earlier eras, everything from beer to ice cream was produced along what earlier native peoples had called "The Great Road." The class structure of early and later industrialism is in evidence as well; the mansions of captains of industry and the rowhouses of ordinary factory workers have shared the street since colonial times—they still do, and are home for 21st-century residents, rich and poor.

FIGURE 1.1 Headstones in the Upper Burying Ground, established in 1692 and used into the 20th century. This is one of the two oldest cemeteries in Germantown; laid to rest in it are blacks, whites, Native Americans, Germans, English, Irish, Catholics, Protestants, adults, children, and over 50 Revolutionary War soldiers.

FIGURE 1.2 Upsala, where part of the Revolutionary Battle of Germantown took place.

Germantown Avenue is also a street on which Philadelphians have worshipped for over 300 years, and it reflects the diversity of traditions that were drawn to William Penn's "Holy Experiment" of religious tolerance. In contrast to the religious conflict that prevailed in Europe and the homogeneity found in the other colonies, Penn extended his vision of radical hospitality to groups along the whole spectrum of faith, even going as far as Europe to recruit religious minorities. Consequently, two denominations were founded by German immigrants here: the "mother churches" of the Mennonites (established in 1690) and the Brethren (1723), both of which still stand and have active congregations. Some of the first houses of worship in the New World for Lutherans, Presbyterians, Episcopalians, and Quakers are still in service on this street. Through the efforts of a pious and precocious 16-year-old, Eliza Shirley, the Salvation Army in the United States was founded in 1879 where 11th Street meets Germantown Avenue.

FIGURE 1.3 Marker in the stone wall on Germantown Avenue in front of the Concord School, established in 1775 as an early English-speaking school.

History oozes out of the stone walls, stuccoed colonial buildings, burial grounds, and old storefronts. Historical markers sprout along the street, planted by a vibrant Historical Society that has dubbed the area "Freedom's Backyard." Indeed, many seeds of the city's and the country's history are found along this route. But this one street is also a microcosm of present-day Philadelphia. Germantown Avenue connects the most affluent neighborhood in Philadelphia with the poorest. Chestnut Hill, a predominantly white neighborhood in the northwest corner of Philadelphia, is known for its luxurious homes and quaint shopping district full of boutique shops, upscale restaurants, and banks. But looking out the window of the #23 bus as it travels down Germantown Avenue, one sees the dramatic demographic shifts. Moving toward the center of the city, the 23 passes through the Mt. Airy neighborhood. Here one sees a mix of skin colors, commercial establishments (both upscale and not so much), and a housing stock that is over 300 years old. For the past 50 years Mt. Airy has enjoyed a reputation as a successfully racially and economically mixed neighborhood and has often caught the attention of urban researchers and journalists. There is a noticeable change as one travels farther down the Avenue into Germantown: the busy sidewalk traffic becomes predominantly African American. Shops in this bustling commercial strip are protected at night by metal grates. The discount clothing shops, and hair weaving and nail salons share blocks with structures where George Washington lived, drank, and worshipped. Moving south and east, the Avenue slices through the Nicetown and Fair Hill neighborhoods, and more abandoned buildings and weedy lots appear. Drug dealers gather on corners and wander over to visitors unselfconsciously. However, this is not a consistent trajectory of downward social mobility moving down the Avenue. Suddenly, one enters a three-block urban oasis that is a hub of activity, as Muslim shoppers pour into the streets after prayers into attractive shops, or socialize around the vendors of oils.

The 23 bus makes its way down Germantown Avenue a bit more efficiently than its predecessor, the much-beloved trolley. Driving through Nicetown, there are signs of development—new townhouses, an apartment building, and office space—fruits of the labors of the Nicetown Community Development Corporation. A mural sparkles with glass mosaic, and enticing smells of jerk chicken waft onto the street from an exuberant-looking bright yellow Caribbean restaurant. Crossing Hunting Park Avenue, one cannot miss Triumph Baptist, with its modern stucco structure. Across the street are

Ford Memorial Church and Nazarene Baptist—vital congregations themselves. Worshippers are offered a smorgasbord of possibilities. Soon, Broad,
Erie, and Germantown Avenues collide, creating a congested shopping district with clothing, food, and sneaker stores. On Sunday morning, it will be
vacant, except for a few men walking on the Avenue. Germantown Avenue
curves at Glenwood, then suddenly makes a straight pass through Fairhill,
with churches and businesses on the west side and the lush Fair Hill Burial
Ground on the east side of the street. The historic cemetery is surrounded by
an iron fence that shelters children playing within. Close–by, buildings next
to brown fields are decorated with colorful murals and the sounds of Latino
music begin to filter onto the street.

Approaching Temple University, the 23 cuts over to 12th Street, which
parallels Broad and continues until it ends up in South Philadelphia. To stay
on Germantown Avenue all the way to the river, one has to walk, bike, or
drive. After passing Norris Street, Germantown Avenue runs into Cousins'
Supermarket and continues through the parking lot—a clever marketing
scheme if there ever was one. The Avenue travels through North Philadelphia
and Kensington, passing by where Eliza Shirley founded the Salvation Army,
and the former Breyer's Ice Cream Factory sits vacant, now covered in graffiti. The bus continues through blocks which lack coherence—there are lots
of lots, both overgrown and cleaned up. A few small businesses appear—old
car or tire lots behind razor wire, and some open doors and signs advertising
enterprising car repairmen. Homes, warehouses, and small churches are present, but without any one organizing principle dominating—commercial, residential, or even blight. Yet people live here, in the side streets off the Avenue,
which form a capillary grid. On the west side of the street the old Gretz brewery, shuttered in the 1960's, is slowly deteriorating. Perhaps it will alert some
future archaeologist to Philadelphia's history with beer—before Prohibition,
there were 90 breweries in the city. *true*

A century ago, as commuters hopped on the 23 trolley and traveled down
Germantown Avenue, they would have seen a different cityscape. Neat row
homes, which housed factory workers, lined the Avenue. Residents could easily hop on the trolley and get to work at Gretz or Schmidt's breweries, to
the large Stetson Hat factory, or to the other factories on the Avenue: furniture, wire and iron, early refrigerators, and several candy manufacturers. They
might have worshipped at St. Vladimir's or St. Edward's Catholic churches or
at the synagogue, near where Cousins' Market now sits. There were numerous

FIGURE 1.4 The abandoned Gretz brewery, across the street from Al Aqsa, reflects the signs of blight still present in Kensington.

theaters and clubs, no doubt supplied by the breweries and keeping the Salvation Army busy. The Washington Hotel towered over the intersection where Dauphin and 7th cross. Today its footprint is a vacant lot, tidied up with grass and a low fence, facing Evening Light Apostolic Church on the other side of the Avenue.

Germantown Avenue bears the history of the city—its glory days, its deterioration, its struggles, its innovations, and glimpses of rebirth. Coming through the dreary blocks as North Philly gives way to Kensington, a gleaming mosque emerges as a welcome anomaly on the scene. It did not always gleam.

Germantown Avenue peters out in Kensington, a historically working-class neighborhood now touched by gentrification. Eventually it dead-ends at the river as I-95 traffic whizzes overhead. At the end of Germantown Avenue, one can see the Delaware River and Ben Franklin Bridge into Camden, New Jersey, and the encroaching gentrification of the Northern Liberties neighborhood.

Sociologist Elijah Anderson brilliantly mapped the changing social codes of Germantown Avenue in the first chapter of his book, *Code of the Street* (1999). But Anderson makes only slight reference to the many houses of faith along the Avenue. They are old and brand new, large and small, Muslim and all manner of Christian—each week gathering hundreds of worshippers to celebrate the Divine in the midst of, and sometimes in spite of, their urban

FIGURE 1.5 Chestnut Hill Hospital.

FIGURE 1.6 One of the few practicing physicians on the lower end of Germantown Avenue. Most poorer residents rely on emergency rooms for primary health care.

context. They draw meaning and energy from the city life around them and give it back as well. However, few have appreciated the *agency* these congregations have in their relationship to the street, which is my focus.

The central argument of this book is twofold. First, *place matters*. The proverbial three principles of real estate apply to communities of faith as well: "location, location, location." It matters whether there is a Starbucks or a "drug corner" outside the church doors. It matters if businesses are closing or new apartments are being built nearby. The prayers, sermons, programs, and worldviews of congregations are not immune to their physical contexts. In fact, they are greatly impacted by what is going on in both their immediate and wider worlds. But how religion is produced and reproduced is more than a result of geographic location. *Faith matters, too*, in shaping this diverse and dynamic urban corridor. A new thriving congregation on the block might inspire a real estate developer or discourage criminals. It might encourage young artists or budding politicians. It might attract newcomers to the neighborhood or encourage current residents to stay and put down roots.

This book builds on the ecological approach to understanding urban religion particularly as developed by Lowell Livezey (2000) and Nancy Eiseland (2000), both of whom died far too early. They were continuing in the legacy of the Chicago school of sociology, which had introduced an ecological approach to understanding cities in the 1920s. Robert Ezra Park, the primary architect of the model, saw cities as dynamic environments where physical space and human experience interact in a symbiotic relationship that produces shared meanings—a "human ecology." Drawing on the biological model of Darwinian theory to explain the organization of cities, Park understood that competition between social groups produced different patterns of mobility and spatial segregation. Park and Ernest Burgess developed the "concentric zone theory," which mapped cities in terms of cultural and socioeconomic factors (1925). Aided by transportation and communication systems, upward mobility led to movement away from the core of the city. Institutions, such as schools and churches, become important components in the urban ecology primarily in dealing with social problems created by "disintegrating influences of city life."[1] The Chicago school, and particularly the concentric zone theory, has been widely critiqued as being deterministic. Still, Park has cast a long shadow in urban sociology in cultivating an appreciation for the myriad social processes that create dynamic, interdependent webs that produce and reproduce cities. Although Park and his associates did not consider communities of faith as particularly influential players in the urban ecology, his foundational work continues to inspire those examining the presence of congregations within it. The engagement of faith and urban space is a growing area of research, particularly sparked by the work of Livesey, Eiseland, and Robert Orsi (Williams, 2002). A more recent contribution that grows out of the ecological approach is that of Robert J. Sampson in his widely praised— and controversial—book, *Great American City: Chicago and the Enduring Neighborhood Effect*.[2] Sampson's argument is with those who would reduce social phenomena to individual actions or ascribe them to broader social and economic forces undermine the effects of neighborhoods. The spatial contexts of neighborhoods, he argues, shape social actions and trends. In that sense, we share similar perspectives.

When applied to the study of religion, this contemporary version of the ecological approach goes against the grain of thinking both inside and outside religion itself. Denominations and traditions have largely considered worshipping congregations to be immune to context, assuming that religious beliefs and practices are universal, are transferable, and should be immune to the "corrupting" effects of any environment. Similarly, research on religion has often focused on congregations, or even individuals, as isolated units of study—counting members or surveying beliefs—without consideration for their participation in larger contexts.

Further, policymakers have appreciated the "stabilizing influence" of congregations but not their cultural, social, and even economic power in neighborhoods. Congregations have often been seen as benign by-products of larger social and economic trends. What is new here is an appreciation of the ways in which congregations and their surroundings are in constant dynamic interaction, shaping and being shaped by each other. The basic premise of the ecological approach is that congregations do not develop in isolation but "at the nexus of religion and urban life," as Livezey phrased it. They, like their environments, are always changing, not separately but in complex relationship with their contexts.

Of course, definitions need to be clarified. "Context" can be as local as the block around a house of worship or as expansive as the entire world.

Global forces do affect local city neighborhoods, as they push and pull populations and restructure the economic order and social structures. Context incorporates the history of the place, the narratives that have given substance to community identity. Context includes the larger social meanings of socioeconomic class, race and gender as well. All of these external realities are part of the contexts in which the congregations along Germantown Avenue are located. They transcend the particular space and time of the gathered faithful, yet do not determine the shape of local congregations. Still, they contribute to their unique identity, experience, activities, and in some cases, beliefs.

During my research, a number of events and shifts in Philadelphia and the country as a whole impacted the communities of faith on the Avenue. The Great Recession of 2008 had cascading effects, as evidenced by spikes in unemployment, poverty, hunger, and violence. Parts of the Avenue were in the First Congressional District, which was designated as the second hungriest district in the United States. Citywide, those considered "food challenged" hovered between a quarter and a third of the population.[3] Gun violence continued to increase, with around one gun death per day by 2007, earning Philadelphia its designation as the most violent large city in the country.[4] The public school system continued to decline; despite essentially being in state receivership, severe budget challenges created tensions between teachers and parents, and resulted in poorer education for its students. During the research period, Philadelphia elected and reelected a popular mayor, Michael Nutter, and Barack Obama became the first African American president—two events that reached the shores of religious communities on the Avenue as something between a cultural ripple and a tsunami.

It is critical to keep in mind that the interaction between congregation and context goes in both directions. Each section of Germantown Avenue is changed, to varying degrees and in a variety of ways, by the presence of religious groups. It would be a different urban environment if the apocalyptic "Rapture" occurred and the congregations disappeared. These religious groups affect their neighborhoods in tangible and intangible ways. They participate in creating and maintaining the physical space and the local economy. They can also convey meaning and a sense of sacredness to the otherwise secular street culture. They bind wounds and speak out against those who caused them. They contribute to social control and social connections in

FIGURE 1.7 Signs of urban blight become more prevalent as one moves southeast down the Avenue.

FIGURE 1.8 A section of the Avenue which has been cleaned up and economically revitalized since the Germantown Masjid moved onto the block.

neighborhoods marked by dysfunction and isolation. In a word, congregations have agency—they are not an invisible, benign, or neutral presence. Yet they are not immune to economic, political, cultural, and social forces, nor are they defined by them. As social institutions they act on the environment. Ironically, producing a hope of individual agency among their members is at the heart of the religious enterprise. Congregations' message to adherents, through different languages and traditions, is that "you do not have to be who society says you are."

This book focuses its analysis on this synapse between communities of faith and communities at large on one street in one city. Like studying a tree by boring into the center of its trunk and analyzing one small sample dowel this research seeks to examine the dynamics of faith communities in their interaction with the urban ecology by focusing on Germantown Avenue. These social processes can be subtle and nuanced, so in order to capture them, a varied research methodology has been used. To begin, we had to determine who was there. Over a six-year period, between 2004 and 2010, I, together with research assistants, students, and a photographer, conducted a continuing census of religious congregations. That is to say, we have walked up and down Germantown Avenue innumerable times cataloging the changing population of religious practitioners.

Identifying congregations on one street for inclusion in the study sounds easier than it was. To clearly delineate the universe for study, we included only those groups that meet basic definitional criteria as a worshipping congregation, and whose place of worship fronts, or even just touches, Germantown Avenue. (In other words, those facing a side street with property abutting the Avenue were included.) University of Pennsylvania professor Ram Cnaan has studied congregations in Philadelphia extensively. For purposes of continuity with his research, we have worked with the definition of a congregation he developed for his study (2006). To be considered a congregation, a group must have some social cohesion as evidenced by sharing a religious identity, including an official name. It must meet regularly and on an ongoing basis, in a designated place, for the purpose of religious worship or spiritual practice. Members should participate on a voluntary basis rather than as a result of living together. There must be some administrative structure (however simple) and designated leadership. This definition excludes many religious groups that also contribute to life along the Avenue: convents, schools (including a college, a seminary, and several parochial schools), study groups, prayer circles, faith-based social services (such as nursing homes) or ministries, and gatherings for non-religious ritual. However, it includes gatherings of all religions, even those that do not identify with the term "congregation," such as mosques (or the Arabic term, masjid). All that meet the definitional criteria are considered congregations for purposes of this study.

Using this definition, beginning in 2004 we identified 83 congregations along Germantown Avenue—almost 10 per mile. This was remarkable not only in terms of the density of the religious marketplace but also because this was during a time in which Philadelphia's population was again shrinking. Between 2000 and 2008, Philadelphia, then the sixth largest city in the country, was one of only four of the 25 largest cities to lose population. In fact, it lost 70,000 citizens, giving it the dubious distinction of having the sharpest decline in population of any of the big cities, a drop of 4.5%. For Philadelphia, this is a familiar story. After decades of growth, the City of Brotherly Love ("and Sisterly Affection," which is often added) peaked in population in 1950 at over 2 million people and ranked third in size among US cities. However, a combination of deindustrialization and white flight resulted in a loss of more than 500,000 residents. By 2000, Philadelphia had slipped to fifth largest among American cities. The loss of the manufacturing jobs that had been the bedrock of working- and middle-class neighborhoods, delivered a devastating blow. The proportion of those living below the poverty level increased from 15% in 1970 to 25% in 2010. The latest chapter of outmigration, since 2000, saw middle-class people, both white and African American, move away from the urban core. This has been offset only slightly by a modest increase in population by 2010, largely due to increased numbers of Latino and Asian immigrants moving to Philadelphia. The result of the ebb and slight flow is that poverty continues to be geographically consolidated in African American and Latino neighborhoods. Even after the first wave of the Great Migration north (1910–1930), African Americans accounted for only 13% of the population of the city in 1940. By 2010, 42% of the city's population was African American and Latinos accounted for 12% (up from 8% in 2000).[5] In spite of Philadelphia's ideal of sibling love, the numbers in Figures 1.9 through 1.12 tell the story of population shifts and the flight of the middle class—especially the white middle class.

The census of religious congregations, however, does not follow the same trajectory, as we will see in more detail later in the book. To summarize

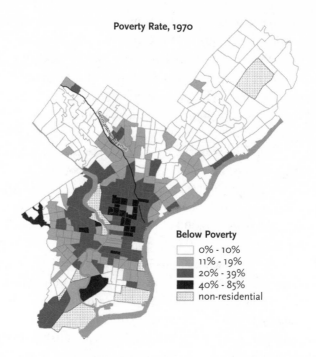

Poverty Rate, 1970

Below Poverty
- 0% - 10%
- 11% - 19%
- 20% - 39%
- 40% - 85%
- non-residential

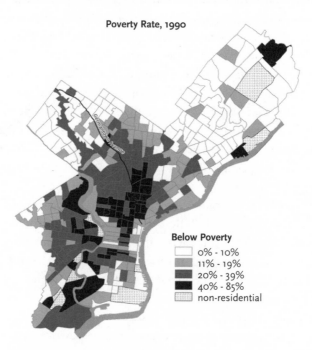

Poverty Rate, 1990

Below Poverty
- 0% - 10%
- 11% - 19%
- 20% - 39%
- 40% - 85%
- non-residential

FIGURE 1.9 Poverty rates 1970–2000.

Poverty Rate, 1980

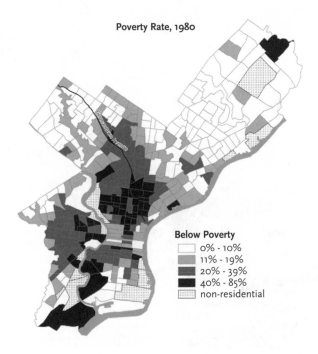

Below Poverty

- 0% - 10%
- 11% - 19%
- 20% - 39%
- 40% - 85%
- non-residential

Poverty Rate, 2000

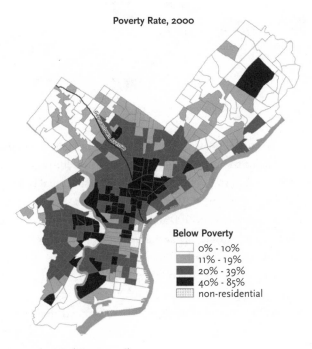

Below Poverty

- 0% - 10%
- 11% - 19%
- 20% - 39%
- 40% - 85%
- non-residential

FIGURE 1.9 (Continued)

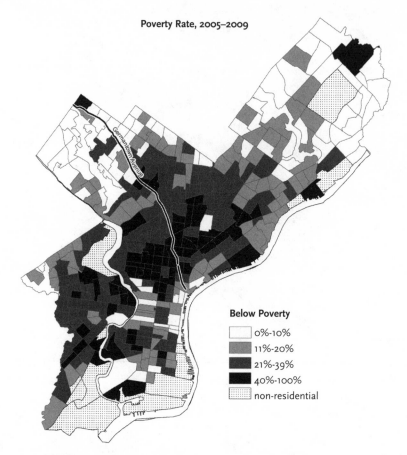

FIGURE 1.10 Poverty rates 2005–2009.

the trend: after losing population for 50 years, Philadelphia experienced a slight increase, 6%, in the first decade of the new millennium, which Mayor Michael Nutter declared to be "spectacular." [6] More spectacular was growth in the number of congregations, at least on Germantown Avenue (Figure 1.13).

During the period between 1990 and 2000, some congregations could not sustain themselves and, in fact, closed, consolidated with others, or moved with their members to the suburbs. But other congregations were newly organized, and the net population of congregations along Germantown Avenue actually rose to from 83 in 2004 to 93 in 2009—a 12% increase. Change could be seen weekly as new congregations announced their presence with

Racial/Ethnic Composition, 1950

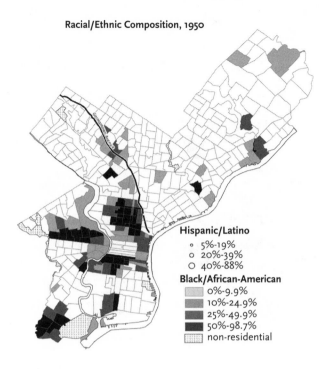

Hispanic/Latino
- ° 5%-19%
- ◦ 20%-39%
- ○ 40%-88%

Black/African-American
- 0%-9.9%
- 10%-24.9%
- 25%-49.9%
- 50%-98.7%
- non-residential

Racial/Ethnic Composition, 1990

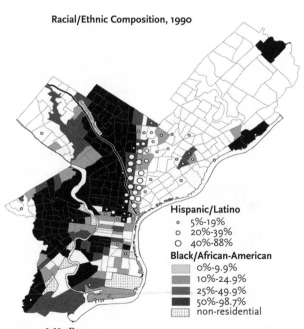

Hispanic/Latino
- ° 5%-19%
- ◦ 20%-39%
- ○ 40%-88%

Black/African-American
- 0%-9.9%
- 10%-24.9%
- 25%-49.9%
- 50%-98.7%
- non-residential

FIGURE 1.11 Race 1950–70–90–2000.

Racial/Ethnic Composition, 1970

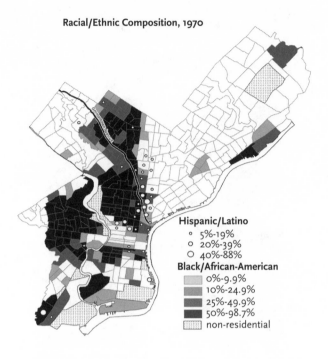

Hispanic/Latino
- 5%-19%
- 20%-39%
- 40%-88%

Black/African-American
- 0%-9.9%
- 10%-24.9%
- 25%-49.9%
- 50%-98.7%
- non-residential

Racial/Ethnic Composition, 2000

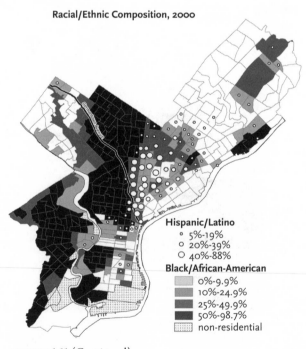

Hispanic/Latino
- 5%-19%
- 20%-39%
- 40%-88%

Black/African-American
- 0%-9.9%
- 10%-24.9%
- 25%-49.9%
- 50%-98.7%
- non-residential

FIGURE 1.11 (Continued)

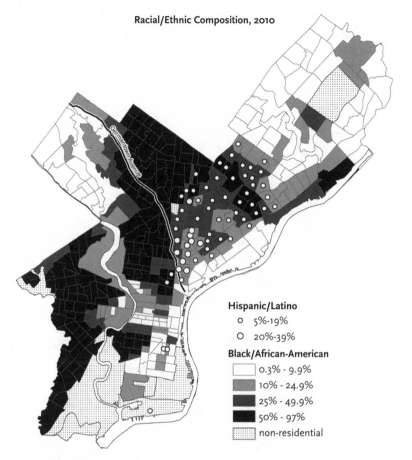

Racial/Ethnic Composition, 2010

Hispanic/Latino
- ○ 5%-19%
- ○ 20%-39%

Black/African-American
- ☐ 0.3% - 9.9%
- ▨ 10% - 24.9%
- ▨ 25% - 49.9%
- ■ 50% - 97%
- ▦ non-residential

FIGURE 1.12 Race 2010.

banners on the same block with churches that have held worship services in the same location for 300 years.

The juxtaposition of population loss and modest gain, and the increase in the number of religious congregations on the Avenue raises the fundamental question, "What's going on here?" It is certainly possible that we got better at identifying congregations, which can often have a small, if not invisible, public face. Barring that, a number of explanations could account for the trend: Were new immigrants coming in to occupy urban space vacated by former residents, and planting their congregations in the process? If the continuing outmigration of middle-class folk is consolidating poverty in the so-called

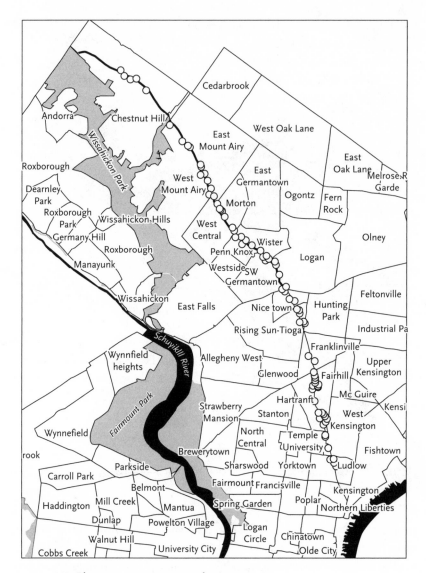

FIGURE 1.13 Plotting congregations on the Avenue.

inner city, are the poor increasingly turning to their faith to help them survive the brutal economic conditions exacerbated by the Great Recession? Do the trends stem from outsiders' evangelism or religious revival among city dwellers? Who are the members of these groups and what is driving the seeming proliferation of congregations?

National trends would not have predicted the increase. Robert Putnam and David Campbell rocked religious observers and leaders with their widely reported findings that religious participation had declined significantly in the first decade of the millennium and in fact had picked up steam after 2005. The numbers of those claiming "no religious preference" (the "nones" as they are often called) or reporting religious participation climbed across the demographic and religious spectrum between 2005 and 2010 but was most dramatically seen among young adults (Putnam and Campbell, 2010). Further, the Gallup polls found that during 2008–2009, there was no significant increase in religious participation—in other words, the hardship created by the Recession had not inspired folks to seek refuge in communities of faith (Gallup, 3/23/09). Other research shows that although poverty and religious adherence move together in other countries, this not so in the United States, unique among affluent nations for high levels of religiosity. Here, poverty is not a predictor of increased religious participation. So, given the demographics along the Avenue, as well as national trends of declining religious participation during the research period, it was curious to see the numbers of faith communities increasing here through 2009.

In order to tease out the reasons for these dynamics I developed a survey to capture some basic information about each congregation, including why they came to be located on the Avenue and how long they had been here.[7] The information gleaned about the age of the congregation, space use, and the demographics and distribution of the membership as well as the scope of their ministry provided a snapshot of each congregation. Aggregating the data provided a sense of where members are coming from and how they were engaging their contexts. Survey interviews were usually conducted with the clergy of congregations and took between 45 minutes and two hours, depending on the loquaciousness of the informant. Some interviews were easily scheduled, but in many other cases four or five visits were required. This was often because clergy were busy with other jobs and only came on site during worship times; there was no "church office" to receive calls and most of the congregational communication took place among members themselves. Still, the survey interviews were rich and often opened the possibility to more in-depth research.

An overview of the congregations shows that they are diverse in some ways, but not all. For example, there are no longer Catholic or traditional

Jewish congregations on the Avenue, as there were earlier in the street's history. When the study began, a large gray stone Gothic cathedral, St. Ladislaus Roman Catholic Church, dominated the corner of Germantown Avenue and Hunting Park Avenue. For 98 years its majestic twin spires had been the spiritual home of a proud ethnic-Polish congregation. However, in 2004 it was demolished to make way for the growing mega-church, Triumph Baptist Church, whose journey is described in the final chapter.

It was surprising not to find any traditional synagogues along the Avenue, especially as it veered into Northwest Philly, home to a large Jewish community. There are several syncretistic groups that incorporate elements of Judaism, as described in Chapter 6. One humble commercial building in the Southwest Germantown section of the Avenue appeared to have a subtle Star of David in the masonry of the facade. After researching many land use maps and a century of deed transfers, no Jewish usage was apparent. It had been a fire station at the turn of the 20th century, but could it have possibly been a Jewish fire station in this parochial city? A historian in the fire department explained the mystery: the star was actually a symbol of firefighting, incorporating the sign for fire (an upward pointing triangle) and the sign for water (the downward pointing triangle).

Despite the absence of Jews and Catholics on the Avenue, diversity abounds. Many of the older Protestant congregations left the city in earlier waves of white flight, leaving buildings now occupied by newer congregations. Still, there are 11 of the so-called Mainline Protestant churches remaining, rewriting the earlier narrative of urban flight, when congregations in these predominantly white denominations were shuttering their urban sites as African Americans moved into "their" neighborhoods. Instead, these 11 churches have remained in place and adapted to the changed context by creating ministries their forebears might not have been able to imagine or understand. The three congregations from the Peace traditions (Mennonite, Quaker, Brethren) are the oldest on the Avenue and continue to work for social justice, conflict resolution, and non-violence. At the start of the study, there were three mosques on the Avenue, all relative newcomers, but one has relocated. There were seven Latino congregations in 2004, mainly small, independent (non-affiliated), and within the Pentecostal tradition. Smaller denominations maintain their distinctive traditions, including the Seventh-day Adventist and the Hurleyites (a spiritualist sect). There is an African Hebrew Israelite congregation and two diasporic African groups that draw on the Abrahamic traditions, bringing together unique religious syntheses. By far the largest proportion of

FIGURE 1.14 The Presbyterian Church of Chestnut Hill.

congregations is African American, but this is not a monolithic category by any means. There are three mega-churches (with memberships above 2,000), all predominantly African American but distinct in their approaches. There are those affiliated with the historic black denominations, such as African Methodist Episcopal (AME), Church of God in Christ (COGIC) and several Baptist groups. Then there are the storefront churches, those smaller independent congregations in former commercial buildings; these account for almost half of the congregations in the study. Some are small, struggling to pay their utility bills but celebrating Jesus nonetheless. Others are solid,

FIGURE 1.15 Greater St. Thomas Baptist Church in the Fairhill section.

stable congregations, often Baptist or Pentecostal in theology and style and independent in structure.

As can be seen in Figure 1.12, congregations are clustered more closely along the Avenue as it moves through more predominantly African American neighborhoods. Congregational presence also corresponds to patterns of poverty (which is highly correlated with race as can be seen in the maps). Yet, surprisingly, even in these neighborhoods the congregations are not as homogeneous as might be predicted. Researchers in the past decade have found that over 90% of congregations in the United States have memberships in which one racial or ethnic group makes up 90% or more (Emerson and Smith, 2000). The congregations on Germantown Avenue, however, are somewhat different. In a city in which poor African Americans are increasingly isolated by outmigration of people, jobs, and services, many of the congregations on

the street stand as stalwart oases of relative multiculturalism. In this regard they do not completely reflect their demographic context and perhaps are even chipping away at the social isolation on their particular corners of Germantown Avenue. Is that a result of moral intentionality, historic imperative, changing demographics, or an accident of congregational history?

Given complex dynamics that the survey findings only hint at, it became apparent that the heart of the study would be ethnographic. In trying to understand "what's going on," researchers were embedded in congregations for weeks, and sometimes months, at a time. Immersing ourselves in congregational life, we participated in worship services, helped with summer Bible schools, shared meals, went to Bible studies and prayer meetings, celebrated health fairs, generally "hung out," and had dozens of conversations (some were scheduled and structured interviews, but many more were spontaneous and informal). We heard stories about faith, community, and life in the big city. Often we had a photographer in tow, who respectfully and artfully documented faith on the Avenue at this moment in time.[8] We are deeply grateful for the trust extended to us as we were allowed windows into the varieties of religious experience, congregational life, and ritual practices that make life meaningful for the hundreds of faithful who gather on Germantown Avenue each week as they have for centuries.

As the book unfolds, we allow the voices and stories from the ethnographic research to structure our analysis. In some cases hypotheses were posited and tested. More often, however, what Robert Orsi (1999) has called the "lived faith" of these urban congregations raised unanticipated questions. Where social dysfunction might be expected, especially in poorer, underserved neighborhoods, the continuing generation of social capital continued to surprise us. Bonding social capital was evident in tenacious connections between people on a block challenged by disintegrative forces. Further, communities of faith often maintained significant connections with organizations and institutions beyond the community, which widened their perception and helped attract resources. Communities of faith along the Avenue are quietly generating the type of bonding and bridging social capital that is so critical for community well-being (Putnam, 2000). Congregations in Mt. Airy and Chestnut Hill are swimming in a pond of social capital already; but for those in other neighborhoods, such connections in otherwise isolated contexts seem nothing short of miraculous.

There were other surprises. While we expected competition for space and truth claims, we found instead subtle negotiation and mutual respect. There was empowerment where powerlessness was expected and lethargy among those with power. Congregations are resilient and self-defining, and can certainly not be reduced to neat models of social predictability or the hypotheses of social scientists. While the findings of this project are often compelling, they are not easily generalizable to other times or locations. That is the nature of ethnographic research, which seeks the "thick description" of cultural dynamics. The research is enhanced, and limited, by the particularity of Philadelphia and even Germantown Avenue. Not many streets have the historic significance of, say, a Revolutionary War battle! But that is not to say the data do not shed insight into the faith on other avenues in other urban contexts. My hope is that they will. But fundamentally, this research offers a model of studying how religion functions in a dynamic urban ecology that can be replicated in other places. The findings have theoretical implications as well for the ways we approach the consideration of faith communities in contemporary cities.

We begin with the most visible, concrete aspect of religious life on Germantown Avenue: the physical space these congregations occupy. The first question is how congregations literally fit in the urban space. Further research presented here, both ethnographic and quantitative is equally spatial and explores the social dynamics of communities of faith and the neighborhoods in which they are located.

The argument developed here is both simple and nuanced: just as neighborhoods cannot be reduced to aggregated individual action nor a result of external forces, so too must congregations be studied within their contexts. As agents in the urban ecology, congregations are both imprinted by and impacted by their environments in diverse ways—physically, economically, culturally, and socially. They have helped shape the physical streetscape, and have been influenced by the surrounding infrastructure as well. Economic trends can greatly influence the identity and mission of a congregation. They are the first to feel the impact of larger trends of job loss, inaccessibility to health care, deterioration of public education, fluctuations in crime, the migration of people, and the cutbacks in publicly funded programs. But congregations also influence the local economy in a variety of direct and indirect ways. Measuring the economic impact of congregations is complex and a research question that is just emerging. Our findings contribute to that exploration.

In response to economic challenges and human needs, people of faith pray and they create social programs. They cultivate civic engagement by ad hoc training in public leadership and by looking for resources and support for their mission. Economic necessity does breed innovation as will be seen in the myriad outreach programs being generated. This is not to romanticize the congregations on Germantown Avenue or to exaggerate their impact on their block, corner, neighborhood, or city. But it is to contend that there is a dynamism in the social processes of communities of faith, and a complexity as they interact with their contexts that is largely invisible to those outside the neighborhoods in which they exist. The hope contained in this project is that it might expand awareness of religious congregations within the urban context, beyond considering them to be merely a benign presence, if considering them at all. To that end, this book is addressed to urban policymakers, developers, and those in the media. But this is also critical, or applied, research, and so a further hope is that congregations from a variety of religious traditions might see themselves in this book, whether in Philadelphia or not. In finding their story in these stories, they could develop a more realistic sense of who they are, and could be, as neighbors on a city street and citizens of the world.

2 CONSTRUCTING THE SACRED IN SPACE AND PLACE

The city possesses a moral as well as a physical organization, and
these two mutually interact in characteristic ways to mold and modify
one another.

—ROBERT PARK, 1915

The space within becomes the reality of the building.

—FRANK LLOYD WRIGHT

The pastor enjoys giving tours of the funeral-home-turned-church.
The tiled embalming room, the chapel, the marble reception area
used for the viewings of many Philadelphians over the centuries,
and the rickety, rope-operated casket elevator—all remain intact,
at least physically. But their meanings have changed with the new
occupants. Pastor pointed out a photograph on the wall of the old
space they had outgrown, a former nuisance bar in another neighborhood. The relocation to this building at this particular intersection had been intentional. He loves the idea and the irony of such
transformations: buildings that had promoted substance abuse and
ritualized death could be adapted as places where people could find
freedom from addictions and life would be celebrated. "It's just like
God, don't you think?" he adds with a chuckle.

Any consideration of religious presence in a particular context
begins with the physicality of that presence—that is, the *place* and
the *space*.

Whether a house of worship is located on a busy street with
screaming sirens and honking horns or in a quiet setting where
birdsong provides background for silent prayer, its place both
expresses and shapes the experience of the faithful. The economic
vitality, demographic diversity, cultural milieu, and myriad other
social dynamics all contribute to the soil in which communities
of faith take root and thrive, or shrivel up and die. The theological understandings of the gathered faithful are not received from
disembodied traditions but are filtered through their contexts.

One member of a small independent Pentecostal church drove from a leafy first-ring suburb to worship in a neighborhood the police had nicknamed "The Badlands." "When you come to church down here, you know, there's a graveyard right outside. There's people selling drugs right over there. And you remember how God saved you. It's not like going to a church on a hill in a gated community." While one might certainly take issue with his view of the neighborhood, clearly the context was shaping his religious experience.

Similarly, space also matters. Bricks and mortar, doors and windows, steeples and altars are not neutral or random elements of a shelter for a worshipping people. Rather, all these elements are dynamically related to the religious identity of the faith community. They both express a piety and contribute to shaping and defining it. Congregations are housed in buildings as diverse as the religious practices themselves. The varied shapes, sizes, and décor of the worship spaces along Germantown Avenue not only attest to rich religious diversity, but also help keep it alive. There are grand Gothic buildings and simple meetinghouses that have served sacred purposes for over 300 years. Some have housed a single continuous congregation over the years while others are now spiritual home to congregations of another tradition. Many are residential or commercial buildings that have been adapted into houses of worship. But in all cases, sacred meaning is constructed within a confluence of stone, wood, wires, pipes, and plaster on an ordinary parcel of land. This raises an obvious question that nevertheless usually escapes our imagination as we pass by so many houses of worship: what makes space sacred, and how does it happen? Germantown Avenue, with its diversity of worship spaces, traditions, and peoples offers a rich opportunity to explore how the sacred is constructed in the dynamic urban ecology.

Theoretical considerations of "sacred space" have rarely looked closely at the importance of these spaces within urban contexts. Traditionally, discussion of the sacred begins, and sometimes ends, with Mircea Eliade and Emile Durkheim, who differed on whether sacred meaning is inherent in an object or space (Eliade) or socially constructed (Durkheim). For both, the sacred is defined as distinct from that which is secular (or "profane").

Those who adopt Durkheim's approach (social constructionists) argue that space is not inherently sacred but becomes so through the work of sacralization—that is, people construct sacred meaning by defining and protecting the pure or transcendent from desecration or violation (Wuthnow, 1994; Nelson, 2006; Chidester and Lenenthal, 1995). In fact, in either a religious or civic space, if there is a shared understanding that it could be violated, this makes it sacred. But sacredness is not simply inherent in the space—it is the result of social processes. Particularly through their rituals, spatial design, control of land, memorializing shared narrative, and iconography, spaces become *inscribed* as sacred by the groups that claim them (Nelson, 2006). Whether an altar, historic house, cemetery, or old desk, those places and artifacts along the Avenue that are deemed sacred are protected from violation and revered because they connect our everyday experience with a greater narrative. This sacred attribute enables us to transcend this moment in time through memory, and this space through higher meanings.

Yet even the more recent work on sacred space has not focused on how and why in densely populated streets, where cultures mix and re-mix, often unassuming buildings such as those on Germantown Avenue can become holy ground. City streets bear the booms and busts of the economy and of demographic shifts. Buildings along those streets are adapted and readapted to new uses over time. Space and the meaning of space is contested in the context of these ongoing social changes. The claim and construction of space as sacred, therefore, takes place in the context of complex and colliding social and cultural dynamics within the urban ecology. The demographic diversity of the people and communities of faith along Germantown Avenue bear witness to the universal human need to find transcendent meaning in daily life and to connect the ordinary with higher purposes.

The religious ecology here is crowded and dynamic. With roughly 11 congregations per mile along the Avenue, there is a spectrum of durability and fluidity. The historic churches have maintained sacred spaces in their footprints for generations. But as commercial areas suffer economic downturns, making affordable real estate available to emerging congregations, small faith communities looking for affordable meeting space move into former commercial strips to form "religious districts" (McRoberts, 2003). In these crowded religious marketplaces, congregations need to more rapidly establish their space as sacred and distinctive. Over the course of six years I have seen some thrive, while others have not, yet more congregations are surviving than aren't. Survival depends on their construction of the sacred.

There are three general categories of religious sacred spaces along Germantown Avenue: congregations that have continued to worship in their original buildings (or on the same sites), which are designated in this study as *historic churches*; congregations that have acquired the former buildings of earlier congregations that have relocated or closed altogether (*"hermit crabs"*); and those which have adapted commercial or residential spaces for sacred purposes (*recyclers*). All construct their understanding of the sacred through different social processes but with the same general result: whether the faithful are entering a grand Gothic sanctuary or a former furniture store, they are stepping onto holy ground.

The Historic Churches of Germantown Avenue

Traveling down the Avenue, one is struck by the number of old, historic churches, most of which have continued to house worshipping congregations in buildings that have been lovingly maintained for generations. William Penn, a Quaker, established the new colony as a haven for religious freedom; and Germantown Avenue began to reflect the early experiment in religious pluralism. The Quakers and Mennonites established their meeting houses at the end of the 17th century (1690 and 1683, respectively). The Brethren and the Lutheran congregations, both established by German immigrants, soon joined them (1724, 1737). Ironically, the Anabaptists (Mennonites and Brethren) were fleeing persecution by the dominant churches in Europe, including the Lutherans, during the Thirty Years War. As neighbors on Germantown Avenue, however, the old tensions dissolved as they were all striving to acclimate to life on this side of the pond. By the end of the century, they had been joined by the German Reformed Church (Market Square, 1733), and the English-speaking Methodists (First Church, 1796). Instead of continuing their old conflicts on new soil, the immigrants fought largely internal battles, often revolving around language, as younger church members pushed for religious services in English rather than German. (We see similar conflicts in Korean or Latino congregations today.)

The timeless ecclesiastical instinct to split rather than change resulted in a number of spinoff congregations. As the 19th century dawned, Market Square begat First Presbyterian of Germantown (1809) and St. Michael's begat Trinity Lutheran (1839). They joined the English-speaking Episcopalians at St. Luke's (founded in 1811). As the century progressed, Germantown Avenue became an ecumenical corridor, with grand Protestant churches sinking their footprints up into Chestnut Hill. Two more Presbyterian churches were built—in Chestnut Hill (1852) and Mt. Airy (1883). The Baptists, on fire from the Great Awakenings, organized congregations in Chestnut Hill (1834) and Germantown (1865). The Methodists had also been energized by the revival movements and established their church at the "top of the hill" in 1848. The Lutherans planted a church in Chestnut Hill in 1861 and later a denominational seminary (1889) on the former estate of William Allen, a prominent citizen, philanthropist, and political leader in colonial Philadelphia—grounds where the first shots were fired in the Battle of Germantown.

This history is rich, but for our purposes it is the *relevance* of that history on Germantown Avenue today that is important. The physical presence of these congregations has provided cultural, economic, and architectural grounding for the development of urban life along, and radiating out from, the Avenue. These churches have provided links with colonial history and have been a source of continuity through generations of new residents and waves of social changes.

The historic churches of Germantown Avenue enumerated—the Friends, Mennonites, Brethren, three Lutheran, two Methodist, two Baptist, and three Presbyterian and Episcopal—have much in common besides location. Although church fires and expanding congregations have necessitated rebuilding, almost all of them stayed on their original parcel of land. The Mennonites, when bursting at the seams of the small meetinghouse built in 1770, moved to another location just a block away. They decided to preserve the original structure as a historic site but return annually for services in Advent. The Presbyterians of Chestnut Hill also outgrew their original building and moved across the street in 1953. Their former building is now home to a vibrant Seventh-day Adventist congregation.

As simple wood structures gave way to more elaborate worship spaces, most gravitated to the imposing Gothic architectural style. The arched windows, vaulted ceilings, and imposing steeples were constructed out of grey schist, which was quarried locally. The architecture reflected and inspired the styles then used by schools, clubs, libraries, and other institutions along the Avenue. By contrast, Germantown Friends Meeting and Chestnut Hill Baptist opted for plain, stuccoed structures. The austere Federal style of the Chestnut Hill Baptist echoes that of the many colonial houses that still pepper the Avenue. Just up the street, the Presbyterian Church of Chestnut Hill is an imposing structure and incorporates both the clean, simple lines of Quaker meetinghouses with the majestic feel of Gothic churches in a tasteful brick colonial revival. All of these churches continue to add to the aesthetics of a busy city street. Inside, whether in dark, stone sanctuaries with the jeweled light of stained-glass windows, or entering the plain, airy spaces that allow brilliant sunlight in, one's sensory experience expands. This is sacred space, which invites thought away from the immediate and mundane to a transcendent experience of the holy. The worshipping members are not the only beneficiaries, however. The historic churches lend a sacred dimension to their immediate contexts. Often history itself imbues a sense of the sacred to both space and place.

Germantown Avenue bears the civic sacred history of the country itself. Patriots fought for freedom on this street, sacrificing their lives and preparing for the long winter at Valley Forge. Here too was the stage for local struggles around race, health care, and freedom of expression—all core to the national narrative, and American civil religion. Many of the congregations not only have been actors in that history but now provide portals for accessing it and act as conveyers of that narrative. Children play in the "living burial grounds" at Germantown Friends Meeting and Historic Fair Hill, touching the low headstones of those who lived in their neighborhood generations ago. St. Michael's Lutheran Church held a memorial service in 1986 for the unknown soldiers buried in their grounds and facilitated the reinterment of a British soldier whose remains were found on their property. In subtle but significant ways, the historic churches connect the current residents of Northwest Philadelphia with their local and national origins.

Race has been an ongoing struggle for the country, the city, and its neighborhoods. It is woven into our national narrative and consciousness, reflecting the most despicable, as well as the most noble, in the American experience. The houses of worship along the Avenue offer connective tissue that binds Philadelphians to both the sacred and shameful. Almost 350 years ago the fragile new meeting of Mennonites and Quakers broke up over the issue of slavery. Despite the small group who broke away to protest human bondage, it would be another hundred years before the Quakers took a formal position against slavery. They then became the epicenter of abolitionist activism. The physical continuity of the Germantown Monthly Meeting has provided an arena for revisiting and replaying the issue of race, which was originally framed as a struggle around slavery. Informants revealed that there is still tension between "the families" (descendents of the original 13 families who founded Germantown) and "convinced Quakers" (those who were not born into the faith but converted). Of course, the tension between old-timers (especially founders) and newcomers is universal in religious communities. What is unusual here is that this tension has been sustained over three and a half centuries.

A few blocks down the street is Historic Fair Hill, a Quaker burial ground. Here the low headstones and verdant, pastoral 4.5-acre lot is in stark contrast to the urban neighborhood that surrounds it, once known by police and portrayed in the local media as "the Badlands" because of high levels of drug-related crime in the 1980s and 1990s. This is holy ground for the Friends, as a number of well-known Quaker abolitionists, including Lucretia Mott, are buried there. The grave of Robert Purvis, an African American who was known as the president of the Underground Railroad is also there.

Connection to this place and its history has inspired activism in recent years. Quakers involved with the burial ground joined forces with local African American and Latino neighbors and congregations to stand up against the drug dealers who had earned the neighborhood its nickname. That chapter of resistance to the enslaving power of drug addiction and those who would propagate it was as empowering for the contemporary advocates as the work of resisting slavery was for the abolitionists. David Young, local historian and director of Cliveden, the historic trust and site of the Battle of Germantown, is fond of the saying that "History doesn't really repeat itself, but it often rhymes." Communities of faith are often conduits for the sacred past, knowingly or unknowingly rhyming with earlier events.

FIGURE 2.1 Historic Fair Hill Burial Ground.

Today congregations up and down the Avenue are often focused on filling gaps in public services, especially in health care. As access to health care is declining for many Philadelphians, faith communities along Germantown Avenue have increasingly been organizing health fairs, providing free flu shots and screening for HIV/AIDS (human immunodeficiency virus/acquired immunodeficiency syndrome). Some clergy have publicly led the way in getting tested for the virus. These efforts are echoes of earlier faith-based responses to health crises.

In the Yellow Fever Epidemic of 1793, churches played a critical, and unique, humanitarian role. Panic around the epidemic caused those who could to relocate outside of Center City. George Washington, Thomas Jefferson, and other political leaders moved onto Germantown Avenue near Market Square to wait out the epidemic, part of an exodus of 20,000. Between August and November of 1793, as the epidemic swept through the crowded neighborhoods of those left behind in Center City, 10% of Philadelphia's population died from the fever. Members of the fledgling African American church were involved in caring for and burying the victims when few would risk touching infected bodies.[1] It is believed that the Brethren Church on Germantown Avenue opened their new burial site for those outside of their faith who had succumbed to the disease and were in need of a final resting place, although it is not clear how the bodies were transported up to Germantown. It is clear, however, that burial grounds in Center City were, no doubt, filling up and that it took a certain moral and civic courage to care for the victims.

The narrative of the struggle for racial justice continues to resonate as well. From the earliest conflict over slavery within the Quaker community, and their subsequent public protest in 1688, through the Underground Railroad stops along Germantown Avenue and its connection to the abolitionists, there is sacred history embedded here. Historic sites and markers remind those who travel the Avenue of this history; however like so much "street furniture," they are often unnoticed. (For example, even though Fair Hill Burial Ground has been very active in passing on this sacred history, its low gravestones led many in the neighborhood to believe that it was a pet cemetery.) Even so, many congregations do connect with the sacred story of the struggle for racial justice and draw on that narrative for inspiration and clarity. A church-based drill team marched up Germantown Avenue for the Juneteenth Celebration of emancipation in front of Johnson House—a stop on the Underground Railroad—one example of how religious and racial sacred stories intertwine.

FIGURE 2.2 Enon Baptist Church Drill Team participates in the Juneteenth Celebration, in front of Johnson House and Brand New Life Christian Center.

The elegant and well-endowed St. Luke's Episcopal Church embodies the history of race relations in the city and country. In the early 20th century, the affluent, white congregation, known for its missionary work, acquired a church building in Germantown for Episcopalians of African descent. This congregation, St. Barnabas, was housed in a much simpler structure and grew in numbers and in outreach programs. Decades later, as more African Americans were moving into Germantown, white members of St. Luke's started moving out of the city. Wanting to keep the impressive campus of Gothic buildings "in the family," the congregation of St. Barnabas was invited to merge with St. Luke's. In a symbolic march from their church in 1968, just weeks after the assassination of Martin Luther King Jr., the now-larger congregation of St. Barnabas walked up Germantown Avenue to St. Luke's. Today the church is almost exclusively African American and many members still proudly identify themselves as being from St. Barnabas, 45 years after the merger. The experience of exclusion still lingers in the collective memory, but the story told is one of enfranchisement, of being on the first wave of racial integration. A current priest reflects the tensions inherent within the congregational story and struggles with the presentation of the narrative:

The fact that these parishes set up mission churches for black people was a cultural wrong that was manifested in society during those years, but was not specific to St. Luke's....Certainly, I have heard others characterize the merger as ironic, given that the church that was set up to keep black people OUT of St. Luke's was now being invited back IN to save it, but would that be a "black power" issue? I also wonder whether it would make any sense to try to present the story at face value—that during an era of social change, a suggestion arose to bring two churches together that had similar worship styles to address needs that each church had. The uniqueness of the shared leadership, the fact that a merger of a black and a white congregation was virtually unheard of at the time…

This narrative reemerged at St. Luke's as part of "Germantown Speaks," an intergenerational oral history project based in three congregations along the Avenue. Students from Germantown High School—a public school on the Avenue noted for high dropout rates, a revolving door of administrators, and incidents of violence[2] —conducted focus group interviews with elders from the churches. The students had been preparing for these interviews and

FIGURE 2.3 St. Luke's Episcopal Church.

were ready with questions, note paper, refreshments, and a video camera. Shyness gave way to wide eyes as the older people from St. Luke's told stories of Germantown High School in the 1940s through the 1960s when black students were denied access to many of the opportunities white students had. They brought pictures of their younger selves and told stories about proudly breaking color barriers in the band, student government, and cheerleading. As students they had marched down Germantown Avenue to the School Board to demand the inclusion of black history in the curriculum. Finally these elders turned the tables, asking students about their experiences in school and in the community. Sitting around tables in the St. Luke's parish hall, something momentous was occurring: the sacred narrative was being handed to a new generation. Past and present were connected through the efforts of this community of faith even as its members might have been ambivalent about the struggle within their own congregation.

This is not to say that religious groups are the only source of connection to the deeper sacred narratives of social history. Particularly in Northwest Philadelphia there is an active network of historical societies and sites that work in creative ways to dust off the traditional museum approach and make history more relevant and accessible to the current residents of the area. Dr. David Young, in his oversight of the historic site, Cliveden, is seeking to liberate history from being a rarefied and often uncritical set of facts to create a sense of engagement with a "shared history." The historic churches on the Avenue are a critical component of this process. Their buildings offer a direct connection to the historical context of Northwest Philadelphia, and indeed the nation. But their people are also conduits of the sacred story, conveying the values that imbued struggles for freedom and for justice. There are also spaces deemed sacred in terms of civil religion: George Washington's summer house, Johnson House (a major stop on the Underground Railroad) and Cliveden (home to a slaveholding magnate but also the site of the most intense fighting of the Battle of Germantown, reenacted each year). Their sacred symbolic value is not only meaningful to history buffs and members of the historic churches but also contributes to the sacred sensibilities of new residents and new congregations. One Pentecostal preacher, whose congregation consists predominantly of new arrivals from the same Caribbean island that still echoes in his own accent, spoke of the historic context in which he found himself and how it informs his church's identity. "This neighborhood is one of the most racially integrated in the whole country. And one reason is right there (pointing to Johnson House). I try to get that in my sermons a couple of times a year."[3] Still this is not the whole story. A middle-aged woman from another church on the Avenue voiced a caveat: "There was slavery in Philadelphia, and in Germantown. People want to forget that. They all remember that Germantown was a stop on the Underground Railroad, but it's a more complicated story than that." Historic sites like Johnson House offer conduits to sacred memory and opportunities for contemporary critique.

The more recent racial history of "white flight," when those of European descent left the urban core for the suburbs in the 1960s through 1980s as African Americans were migrating into the city, is reflected up and down the Avenue with varying degrees of intensity. Although neighboring Chestnut Hill has continued to have a predominantly white population, the Mt. Airy neighborhood has been a study in racial and economic diversity. Blockbusting and panic selling in real estate, and redlining practices by lenders, were not allowed to take hold here. Jewish and Christian congregations were proactive in resisting these practices during the 1960s. The historic churches along the Avenue, if not as politically active, were perhaps no less influential in maintaining the stability of Northwest Philadelphia. The roots of these congregations, ensconced in stone, ran deep. As the old children's Sunday School song says, "The wise man built his house upon the rock … and the house upon the sand fell flat." The original 14 historic churches (11 from the so-called Mainline Protestant traditions and three Peace churches) consequently have been joined by at least 20 other faith traditions. This diversity does not currently include Roman Catholics (although there are two very active parishes just off Germantown Avenue). There is certainly a strong Jewish presence in Northwest Philadelphia, including the Germantown Jewish Center, which is located a half a mile off the Avenue. However, on the Avenue Jews are now represented only by the small black Hebrew congregation, Beth Hephzibah Philadelphia Extension of the Kingdom of Yah. Even so, the religious diversification of the past half century has been significant.

The historic churches in many ways serve as anchors in the rapidly changing urban ecology. Despite the many social, cultural, and economic changes since the earliest believers first established worshipping congregations in the late 1600s, these churches have been a strong source of continuity. Certainly, architecturally they contribute to the aesthetics and sense of stability. Culturally, they are not only islands of religious sacred space, but mediate sacred civic narratives and the values embedded in them. Many times, the historic churches intentionally cultivate this role (such as in the Germantown

Speaks effort). But more often, production of sacred space within the urban ecology is something that occurs unconsciously in daily life on the Avenue.

Inheriting the Shells of Others: Hermit Crabs

Within communities of faith, change is as much a reality as is continuity. Congregations grow or shrink or split and their buildings can become inappropriate for their needs. When the original congregation leaves a building, however, it is more likely to be acquired by another community of faith than it is to be destroyed or converted to secular use. Just as hermit crabs that have outgrown their shells scavenge the beach for larger shells to move into, so do newer, growing congregations move into the shells no longer needed by other religious groups. Even though there is discontinuity in terms of particular congregations, the continuity of sacred purpose contributes value to the neighborhood. Indeed, the practice of emerging religious movements settling into others' discarded sacred spaces is an ancient one (Van Der Leeuw, 1986).

This is much more prevalent moving down the Avenue from Chestnut Hill and Mt. Airy into Germantown and Nicetown. Here we have identified 16 such hermit crab congregations. In some cases, their buildings were home to Protestant congregations in neighborhoods that were much more vulnerable to white flight. Despite the fact that many of the denominations have been criticized for "abandoning the city," younger, growing congregations from different faith traditions are the beneficiaries. For example, the historic Market Square Presbyterian Church, located across from the George Washington's Germantown residence, had seen its congregation dwindle to a handful of faithful worshippers by the 1980s. The building is now home to a dynamic congregation, Impacting Your World Christian Center. The pulpit that had once hosted legendary revivalist George Whitfield is now occupied by the Reverend Ray Bernard, who preaches a "prosperity Gospel" to his predominantly African American congregation.

Buildings that might have fallen into disrepair, deteriorated, and contributed to urban decay are now being cared for by another generation of worshippers—an obvious contribution. Impacting Your World has carefully maintained its imposing structure in historic Market Square. Still, caring for these older buildings can be a mixed blessing, as the members of Second Baptist found out in the spring of 2010. Having acquired the former Mt. Carmel Methodist Episcopal Church (built in 1895), they were able to make attractive cosmetic renovations to the building. However, the smell of mold in the sanctuary betrayed the rotting timbers of the structure. During a funeral for a neighborhood man who had been shot, the additional crowd taxed its beams and the floor collapsed. "'I heard a loud crack, then the floor dropped and the pews fell' toward the center of the sanctuary, said mourner Nikki Smith of North Philadelphia. 'Everybody panicked.'"[4] Fortunately, all 250 in attendance escaped without injury, but it did underscore the challenges of maintaining grand old houses of worship. The congregation did repair the building and continues to worship there.

In acquiring the sacred spaces of other traditions, new occupants need to make them their own. In adapting spaces to their own worship needs they have demonstrated a notable respect for the original design. For example, St. Mark's Outreach Baptist Church acquired the old Quaker meetinghouse that sits on a small grassy knoll overlooking Fair Hill Burial Ground. Many of the straight-backed wooden benches in the austere sanctuary remain intact. But the Baptist congregation has added a raised pulpit, musical instruments (piano, drums, and keyboard) as well as flower vases, none of which would have graced the space when the Quakers met for silent meeting. Perhaps some might be spinning in their plainly marked graves across the street; more

FIGURE 2.4 Impacting Your World Christian Center, originally Market Square Presbyterian Church.

likely, though, they would look kindly on those who have found their own inner light.

The historic churches have decades, sometimes centuries, of sacred meanings infusing their worship space. History itself becomes an element of the sacred—internally and in relation to its local ecology. Those who have acquired houses of worship from their original owners draw from the history of the building as well, in creating space that becomes sacred for them. But the most creative production of the sacred occurs in buildings intended for other uses.

Reduce, Reuse, Recycle

Entering the old furniture factory, Muslim worshippers quietly slip out of their shoes before finding a space on the prayer carpet. Not far up the Avenue, Mennonites silence their animated greetings as they enter the renovated iron works warehouse and retailer, and transition into private meditation in preparation for worship. A few blocks away, the simple altar in the former shoe store, adorned with plastic flowers around the wooden cross, inspires no less reverence than the majestic Basilica, as Pentecostal worshippers whisper, and then shout, their adoration of God. On this one city street, ordinary space becomes holy ground—all without the assistance of traditional architectural forms. Here, the Divine is encountered not in ethereal stillness but as sirens screech up and down the street outside. Spirits soar not beneath vaulting ceilings with dim lighting but under drop ceilings and fluorescent lights found in every other store on the block. That which is sacred is not apart from, but seemingly embedded in, this city street.

These urban buildings, whose original purpose was secular, but which have now been reconstructed as sacred, offer case studies of the adaptive reuse of space. This is much more the norm on the Avenue—of the more than 83 active congregations (the census is fluid), between 56 and 58 worship in buildings that were originally built for commercial use. The entrepreneurial spirit and creativity of congregational leaders is evident in the wide variety of buildings that have been recycled for sacred use: banks, liquor stores, theaters, factories, stores of all types, a blood bank, a school, and a funeral home are now serving as worship spaces. Some of the buildings have also been residential but it is commercial buildings that are more often, and more easily, adapted. People of faith pour sweat equity into transforming market space into holy ground. Ordinary materials, in ordinary buildings, through volunteer labor, create space that becomes inviolable. Speaking in his church which was once a plastics factory, the Reverend Rodriguez was clear:

> We make the space holy. The altar is made of wood, the walls of cement but this is where the word of God is preached and that is why this is a holy place. I don't allow selling or eating or drinking in this space. We have designated places for that.... If we are working in the church, and it is necessary [to go to the altar], then yes. But while in worship it is designated for who will be preaching and any invited ministers, the "generals of God."[5]

The adaptive reuse of commercial space is labor intensive and often involves not just wood and cement but murals, special lighting, and ubiquitous glass bricks arranged in the shape of crosses. In describing the transformation of commercial buildings into sacred space, one of my research assistants marveled:

> I am struck by the fact that no matter how shabby storefront churches might look on the outside, I have yet to visit one that isn't beautifully maintained on the inside. At St. Luke's the carpet is red, the walls are painted pristine white.... The altar area is fenced with a carved railing of blond wood, and on it three carved wooden chairs form a row behind the pulpit. On the small altar under the pulpit, there is a large candle and a bouquet of roses. Nothing about the exterior is elegant; nothing about the interior is shabby.[6]

In such spaces, the religious experience is no less transcendent than it is in Gothic sanctuaries with stained-glass windows and marble altars that create a boundary between sacred and secular space. Yet in the transformed structure, making it *sacred* is not just a matter of rehabbing an old property but an ongoing process of reinforcing inviolability, such as not allowing eating and drinking in the worship space. There is also a creative tension in the reworked construction of the sacred as both *over-against* the secular/profane and *in relationship, or negotiation,* with it. That is, sacred space within adapted buildings is "in but not of" the urban ecology, at once holy ground and embedded in the urban context.

The social dynamics embedded in the processes of construction of the sacred in the urban ecology can be seen in two congregations on the same intersection on Germantown Avenue, both of which appropriated commercial buildings for religious use. In what ways did the physical space both express and shape the religious identity of the two congregations? How have these two buildings *become* sacred spaces at the busy intersection they share on Germantown Avenue? How do boundaries function in the construction of congregational identity vis-à-vis sacred space? To what degree is exclusion and differentiation from the secular/profane incorporated into a high sense of religious identity?

A Quiet Witness

Germantown Mennonite dates back to the earliest Mennonite German settlers in North America—the original 13 families who settled Germantown in 1683. This early group comprised both Quakers and Mennonites who formed a single meeting (congregation), but they soon split over the issues of ordaining leaders and condemning slavery. Four within this early congregation did issue a public statement against slavery in 1688, written and signed in the home of Thone Kunders on Germantown Avenue. It was the first such faith-based condemnation of slavery, argued on the basis of the Golden Rule. Although none within the meeting were slaveholders, there was a hesitancy to embrace the position, given the economic importance of slavery and, at least for those from England, a familiarity with "indentured servitude." For the Dutch and German immigrants, the ownership of another human being contradicted the core beliefs of the Friends (Quakers).

After the meeting split, the Mennonites incorporated Dutch and Swiss Mennonites into their circle, then built a meetinghouse from logs. In 1770 they built a small stone meetinghouse that was home to the congregation for over 200 years. The table on which the anti-slavery statement was signed remains in that space as a sacred object, connecting believers to their sacred past. During the 1970s, the pacifist congregation of Germantown Mennonite began attracting peace activists who shared "a vision for Mennonites who loved the city and felt a spiritual calling to live in an urban setting." Consequently, by the 1990s they had outgrown the meetinghouse and were nomadic for several years (primarily sharing worship space in other congregations) until landing in their current location. They chose another historic stone building along the Avenue, not far from the old meetinghouse that they maintain as a historic trust. The large colonial-era structure first served as a women's club in the 19th century, a place where Grace Kelly is said to have danced, but then had become a well-known ironworks retailer known for its dusty, cluttered collection of fireplace irons.

The building cost $250,000 to buy and renovate—a source of controversy in the congregation. Some members felt that even this relatively small sum was an extravagance, and the money could better be spent on programs for the poor in the community. A majority prevailed, however, and there is no sign of hard feelings. The congregation undertook much of the renovation themselves and takes justifiable pride in having transformed the dark, attic-like space into a sun-drenched worship area, elegant in its utter simplicity.

There was minimal formalized ritual to mark the transition into the new building—a brief dedication service that seemed forgettable to those interviewed. But the real work of sacralization was literally a social construction, through the sweat equity invested by members during the process of renovation. One long-time member said, "What really made this place sacred for me was all the work we did on it—getting rid of all the junk, all the garish colors,

FIGURE 2.5 Original Germantown Mennonite Meetinghouse.

FIGURE 2.6 Current location of Germantown Mennonite Meetinghouse.

FIGURE 2.7 Mennonites at worship.

and making it so peaceful and beautiful."[7] The renovations in both process and result reflect the deep commitments of these Mennonites to humility and hard work. The result is an uncluttered space that both expresses and enhances the peacefulness of the worship. No crosses or religious icons are to be found in the sanctuary. The "altar" changes regularly but normally incorporates candles, woven cloth, and fresh flowers in different configurations. There are no stained-glass windows, carpeting, elevated pulpit, or organ, and plain wooden chairs are used instead of pews. For some religious traditions, this would appear to be a plain and empty shell. But when you hear the rich four-part singing of hymns or the heartfelt time of sharing, it is clear that this former ironworks store has been transformed into sacred space by the "work of the people." While the old meeting house still stands and is preserved for occasional services and as a museum site (receiving around 600 visitors per year), the members of Germantown Mennonite primarily experience the sacred in their new space.

Brand New Life: Taking It back

Just across the street, in stark contrast to the quietness of Mennonite worship, is a Pentecostal church whose services are ecstatic, celebratory, noisy, and emotional. A jazzy organ provides background not only for singing but also for prayers, preaching, testimonies, and even announcements. The keyboard is usually joined by piano, bongo, and a full drum set, expertly played by a surprisingly competent four-year-old boy. Those who come forward for anointing are often "slain in the Spirit," fainting into the waiting arms and blankets of church nurses. Others are energized by the spirit, breaking into dance and twirling Mylar streamers. Singers lead in a reggae-rhythmed welcome song, as newcomers are hugged and kissed by almost every person in the congregation. The preacher, a mild-mannered Jamaican man, oversees it all, exuding acceptance and encouragement. His sermons stress a personal relationship with God, and those who testify focus on the divine power which has enabled them to overcome despair, drug addiction, and assaults on their dignity.

Like the Mennonites, this congregation outgrew its former building—a renovated and rehabilitated bar in another part of the neighborhood. But when looking for another site, members were drawn to the historic building on a busy intersection that had been, until recently, home to the oldest funeral home in the United States. The name of the congregation is ironically—and consciously—Brand New Life Christian Center.

Unlike the Mennonites, the Pentecostals initiated their physical and spiritual move into the new space with an elaborate set of sacralizing rituals. Members were adamant that all traces of the "funeralizing business" be removed. They then went through every room and "anointed" it, driving out demons and inviting the Holy Spirit in. Eight years after moving in, the pastor and lay leaders of Brand New Life still gather early each Sunday morning and walk through the sanctuary, touching each chair, praying out loud in English or in "tongues" for the Holy Spirit to drive out demons and to occupy the space. Demons can still come in from the outside, they believe. This ongoing cleansing ritual continues to sacralize this space and claim it as holy ground.

The irony of the name is not lost on the congregation. Most say they do not think about its former life as a funeral home very often, but they also like the fact that it was "once a place of death, but now it's a place of life." The motto of the congregation is drawn from an obscure passage in the Hebrew Scriptures and is simply, "Taking it back." For some, this signifies taking life back from death, particularly through recovery from drug addiction. For others it means taking back anything that was "snatched away by the enemy," including health, wealth, respect, love, and education. Yet the motto does not signify the entitlement conveyed in the prosperity churches but a claim of empowerment to resist demonic forces.

For a Pentecostal church there are surprisingly few religious icons demarcating the space as "Christian." Crosses are etched into the glass doors of the side entry and appear on the pulpit. In the renovation process, the original design was respected. Few changes were made to the funeral home, despite the need to cast out death from the premises. Rather, improvements focused on accentuating the elegance of the marble, adding more chandeliers, and installing overstuffed brocade and gilded furniture at the front of the sanctuary. Symbols of the sacred, therefore, are not necessarily explicitly religious but are decorative and ornate. "Taking it back," it would seem, is aesthetic as well as spiritual, psychological, social, and cultural. But taking back what God gave and intends for faithful followers is still qualitatively and quantitatively different from claiming new real estate or luxury cars, which pure prosperity-gospel churches claim to be God's will for believers.

FIGURE 2.8 Brand New Life Christian Center.

At the Crossroads: Germantown Avenue and Washington Lane

It would seem that these two congregations have very little in common, yet there are remarkable similarities. Both Brand New Life and Germantown Mennonite made conscious choices to base their congregations at a busy and somewhat gritty intersection on Germantown Avenue. Growing congregations tend to move *away from* the urban core, yet they chose to move *into* it. Despite their very different congregational demographics and worship styles, the location decision reflects a shared sense of divine presence. The ancient prophet Jeremiah exhorted the faithful to "seek the shalom of the city," and in so doing, they would find their own well-being (which could be considered the earliest expression of an urban ecological approach). The Mennonite and the Pentecostal churches reflect their belief that God can be found in this densely populated neighborhood in the midst of commercial activity.

Further, neither congregation has tried to differentiate their buildings as sacred in contrast to the secular character of surrounding structures. No major changes were made to the facades, nor were steeples added. Signage and iconography are subdued. Both congregations were respectful of the historic character of the buildings they moved into.

The two congregations have taken their place within the urban ecology seamlessly, it appears. They have adapted commercial spaces for sacred purposes but without asserting a holiness as over-and-against their immediate context. Partly this is due to the preexisting historic and sacred nature of the Avenue, particularly at this intersection. On the corner abutting the Mennonite Church and directly across from Brand New Life is a building sacred because of its historic role: Johnson House, a stone colonial-era private home, well known as a stop on the Underground Railroad. It is well maintained by a non-profit board and serves as a museum and field trip destination for Philadelphia schoolchildren. The role it played in the history of the anti-slavery movement makes it an important symbol for Quakers and others from pacifist traditions as well as for African Americans and other people of color—two groups with deep roots and a continuing presence in Germantown. Therefore, Brand New Life and Germantown Mennonite derive a degree of historic sacred identity from their revered neighbor. Johnson House symbolizes the highest values of both communities—the costly struggle for liberation from slavery and the courageous sacrifice of pacifists of European descent. The minister of Brand New Life incorporates the witness of Johnson House into his sermons. Germantown Mennonite was the venue for the premiere of a musical interpretation of the Underground Railroad.[8] Both congregations engage Johnson House—it is not an accident of location.

This is not to say that the congregations' sense of sacred is derivative; indeed, sacralizing work is continually being done in each location out of their respective spiritual needs and experience. Despite their differences, along racial and socioeconomic lines (Mennonite worshippers are predominantly white, those at Brand New Life are almost exclusively Caribbean and African American), both congregations can be seen as *exilic*—people who have been excluded or displaced—and in need of a sacred sense of home. Germantown Mennonite, the mother church of the Mennonites in the United States, was expelled from the denomination they had founded because of their public stand for civil and ecclesial rights for gay/lesbian/bisexual/transgendered people. The congregation comprises largely middle- to upper-middle-class professionals, most of whom are of Mennonite pedigree. Despite the expulsion, their sense of Mennonite identity is unshaken. They continue to contribute money to the denomination, subscribe to the literature, and speak of Mennonite values and history. Despite the stinging awareness of their

FIGURE 2.9 Comer's Paper Products at the corner of Germantown and Washington Avenues.

ostracism, at worship they are at home in their familiar Mennonite tradition. Across the street, many of those who gather at Brand New Life have been displaced through addiction, immigration, or poverty, or all three. Through prayer, healings, preaching, and testifying, their ritual life focuses on "taking it back," or claiming a home for the displaced.

Gerardus van der Leeuw argued that "house and temple...are essentially one."[9] It is no accident that religious buildings are referred to as *houses* of worship and that both home and temple provide physical and psychic sanctuary. The center of power in the home is the hearth, the source of eating and drinking. The parallels with rituals at many altars—partaking of bread and wine—is clear. The power of sacred places, both religious and domestic, is that they ground us in a sense of identity, or place in the world, even as they connect us to the transcendent. Both Brand New Life and Germantown Mennonite, through very different liturgical practices, produce a sense of spiritual at-home-ness in members. Their physical spaces *become sacred*, therefore, when they are identified as a spiritual home, giving worshippers a sense of place and power in a social context that has not always been welcoming to them.

Throughout the work of sacralization, it is clear that the two proximate physical spaces—which have been designed and decorated in such very different ways—have become sacred in a functional sense. They become holy ground

FIGURE 2.10 Johnson House, an important stop on the Underground Railroad.

because that which is holy happens there. The objects considered sacramental are not crosses, chalices, or even the buildings, but the people within them. The physical space is not inscribed with sacred status apart from the people who engage in the ritual of home-claiming. The building is transformed from ordinary to extraordinary only when the people themselves are transformed. The lived theology of the buildings is therefore instrumentalist. It is the faith of the people transformed, whether through individual miracle for the Pentecostals or in solidarity working for social justice for the Mennonites, that is transcendent. Often, that transcendence is not that different for these two congregations, despite differences in social location and styles of worship. On one Sunday morning, for example, a similar ritual took place on each side of Germantown Avenue. At Brand New Life, congregants were invited forward to be anointed with oil during a prayer of healing. As leaders prayed for those who came forward, some were overcome, some spoke in tongues, some wept,

FIGURE 2.11 Altar in Mennonite worship space.

FIGURE 2.12 Worshipper at Brand New Life Christian Center.

but all seemed to go into the deepest recesses of their souls. The sanctuary, splashed in light from its chandeliers and filled with the riffs of the jazz combo, was holy ground. Across the street, the Mennonites were also having prayer for healing. People were invited to come forward to seek healing for themselves, or someone else, or on behalf of a conflict somewhere in the world. They were anointed with water in the silence of the sanctuary. This moment of longing and solidarity reinforced an awareness that this too was holy ground. In both cases sacredness was conferred not on the space but *through* it.

Boundaries of Sacred Identity

In much of the literature on the establishment of religious identity there is an emphasis on the social construction of boundaries. Religious groups need to establish themselves as being *over against* the secular society, other religious groups and institutions. Sacred space and religious identity must be differentiated from that which is sinful, profane, worldly, or in a word, "not-us." To varying degrees, therefore, congregations must become exclusive in order to reinforce the distinctiveness of those within the flock. Yet how do congregations construct and perhaps negotiate such boundaries in the fluid dynamics of urban neighborhoods?

At the corner of Germantown and Washington are two congregations with distinct identities and sense of place. Yet their boundaries are not impermeable, but porous. The establishment of religious identity, in other words, is not dependent on rigid, exclusionary borders but can be constructed as fluid and interactive with the context. These congregations have "blended in" within their context, but not at the expense of their cultural and sacred identity.

Members going in and out of Brand New Life and Germantown Mennonite on Sunday mornings are generally indistinguishable from pedestrian traffic in terms of dress. Neither congregation has norms that encourage people to wear their "Sunday best." A few men in each congregation can be found wearing ties, and a few of the older women at Brand New Life wear hats. Clergy in both congregations do tend to dress more formally, but they are not set apart in clerical garb. Congregants on both sides of the street arrive in jeans and work clothes, and a few come to the early Pentecostal service directly from their shifts in health care jobs, still wearing their scrubs. The main visual distinction that is apparent in the sidewalk traffic on Sunday mornings is that there are more white people going into the Mennonite church than is reflective of the local population. Worshippers at Brand New Life are predominantly black (Afro-Caribbean and African American), a demographic reflection of the neighborhood.

In their respective rituals and ministries, both congregations bring in "secular" forms and invite the local context into the space. Brand New Life incorporates technology into their education programs and worship services, and services feature jazz and a surprisingly professional level of vocal music given the size of the congregation. For more traditional Afro-Caribbean and/or Pentecostal congregations, these forms might be associated with the devil. But here they are incorporated without explanation or apology. At Brand New Life the face of the devil is much more likely to be associated with addiction. In this sense there is a high level of differentiation between sacred and profane, between being saved or lost, as that which has been taken from them needs to be taken back. Apart from the need to differentiate themselves from the substances that can enslave them and are inherently sinful, there is a comfort level with the cultural stream in which they, many as new immigrants, are now swimming.

Mennonite worship is more reflective of traditional Protestant practices. But here too there is comfortable dialogue with "secular" culture as non-religious themes are easily incorporated into liturgical speech and education programs. For example, the adult education program is structured as an open discussion on contemporary topics such as conserving energy and teaching science in public schools. The language and perspectives shared are not necessarily or distinctively faith-based. What is distinctive is that the conversations are held among those with shared values and Mennonite backgrounds.

There are other, very tangible, ways that the two congregations invite the context into their space. Both have day care programs that rent space the congregations have renovated and can use on Sundays. Further, Brand New Life rents office space to both a neighborhood non-profit organization (Victim Assistance Program) and a small for-profit investment program. The Mennonites participate in an interfaith program in which they host homeless families for extended stays. They are proud of the bathrooms with showers they have installed especially for these families.

By all indications the cultural interaction with the neighborhood context flows both ways. The incorporation of local context into the space is reciprocated by a social acknowledgment of respect from the neighborhood. One small social indicator of the sacredness of these spaces is the absence of graffiti on either building (nor is there any on Johnson House) in a neighborhood that is well-tagged by "informal artists." There is a shroud of inviolability on the church buildings, reflecting respect, if not an overt perception of the sacred by outsiders. This respect extends to the congregations within them as well. Local businesspeople appreciate the presence of the believers who gather on their street. The contestation of urban space often focuses on parking. Yet at the intersection of Germantown Avenue and Washington Lane, local businesses lend their parking lots to those attending services.

Further, the surrounding neighborhood is home to faith-based businesses (such as God's Given Gift Salon). Within this district where crime, including violent crime, is at high levels, signs can be found for a faith-based security company. The sacred spills over into the secular street; boundaries between sacred and commercial are not rigid, but porous.

As both congregations are open systems, maintaining cultural dialogue with their contexts, it is interesting that they do not interact with each other. There is no indication of animosity or even judgment of their fellow Christians on the other side of the street. But the particularity of experience and social location can prove to be more formidable boundaries than perceived barriers between the sacred and the secular.

FIGURE 2.13 Religious meanings are not contained by the walls of worship spaces, but flow into the local street life.

These two thriving congregations have constructed sacred space out of former commercial buildings. Here these exilic faith communities have created spiritual homes that strengthen a sense of place for their members in an often-alienating environment. These two congregations are engaged in the cultural work of producing the sacred in ways that challenge dominant paradigms of Eliade and others, who argue that the sacred is either created or exists in oppositional relationship to the secular/profane. Their *lived religion* challenges this sacred/profane dichotomy in two ways:

• Strikingly, the strong sense of sacred created through human agency is identified with the *people* rather than the *place*. The building becomes a shell for sacred activity; its sacredness is therefore derivative of the human experience it shelters.

• Sacred identity is not constructed *over against* the context but in *relationship* with it. In tangible and intangible ways, that which is sacred—primarily the ritual activity of the people—spills out into the street and invites the city into its walls. The boundaries are not set, but are permeable. In the interaction with context the sacred is not diluted but becomes more clearly defined.

My research in not only these two churches but in many congregations along the Avenue suggests that those communities of faith with more rigid boundaries between sacred and secular are less likely to thrive on this dynamic city street. Several congregations, for theological reasons, do not engage in any "outreach ministries" with non-members, and they are struggling to survive. Further, congregations such as Brand New Life and Germantown Mennonite are challenging notions of the sacred. Sacredness is not associated with exclusivity or the aesthetics of physical space but as part of everyday life within the city; it is not a static state, but an ongoing process.

3 SEEKING THE WELFARE OF THE CITY: ASSESSING THE IMPACT OF URBAN CONGREGATIONS

Build houses and live in them; plant gardens and eat what they
produce…seek the welfare of the city where I have sent you into exile,
and pray to the Lord on its behalf, for in its welfare you will find your
welfare.

— JEREMIAH 29: 5,7

During a typical week on the Avenue, a visitor to Father's House
of Prayer might find a small troupe of boys in white face performing "Christian mime," with impressive talent and skill. At Chestnut
Hill Presbyterian, up the street, members are encouraged to participate in public demonstrations in front of an unscrupulous gun
shop, which is enabling dangerous handguns to get into the hands
of people who can't pass background checks. At the Church of the
Brethren, the contemplative worship conducted by their 18th-century
forebears has evolved into exuberant praise over the generations.
On one bitterly cold Sunday in January, an old woman praises God
for the support she got from church members to successfully challenge the utility company seeking to cut off her heat. Farther down
the Avenue, a Lutheran church is announcing free HIV testing and
an affluent mega-church is publicizing free flu shots. At the same
time, a storefront preacher is praying fervently to "God, the Great
Regulator," to bring Mr. Smith's blood pressure down to 120 over
70, as long as he stays away from salt and takes his walks. Those
gathered at St. Luke's Second Born Early, who are challenged by
poverty, unemployment, and hunger, nevertheless sing with gusto,

> I need you, you need me.
> We're all a part of God's body.
> Stand with me…
> You are important to me,
> I need you to survive.
> I pray for you, You pray for me.
> I love you, I need you to survive.

For many in these communities of faith, congregational life fulfills many needs; it can become the primary source of preventative health care, participation in the arts, moral support (if not therapy), friendship, education, leadership training, and political power as well as spiritual nourishment. Increasingly, congregations are sources of physical nourishment as well. As hunger in Philadelphia spiked in 2010, affecting almost one third of the population, faith communities scrambled to open, stock, and sustain food pantries to keep pace with the demand at their doorstep.[1]

Despite the many ways in which congregations are providing a whole range of services, these communities of faith in cities are invisible to urban planners, developers, and politicians. At best, they are considered a benign presence in the urban ecology, harmless and meaningless when one weighs the economic viability of a neighborhood. At worst, they are considered a drain on public resources because they occupy real estate without contributing tax revenue or significant economic activity. Storefront congregations in particular may be seen as signs of blight rather than resources for neighborhoods already at risk. This perspective is by no means unique to Philadelphia.

The Cost of Invisibility

In the fall of 2010, Evanston, Illinois, publicly debated the social value of its houses of worship. A bill was introduced into the city council that would require special-use permits for all houses of worship—that is, new congregations wanting to move into the city as well as existing faith communities that wanted to expand or rebuild would have to apply for a permit. The driving concern for the aldermen was their perception that the proliferation of storefront churches was detrimental to economic development. Alderman Ann Rainey introduced and defended the proposed ordinance: "Seven of anything is too much in one block. It's anti-diverse. It's anti-economic development. It makes no sense."[2] Earlier she had argued that these congregations hamper business development by appearing vacant. "The problem is that they're not vacant, and the fact that they're not vacant won't allow for retail and commercial uses that will liven the street.... We have to start thinking about economic development...why would you want to rent when there is no activity on Howard Street or any other street that is chocked a block full of churches, mosques or synagogues?"[3]

A local organization of African American clergy, the Evanston Pastors' Fellowship, took issue with the move. As the president, the Reverend Mark Dennis explained, the council had proceeded without consulting religious leaders; the pastors suspected that the measure was being driven by developers.[4] Further, they saw the city council setting itself up as gatekeeper of religious groups in their community, as a violation of the First Amendment rights to the free exercise of religion and public assembly. "It was like they considered churches to be unsavory citizens, and not contributing to the public good." After submitting a letter of protest, the small group of pastors was joined by other institutions—interfaith organizations, other Christian churches, a synagogue, civic groups, and even a seminary—to form a broad-based coalition opposed to the proposed law. Lawyers and legal groups volunteered legal interpretations. The pastors researched the zoning code and found that special-use permits were required only of groups that might have "potential adverse impacts" on the city.[5] They felt that the real value of congregations was being misunderstood. The Reverend Dennis testified before the council that houses of worship in Evanston added value to the city rather than having a "negative, cumulative effect.... They are anchors in the community, making it stronger, more welcoming, more peaceful and more viable.... They have more value than can be quantified." His church, Second Baptist of Evanston, is now the largest African American church on the North Shore of Chicago. Like so many thriving congregations, it had humble beginnings; freed slaves had started worshipping on the second floor of the post office. Now, members travel into the city from as far away as Wisconsin, and end up contributing to the local economy by paying for parking and eating in local restaurants. "We have to be more proactive now, telling our story and telling the story of the smaller churches."

Through the efforts of the Evanston Pastors' Fellowship and their allies, the proposed ordinance was defeated, 7–2 after they had threatened legal action, citing violations of the federal Religious Land Use and Institutionalized Persons Act of 2000.[6] The coalition did make a small concession: new religious groups wanting to locate in two particular areas of Evanston would have to get a permit. But if they are denied, the city will have to demonstrate just cause and enable them to relocate in another part of the city.

Evanston is a specific and very public example of struggles over land use, but the perception that economic development and religious development conflict (and are even antithetical) is far from unique. At the root of the conflict are differing understandings of community value: what is best for a community's viability? Does the presence of a commercial strip filled with chain stores necessarily mean that a community is being strengthened? Does a district with a number of religious congregations indicate the decline of that community? How is social value understood? Are tax revenues and real estate values the best measure? How can the social value of communities of faith be assessed and then factored into larger questions of the viability of urban neighborhoods?

The measurement of social value is tricky. How can the provision of much-needed encouragement to a young person struggling in school or to an older person without a job be assessed? How can the neighborhood benefit of a refurbished storefront property be quantified? How can the loss of potential business because of the presence of storefront churches be calculated? How can the social capital generated in communities of faith be evaluated in terms of their contribution to making streets safer, children healthier, and adults less discouraged? The Reverend Dennis was frustrated in trying to communicate such intangibles to government officials used to dealing with cost-benefit analyses. He, like many clergy, had a different understanding of *social* costs and benefits.

If the real contributions of communities of faith are to be appreciated by those who would plan and govern our urban areas, they must first be identified, and, if possible, measured. If social value is documented, it can then be leveraged for public recognition and public resources.

Methodological Challenges in Measuring Social Value

In recent years scholars have shown renewed interest in urban religion. Much of their research has been ethnographic, and notable studies have contributed thick descriptions of the many expressions of religious faith in urban areas.[7] This has contributed greatly to the literature among scholars of religion but has not provided compelling arguments of social value for those who need to be convinced that communities of faith do indeed contribute to the quality of urban life in significant ways. To policymakers and philanthropic foundations concerned about the economic health of urban neighborhoods, these religious communities, which occupy tax-exempt properties, are assessed only through the seemingly crass cost-benefit formulae, the lingua franca of public policy. Like the Evanston City Council, they want quantitative evidence of social value.

In response, a few scholars have taken up the challenge to look quantitatively at the economic impact of congregations in urban ecologies. A well-known contribution in this regard has been the study conducted by Ram Cnaan and colleagues at the University of Pennsylvania. They studied the social value of outreach ministries of congregations by looking at replacement value of the service, that is, what it would cost to replace the human services or programs if the congregation were not there. By putting dollar values on staff and volunteer hours, use of space, utilities, and in-kind contributions, as well as the financial contributions of the congregation itself, they were able to calculate the value of each congregation's social ministry programs. They concluded that the average congregation in their sample of seven cities and one small town contributed $184,000 worth of social services per year.[8] This is a number that congregations can literally take to the bank.

But contribution to the social good through outreach programs is only one dimension of a congregation's impact on the quality of life in an urban context. Recently, Partners for Sacred Places, which sponsored Cnaan's study, took on the challenge. This organization, which defines itself as "the only national advocate and resource for the sound stewardship and active community use of America's older religious properties," developed a calculation of what they call the "halo effect" of congregational presence in communities. The goal is admirable: to be able to present communities of faith as viable agents in the urban ecology, contributing to the public good in significant and measurable ways. But quantifying the myriad ways—often subtle and hidden—that congregations contribute to the social good is a formidable task, which they readily acknowledged.[9]

Following up on an earlier, more conceptual, article introducing the possibility of valuation of the ministries of urban congregations,[10] Partners then tested the approach in a unique pilot study with 12 congregations in Philadelphia. The study is preliminary but ambitious: "The challenge is to assess the value of outcomes such as happiness, rehabilitation, clean air, obeying the law, parenting, neighborhood pride and family reunification, to name a few, and assign them with an appropriate dollar figure."[11] The sample size was small and unrepresentative—only 12 congregations were selected in Philadelphia. Despite the religious and geographical diversity represented, all were stable congregations, housed in historic buildings, and had established relationships with Partners for Sacred Places.

The task of translating the value of the intangibles of religious presence in a community into dollars and cents is indeed challenging, not only in terms of methodology. Even if it is possible, such valuation can also rub us the wrong way: do we really *want* to attach a price tag to "the power of prayer," the impact of pastoral counseling, or the gift of hospitality? Lead researcher Ram Cnaan admits that many will find the approach of attempting to quantify all aspects of a congregation's presence and activity in economic terms "weird."

For example, an important contribution of many congregations to urban neighborhoods—known by neighbors but not recognized by researchers—is green space. In neighborhoods where trees are few and play areas scarce, many congregations have cemeteries, urban gardens, yards, and play spaces. All of these can, and should, be counted. But how do we measure the value of a cemetery? In oxygen produced? Do cemeteries produce a sense of peace among a stressed population (calculated as hours of therapy)? How might the negative impact be factored in, such as when burial grounds become havens for drug dealers? Certainly if a congregation builds a basketball court, people will come—young men who sometimes play into the wee hours of the morning. Beyond counting the number of people who use the court, how can the important value of physical fitness, socialization, self-esteem, and perhaps reduction in attraction to criminal activity be measured in economic terms? Should it be? Should not narrative descriptions of individual transformation suffice in eliciting civic support for a congregation? Arguably, as communities of faith will need to justify their occupation of non-taxed real estate to local government, private developers, or potential funders, then the use of the terms of market value might be appropriate.

The Partners study courageously stepped in where other researchers have not, identifying multiple ways congregations contribute to the common good, many of which have been unrecognized. They then drew on econometric measures of social value, some standard and some they developed. The goal was to get to a final number, a dollar figure, signifying the economic value of a congregation to its context. For policymakers and potential funders, this would provide the basis of a compelling argument for a congregation's worth and their need to support it.

Researchers selected 54 variables in areas including physical resources (green spaces, parking lots, recreation spaces, even trees), programs (space use and volunteer hours), capital (budgets, building improvements), the impact on individuals (rehabilitation, suicide prevention, divorce prevention, etc.), impacts on community (crime rates and real estate values), and bringing people to the neighborhood (out-of-town members, visitors, participants in special events, etc.). Although space does not allow a detailed description of how they calculated each variable, some examples give an idea of their methodological approach.

Congregations generate social capital, both "bonding" and "bridging,"[12] which has economic consequences. That is, as members of congregations interact among themselves (bonding) and develop active relationships with those beyond their walls (bridging) in so doing, they generate economic activity as well. An example of this is that many city churches attract visitors because of their historic value or through annual reunions of past members and friends. Earlier studies have found reunions to be a particular practice in African American congregations (Grant, 2005; Sutton, 2004). Practices can vary widely, as do personal resources, but visitors spend money, contributing to the local economy. But how could the value of this practice be captured and quantified? Clergy in this study were asked how many members regularly came in from outside the neighborhood for worship, and then how much they might spend per visit—an estimate. A sample of commuting members was also asked the same question. Research in tourism was also consulted for measurements of spending for day and overnight visitors for special events. A final estimate of $15 per visit for out-of-town members was used in the calculation. Then, 11 special events were identified—those that would draw out-of-town visitors for an overnight stay.[13] After determining how many events and participants the houses of worship had hosted, and drawing from estimates used by government and tourism sources, a "conservative" estimate of $52.50 for each overnight guest (plus the daily expense estimate) was calculated, resulting in estimates of how much the out-of-town visitors, including commuting members, attracted by these 12 congregations were contributing to the local economy.

Some of the other variables used in calculating the value of an urban faith community were less obvious. For example, the contribution of the trees on religious properties was measured. Trees were counted and their market value was estimated. The researchers measured the circumference of the trunks and ran the data through the iTree software. This accessible public resource was developed by the USDA Forest Service specifically to "quantify and put

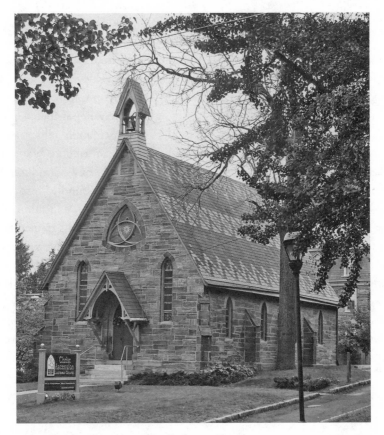

FIGURE 3.1 Tree at Christ Ascension Lutheran Church.

a dollar value on the street trees' annual environmental and aesthetic benefits," including how trees capture carbon and reduce pollution, manage
storm water runoff, contribute to real estate value, and yes, generate oxygen.[14]
Within their sample, the mean dollar value of trees on the property of each
house of worship was $2,749.91, with one particularly wooded church prop-
erty contributing $17,511 of value to its local urban ecosystem.

   Not all the variables proved to be so easily measurable. For example, how
do you calculate the value of "teaching youth civic behavior"? After drawing
on earlier estimates of the benefits of keeping high-risk youth out of a lifetime
of crime and substance abuse, researchers took into account other influences
on young people as well as the fact that most of their congregations were not
serving the high-risk population.[15] They then assigned a value of $2,500 per

There is a value to religious services

youth per year to those involved in church programs. This estimate could be too high, too low, or right on target; but the attempt to put a dollar value on human experience reflects the challenges and the fuzziness of such efforts.

After calculating all 54 variables of the economic value of congregations, from the most obvious economic contributions (programs provided, capital improvement expenditures) to the least tangible (the value of "people finding relationships and networks," for example, $1,200 per family), the Partners study concluded that these 12 communities of faith contribute a whopping $52 million to the common good each year, or a mean of $4.3 million per congregation. The economized social contributions were bundled into three major areas: direct spending (hiring, subcontracting, etc.), education (day care, parochial schools), and "catalytic impacts" (contributions to quality of life through open space, attracting people and businesses, individual transformation, community development, and safety net services). Although this study did not have a representative sample of urban congregations by a long shot, the valuation process is certainly one that could benefit groups like the Evanston Clergy Fellowship as they make a case for the social value of houses of worship in a community. While the Partners for Sacred Places approach will surely generate criticism, it at least attempts to address the question of contributions to the common good that communities of faith make that remain generally unrecognized.

Religious Presence in the Urban Ecology: The View from the Avenue

Undeniably, communities of faith contribute to the social well-being of individuals, neighborhoods, and cities in ways that should be identified and publicly appreciated. Many of these contributions cannot be reduced to a dollar figure. That said, it is important to measure what can be measured, engage in ethnographic research to tease out the nuances of how social value gets generated, and to provide evidence, both quantitative and qualitative, of religious contribution to the common good. Sometimes simple frequencies are compelling data in themselves, such as the number of feeding programs provided by congregations. This quantitative datum gives clues of where ethnographic work needs to be done: who is coming to the soup kitchen, and what are the personal benefits and social connections created? These are important data best captured by observing and listening. This is especially true in smaller congregations, not represented in the Partners study, and with more subtle ways of being present in a community.

This methodological question is at the core of *Faith on the Avenue*. There is a quantitative component to the study in the form of a survey, which gathered basic data about congregations: denomination, membership and attendance, demographics, staffing, budget, programming, building information. Informants were also asked about economic activity (local businesses patronized, renovation costs, etc.) and the impact of pastoral ministry (people who stopped using drugs, found jobs, stayed out of prison, or avoided suicide because of the ministry of the congregation). Even face-to-face interviews only begin to tell the story of the impact of congregational presence in a neighborhood.

I employed the combination of quantitative and qualitative research methods to pursue the same questions of the Partners study: how are faith communities engaged with the urban ecology? As they are present and have agency within their context, how exactly are they contributing value? In what ways are neighborhoods impacted by them—or not?

To begin this process, survey interviews were conducted with leaders of 43 of the 108 congregations recorded over the course of the study. The census of congregations at any one time ranged from 83 to 96 between 2003 to 2011, as some congregations have come and gone. It might appear as if there is a great deal of religious change on the street, but the *presence* of faith groups is actually remarkably stable. The historical churches described earlier serve as anchors in the changing street life. Almost one third of congregations on the Avenue were founded before 1900 and have remained for generations. Over half of the congregations were founded in the second half of the 20th century (1951–1999), a relative boom after minimal new religious starts in the first half of the century. A small percentage of congregations (5%) have been established since 2000.

The distribution of religious groupings has remained consistent over the course of the study. In 2011, there were 9 congregations affiliated with the Historic Black Denominations; 12 in the denominations which have traditionally been designated as Mainline Protestant, 3 Peace Churches, 4 Latino congregations, 5 congregations in "other religions," and 8 groups listed as "other Christian" because they could not be identified with the other categories.[16] In addition, half of the sample (40) were independent congregations, and predominantly African American. Recent research has focused on the rapid growth of independent, nondenominational churches nationally, now the third largest religious group after the Roman Catholic Church and the Southern Baptist Convention.[17] Although it is difficult to pin down an exact number and percentage in the national data, independent churches are predominantly found in metropolitan areas, with the New York-New Jersey-Philadelphia corridor having a heavy concentration.

Germantown Avenue was divided into six sections for purposes of analysis. Boundaries were delineated to keep the distribution of congregations as even as possible while reflecting neighborhood identity.[18] The six sections—Kensington, Fair Hill, Hunting Park, Germantown, Mt. Airy, and Chestnut Hill—are natural designations that are bounded by major thoroughfares, anchored by commercial strips and, in most cases, a shared sense of identity. (Hunting Park actually incorporates a smaller neighborhood, Nicetown, as well.) Kensington has the least density of commercial activity, with some

FIGURE 3.2 Sections of Germantown Avenue with congregations indicated.

small businesses interspersed among row homes and empty lots. Residents in this section of Germantown Avenue do not have a clear sense of neighborhood identity or pride, often just referring to their area generically as "North Philadelphia." This is in contrast with what one finds moving up the Avenue, through the more commercially active and increasingly affluent sections, which have a stronger sense of place.

The religious presence varies by section, as can be seen in Figure 3.3. The Mainline Protestant and Peace church congregations are clustered at the northern end of the Avenue, in the Germantown, Mt. Airy, and Chestnut Hill sections. Similarly, the Latino congregations are found only in Kensington and Fair Hill. Those identified with African American traditions, both Historic Black Church denominations and independents, are represented up and down the Avenue, except for Chestnut Hill, where they are entirely absent. Germantown has a few more of the Historic Black congregations, and Hunting Park has none, but does have many more independent Black Protestants.

Churches that don't fall into any of these categories are found in all sections except for Hunting Park. The three mega-churches are distributed in three different, though contiguous, sections: Hunting Park, Germantown,

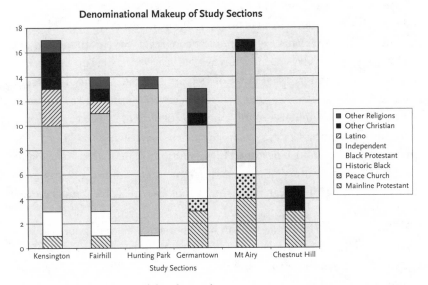

FIGURE 3.3 Denominational distribution by sections.

and Mt. Airy. There are also three non-congregational religious institutions: the Lutheran Theological Seminary and the Neighborhood Interfaith Movement,[19] both located in Mt. Airy, and the Sisters of St. Joseph based at Chestnut Hill College. The Fair Hill Burial Ground is a quasi-religious institution: a non-profit preservation and programmatic group with deep connections to the Society of Friends (Quakers). Although these institutions have not been included in the census of congregations, they each have a significant and growing engagement with the urban context. All four of these religious institutions have provided educational and social service programs that have had citywide and regional appeal as well as local impact in the immediate urban ecology.

The distribution of the religious traditions reflects the racial and socioeconomic demographics of their sections of the Avenue. These congregational clusters draw members from, and participate in, the local ecology, contributing to the construction of local cultures and community identity. Much like the smaller independent congregations densely packed in the impoverished section of Boston in Omar McRoberts's study[20] and the "high status congregations" clustered in the more affluent and low-density neighborhood described in Elfriede Wedam's research,[21] the communities of faith in these six religious districts navigate shared urban space. Through differentiation and competition they offer a diversity of worship options within the districts.

Along with geographical distribution, other differences between the denominational groups are evident. Among those surveyed, Peace churches and Mainline Protestants were the oldest congregations (mean age: 311 and 166 years, respectively). Latino churches were the youngsters on the Avenue, with an average congregational age of 18 years. African American congregations were older (40 years) but had not been on Germantown Avenue as long as the other religious groups, who preceded them by 20 years, on average. The older congregations were clustered in Germantown (163 years), Mt. Airy (136.4), and Chestnut Hill (142.8), and an analysis of variance confirms that they are significantly different in age from those congregations in Kensington (mean age: 21.4 years), Fairhill (21.2), and Hunting Park (59.2). [22]

There was also a lot of variation in size among the denominational groups, as shown in Table 3.1. The mean numbers can be inflated by the presence of mega-churches, so a more accurate reading is at the median point of congregation sizes along the distribution.

Table 3.1 Congregational age and membership size by religious tradition

| | Grouped Religion | | | | | | |
	Mainline Protestant	Peace Church	Historic Black	Independent Black Protestant	Latino	Other Christian	Other Religions
Mean Age of Congregation	166	311	30	40	18	59	75
Mean Membership	263	195	127	306	53	560	35
Median Membership	171	100	70	80	52	30	65

Attendance fluctuates in tandem with size of membership. On Germantown Avenue, the median attendance was 50 worshippers in 2009. If the largest congregations are taken out and only those whose attendance is less than 500 are included, median attendance is 70. This is a more accurate prediction of what is seen in weekend worship in most of the congregations on the Avenue. National data show that overall worship attendance was declining in the first decade of the millennium, dropping from a median number of weekend worshippers of 130 in 2000 to 108 in 2010, across denominational and racial/ethnic lines.[23] Germantown Avenue's preponderance of small independent churches accounts for the smaller attendance figure. Because this is not a longer longitudinal study, it cannot be said for certain whether these congregations are shrinking, growing, or holding their own. In conversations, however, clergy in the study expressed concern that they had seen their numbers decline since 2008 which is reflective of national trends.

As the fortunes of neighborhoods along the Avenue vary greatly, so do congregations' budgets. It comes as no surprise that when asked about the range of their annual budgets, congregations in Kensington and Fairhill were more likely to report annual budgets of $50,000 or less; those farther up the Avenue clustered in the $100,000–$200,000 range, with several reporting more than that.[24] This predictably correlated with size of congregation as well: 60% of those with 50 members or fewer had the smallest budgets (<$50,000). More people means more money—and both could be found "moving up" the Avenue.

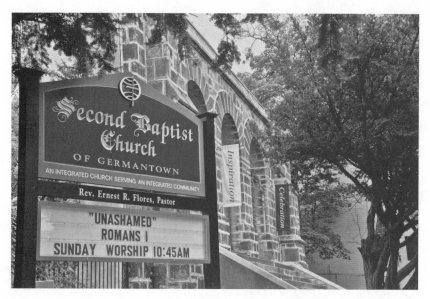

FIGURE 3.4 Second Baptist Church, one of the Mainline Protestant Churches on the Avenue.

FIGURE 3.5 Taylor Memorial Baptist, an independent church founded in 1950.

Such dramatic patterns of stratification are present on one city street (granted, a long one). However, there some ways that the similarities across tradition and section defied prediction and departed from national trends. The maps in the first chapter tell a story of growing poverty and continuing racial segregation; as middle-class people continued to move out of the city, the poor became increasingly consolidated geographically. The patterns of segregation in the United States and the well-documented trend of immigrants to worship in ethnic-specific congregations have continued to support Martin Luther King Jr.'s well-known observation that "11 o'clock Sunday morning is the most segregated hour in America." [25] That comment inspired much soul-searching in white religious traditions, commitments toward diversification based on sacred mandates, and research by social scientists. The results have been discouraging for those hoping that the diversity of peoples of God would be reflective of the increasing polychromatic profile of society. Michael Emerson and Christian Smith (2000) found that in 90% of all congregations in the United States, the membership is at least 90% or more of one race. Along the Avenue, however, such monocultural congregations are far less prevalent: "only" two thirds (65.9%) reported having 90% or more from one racial/ethnic group. This does not indicate a dramatic departure from the national norm, as 84.1% of the congregations still have 70% or more of one group. Still, congregations on Germantown Avenue are not as solidly segregated as elsewhere.

Congregations are voluntary associations and increasingly so. Americans are not as religiously defined by habit and loyalty as they once were; rather, they choose from the options in the religious marketplace whether or where they want to worship. The dynamics of religious segregation are largely dependent on mobility; therefore, the closest congregation is not necessarily the assumptive choice. With the outmigration of middle-class folks to the suburbs, it could be expected that some churches—Mainline Protestant, Historic Black—would have higher numbers commuting in from outside the city while others would draw members from the local context (Latino, Independent Black). The findings on Germantown Avenue offer a different picture of proximity. The survey asked whether members came from the near neighborhood (within 10 blocks), within the city (beyond 10 blocks), outside of the city limits (contiguous suburbs), or outside the region (non-contiguous suburbs). Except for Latino congregations, which are far more likely to draw from the immediate context, and the Peace churches (Mennonite, Quaker, *travel*

Brethren), which had significantly more members living outside the region, there was no significant variation among the other groups in terms of proximity. About one third of members of all the Christian groups and in all sections lived within 10 blocks of their house of worship; about half came from farther away, yet in the city. Mainline Protestants did have more commuters from the suburbs, but the difference was not significant. For who is attending (as opposed to members), the percentage drawn from the 10-block area increased when both religious groups and geographic sections were considered, but the increase was not significant. In other words, in these congregations, a solid base of one third of their followers could walk to worship.

These data are somewhat different from those of earlier studies based on the Philadelphia Congregations Census, with its much larger sample of 1,393 (Sinha, Hillier, Cnaan, and McGrew, 2007). Using the 10-block radius as a measure of close proximity, these researchers identified those congregations with 50% or more of attenders living within that area as "resident congregations." In that study, 42% of the sample qualified. In my study, the proportion was lower (27%), perhaps due to the fact that there are no Catholic churches or traditional synagogues on Germantown Avenue—two traditions that draw higher numbers of members who walk to worship. Further, in the Sinha et al. study, predominantly white communities of faith were more likely to be resident congregations, but that is not so here; in the Avenue study, 28% of Independent and Historic Black churches were considered resident congregations and just 15% of the predominantly white Mainline Protestant and Peace churches were. The resident congregations in my study were much more likely to be congregations with modest budgets in poorer neighborhoods. The earlier study found that resident congregations were located in neighborhoods that were more stable, as measured by home ownership and population gains. This was a correlation, however, and could not explain causality—that is, did the presence of neighborhood stability attract congregation members or did the congregations create it? The direction of the interaction was not clear.

Congregation-Based Social Ministries

One way that congregations contribute to the stability of a neighborhood is through their social ministry programs. These are defined as formalized programs designed to benefit those outside the congregation. Therefore, evangelism programs are not counted. Flea markets offer affordable items to a community but also generate revenue for a church or mosque and help them pay the bills, so they were not counted either. Fee-based programs, such as parochial schools, do not qualify as social ministries in this study, despite the social good they contribute. Even so, along the Avenue, communities of faith altruistically serve their neighborhoods though a wide variety of programs. Congregations surveyed (N = 44) reported 126 different organized outreach programs for their neighbors.

As with previous studies (Chaves, 2004; Cnaan, 2002; Woolever and Bruce, 2002, 2010), food programs are the most prevalent, with over half of the congregations participating in one or more feeding programs. As hunger began to spike in Philadelphia, more and more neighbors were showing up on the doorsteps of houses of worship. St. Michael's Lutheran Church, for example, began a "Holy Hotdogs" program during the summer of 2009 to help with the food insecurity created when school is not in session.[26] It was quickly clear that far more was needed than hotdogs, so by October it became "Holy Hot Dish." They linked with a suburban congregation to help with food preparation and began serving a hot meal weekly to over 100 people. Pastor Andrena Ingram estimates that in 2010, 1,537 meals were served by her small congregation; that increased to 4,465 meals per year by 2011. At another church farther down the Avenue, an older woman described their experience, "We opened our food pantry on Thursday mornings, basically with food we collected from the congregation. But more and more people started coming and we would run out of food by 11 o'clock and have to turn people away. It broke my heart." Like many congregations they tapped into larger non-profits to help stock the shelves and fill the grocery bags as the need continued to increase. Melanie DeBouse, pastor of Evangel Chapel and Children's Mission, located in a poor corner of Fairhill, has a kitchen and storage rooms stocked by Philabundance and SHARE, two local food distribution non-profits. "We do get some contributions (from individuals)," she laments, "but they're few and far between.... I live by faith."

Beyond soup kitchens and food pantries, congregations address hunger in a number of ways: collecting food from the community, having healthy-dinner cooking classes, participating in the "Walk against Hunger," making meals for shelters, providing indoor dining for elders, serving meals outdoors for homeless people, and having fundraisers for food programs. An important function of the standard summer program (often called "Daily Vacation Bible School")

FIGURE 3.6 St. Michael's Lutheran Church, a historic church with a growing food program.

fight hunger

is providing a meal (or two) for neighborhood children. The Archdiocese of Philadelphia has a summer program that provides approximately a million meals to school children at 380 sites throughout the city. Five of the congregations on the Avenue are food distribution sites—two Mainline Protestant and three independent black churches in the Germantown, Mt. Airy, and Fairhill sections. Even if a congregation does not have its own feeding program, it is not unusual in any of the congregations nowadays to see groceries brought to the altar during the offering. A generation ago, providing Thanksgiving turkeys for "the needy" who were served by the 25 soup kitchens and food pantries in Philadelphia was likely the extent of a congregation's food ministry. Today, it is estimated that the city has more than 800 charitable cupboards and soup kitchens—almost all of them in faith communities and staffed by volunteers. The number of Philadelphians dependent on these local resources tripled between 2006 and 2011 (Citysoup, 2012). The congregations along the Avenue—of all sizes, traditions, neighborhoods, and budgets— are very much on the front lines of the city's food crisis.

Collecting and providing clothing and recreation opportunities are the second and third most prevalent outreach programs, whether through organized programs or informal connections. The congregations on the Avenue reflect a national trend documented by the Congregational Life Survey, which showed an increase in the number of congregations that provided "emergency relief or material assistance (food, clothes for the needy)" between 2001 and 2008[27] (Woolever and Bruce, 2002, 2010).

Beyond providing for the immediate needs of food and clothing during a period of economic downturn, the congregations sampled were also highly involved in health care ministries. Almost one in four had, in the last year, been involved in a program that addressed the health needs of underserved communities. Again, congregations had moved beyond sponsoring the occasional blood drive to organizing health fairs, which are increasingly popular and necessary. Live jazz, drill team performances, Zumba demonstrations, barbecue, and face painting create a festive environment where the very serious business of blood pressure and diabetes screening, eye and dental exams, and testing for breast and prostate cancer as well as HIV can be conducted in communities where many are uninsured. Further, the fairs provide opportunities for new coalitions and alliances to be formed across religious and racial lines and with neighborhood health services. Four churches and a mosque in the Germantown district, along with a growing variety of health and social service organizations, have organized one such fair for five years running. Co-chaired by an Episcopalian laywoman and a Muslim leader, the annual event has been held at Vernon Park, a greenspace rich in history. On a sweltering summer day, participants from this unlikely coalition of organizations attracted 500 people from the community to make a party out of basic health care screening on the familiar green where candidate Barack Obama had spoken about universal health care. Prior to the passage of the Affordable Care Act, many without access to health care found their only hope in events like this one. After one year's event, Co-chairperson Hildegarde Freeman said, "Nine people were tested (for HIV/AIDS) that day. I pray we saved a life."

Mega-churches are at an advantage here as they do not need to form coalitions; they can sponsor their own health events. New Covenant Church sponsors both men's and women's health fairs each year on their large campus. In 2011, 75 senior citizens took advantage of the free flu shots they offered. Triumph Baptist Church has been sponsoring a health fair annually for a decade. In 2012 it was co-sponsored with the DeSean Jackson Foundation and had a focus on pancreatic cancer. In the Kids' Corner, children got identification cards and were fingerprinted as well as playing games. Triumph includes regular health care updates on its website with links to the Temple

serious problems

FIGURE 3.7 Enjoying a health fair in Germantown.

University Health System. Both of these large churches have made health a priority in their communities.

In the area of HIV/AIDS, Philadelphia congregations are beginning to make a dramatic contribution. After years of ignoring HIV/AIDS with silence, the black churches of Philadelphia began to engage the epidemic head-on in 2009–2010 through citywide events that inspired local clergy to speak out. Philadelphia FIGHT, an AIDS education, service, and advocacy organization, linked with the faith communities to sponsor interfaith prayer breakfasts and an AIDS summit. Here, challenging information was shared about the virus, which disproportionately affects the African American community. Although infection rates had been linked to drug use (through needle sharing), now the most frequent cause is sex between men. This challenges black churches further, since they have historically considered homosexuality, as well as illegal drug use, to be sinful.[28] Overcoming the stigma and long-held beliefs and moral positions in the interest of saving lives, African American churches have been on the forefront of efforts to get everyone tested, beginning with the pastor.[29] Five of the churches on the Avenue have had public testing events, including during worship—many were surprised when Bishop C. Milton Grannum of New Covenant Church was the first to be tested in front of his largely professional-class congregation.

There are many other types of outreach programs based in the churches along the Avenue—fifteen in all. As well as food, clothing, recreation, and health, congregations are serving their communities through housing and economic development projects, child care, visitation of homebound people in the neighborhood, counseling and rehabilitation services, and programs focused on arts, peace, and environmental care. An emerging area of concern is in prison programming. Five of the churches in the sample have a formalized prison ministry—three of them in Fairhill, one in Kensington, and one in Germantown. All are small, independent churches, but they support the families of prisoners, visit prisoners themselves, and help with their re-entry into society. One congregation works with an outside group but all are staffed by volunteers.

Which congregations are involved in sponsoring social ministries is predictable in many ways. The larger congregations in Chestnut Hill have the highest number of programs, with an average of 6.4 per church. At the other end of the Avenue, the smaller congregations in the Kensington section have the fewest (2.6). Despite the gap, the difference among the sections was not significant. Significant variation appears when budget groups are compared (P = .04). Not surprisingly, those with the largest budgets could afford the most programs: those with budgets of $500,000 to $1,000,000 had 7.6 programs; those with over $1 million had 8. There was one budget group that interrupted the trend: congregations reporting budgets between $200,000 and $500,000 only had 2.8 programs, less than the third of sampled churches with budgets between $50,000 to $200,000, which had more than 4 programs. The groups with the lowest budgets (<$50,000) had 2.4. It seems that the "middle class" in this sample (those in the $200,000–$500,000 budget range) were not directing their dollars to those outside their walls but were focusing on shoring up those walls and taking care of their members. A closer analysis of these better-resourced congregations with fewer programs shows that they are not hard-hearted but there are particular factors at work: some are in old buildings whose upkeep consumes a big share of their budgets; several have theologies that lead them to take care of their own first and provide needed food, addiction services, and emergency support to members; two were in the process of a transition in leadership—new clergy who had inherited inwardly focused congregations but were now in the process of becoming more community-oriented. Religious tradition did make a difference, however. Mainline Protestants, whose congregations had made a very intentional choice to stay in the city when many of their co-religionists were moving to the suburbs, had the highest number of social ministry programs (7.8). The age of a congregation had a significantly positive relationship to the number of programs ($r = .32$, $P = .04$). That is to say, the older congregations that were able to maintain their buildings were able to also invest in outreach programs for less-advantaged communities. Newer ministries with fewer people and resources felt the need to focus energy on building up the congregation. Programs designed for non-members were a luxury they could not afford.

However, formalized programming is only one way that congregations impact their communities. There are myriad ways that congregations serve informally—and, to outsiders, invisibly.

An old woman named Agnes shuffled up to the front of Jesus Is the Way Church on the corner of Germantown and Slocam. She peeked inside and then around the corner to see if Pastor Jackie Morrow's familiar blue van was there. Even though Pastor Jackie said that she is at church "all the time," at that moment she was out with some of the children from the summer program. The woman waited a few minutes before walking away, but she'll be back. "The pastor helps me a lot," Agnes says.

A former schoolteacher, Pastor Jackie is a middle-aged woman who exudes tremendous energy. On the second floor of the brick building originally built as a residence, she runs a Christian school for 10 students from Pre-K through 6th grade. She has an M.Ed. in computer science and has been entrepreneurial in getting donations of school supplies and the electronic resources it will take to close the digital divide for African American schoolchildren. In this one-room school, Pastor Jackie and two other volunteer teachers give individual attention to students learning math, reading through phonics, and the Bible. Her mother, who has Alzheimer's, sits quietly in the classroom as well,

FIGURE 3.8 Pastor Jackie Morrow, Founding Pastor of Jesus Is the Way Church.

occasionally squeezing someone's hand and offering them God's blessing. Pastor Jackie also leads a small flock that meets downstairs, runs a summer program each year for 30 children, and is an ongoing presence in the community. At the prayer table on the sidewalk outside, anyone can write down their prayer requests to be taken to the daily prayer meetings. Besides prayers, Pastor Jackie gives out bus tokens and food to anyone in need who stops by. She makes the small yard out back available to neighbors for their barbecues and for young men to play basketball. Neighbors like Agnes know her as someone who can help them out if they need a hand-up, a listening ear, or a place to hold a funeral. Two things are clear: the non-programmatic presence of Jesus Is the Way Church is an important source of care and connection in its context, but few outside the immediate neighborhood know about it.

Congregations along the Avenue have such agency in their immediate contexts, although it is difficult to document by counting programs or calculating value. Congregational informants who were interviewed discussed how—through informal encounters in their neighborhoods—individuals in crisis who had fallen through the safety net had been helped. One third knew of individuals who had been helped to kick a drug addiction through the congregation. Beyond organized prison ministries, one third of congregations could identify individuals they had helped to stay out of prison. Thirty six percent could name people who had found jobs through the informal network of the congregation—the median number of jobs found was five.

Pastor Melanie DeBouse is an educator by training and temperament. She serves in Fairhill, in a section with the lowest educational attainment in the city—less than 10% of adults have college degrees (Pew, 2012). When her six-year-old granddaughter has an idea she tells her, "Kiss your brain!" and they both kiss their hands and touch her forehead. As pastor to a small congregation of people who are struggling to make it, she is helping people of all ages to kiss their brains. She teaches a rigorous curriculum in her Bible study group, challenging her students to transcend their sense of limitation:

> Most of these guys are so below par academically. In the beginning they would say "Oh, I can't read today. I forgot my glasses." So I went out to the dollar store and got a bunch of reading glasses. "Try these!" Then I purchased Bibles with larger fonts. But I had already started to connect the dots…they couldn't read. But what has happened over the last year is that their reading has gotten better. And that's a God thing!

Some of the informal outreach that occurs on the Avenue not only enriches lives, it can save them. When asked whether through the ministry of the congregation a suicide had been prevented (a difficult thing to know), one third of the informants had moving stories of lives saved.[30] Pastor Jackie of Jesus Is the Way recalled a recent pastoral encounter with a stranger who had contacted the church and was contemplating suicide. The person had gone to the Yellow Pages and looked up "Jesus." She went to meet him and was able to help him through his hour of despair. Another preacher, a large African American man with a warm smile, became quiet and tears filled his eyes. "I tried…but I couldn't prevent it…" he choked out. He was able, however, to conduct the funeral and console the family. Such a compassionate presence in his distressed context is, as they say, priceless.

Whether providing human services through organized programming or informally through their relationships with neighbors and the social connections to link people with resources, congregations on the Avenue play an essential role in their contexts. Earlier groundbreaking research had put a dollar figure on what religious institutions contribute to the common good through humanitarian outreach, and thus ease strain on municipal budgets (Cnaan, et al., 2002). But it is difficult to capture all the social good that congregations contribute daily. Despite the challenges of quantifying organized and informal acts of compassion, it is critical that they do not go unrecognized, especially now. As a result of the Great Recession of 2008 increased numbers of Americans, especially those in urban areas, were experiencing unemployment, hunger, poverty, and homelessness.[31] As social needs grew, state and municipal governments were collecting less tax revenue and so services for the poor were being cut. Many ended up knocking on the doors of the closest house of worship they could find and congregations responded as well as they could. This phenomenon was happening in all faith groups in all parts of the country, although Philadelphians were hit harder than most. As Pennsylvania unemployment rates moved from 5.3% to 8.9% between 2008 and 2010, and that of the United States from 5.8% to 9.6%, Philadelphia trended consistently higher, with the jobless rate going from 7.1% in 2008 to 11.5% two years later (Pew, 2011).

The problem was that congregations were experiencing their own challenges. National data show that the financial health of congregations was dropping significantly (FACT, 2010). In 2000, 31% of congregations of all traditions, sizes, and regions of the country reported that they were in "excellent financial health," but by 2010 only 14% could make that claim. The financial decline that had begun in the first half of the decade accelerated by twice the rate between 2006 and 2010. Not only were collection plates lighter because of smaller donations, but fewer people were putting in their tithes and offerings. The FACT study also documented what was alarming clergy by 2009: attendance was slipping. They concluded:

> Indeed, the prominence of mega-church images notwithstanding, more than 1 in 4 American congregations had fewer than 50 in worship in 2010, and just under half had fewer than 100. Overall, median weekend worship attendance of your typical congregation dropped from 130 to 108 during the decade according to the FACT surveys.

Fewer people with less money encountering increased demand for social services: this is not a hopeful equation. However, the national survey bore out what was observed on Germantown Avenue—people of faith did not stop helping their neighbors. Congregations did, in fact, tighten their belts, but researchers found no decline in social ministry programs as a result of the recession. Even when controlling for the size of congregations, they found there was no withdrawing from social outreach. The Great Recession took a "holy toll" on congregations in many ways, but helping out neighbors was not one of them (FACT, 2010a).

Impacting the Local Economy

As municipal governments look at their tax base, it is natural that they would turn their attention to houses of worship that, as observed earlier, do not pay taxes, generate much commercial activity, or hire a lot of people. Driving down Germantown Avenue on a weekday, many congregations appear shuttered, giving the impression that nothing is happening on these parcels of real estate. Appearances can be deceptive.

My survey found that congregations are active participants in the local economy in important, if sometimes hidden, ways. Overwhelmingly, congregations own their buildings. Those that acquired commercial property chose not to rent, not only because property was affordable for purchase but also because they wanted to be able to renovate and adapt the space for sacred purposes. Most (83%) had done some renovations and improvements on their building in the previous three years; the median amount invested was $25,000. Many of the improvements were quite substantial (including one at a Mainline Protestant church for $375,000—which is why I did not use the mean in reporting the data). Virtually all used a combination of volunteers from the congregation and local contractors. Three quarters of the congregations sampled had capital improvement plans for the coming three years, and one third had already purchased additional property. Generally, the additional properties (including lots as well as buildings) represented the dreams of expanded ministries.

Older buildings present a challenge in terms of maintenance, and at least two of the historic buildings will need major work in the next five years. But overall, the congregations keep their sacred places in good condition, which helps stabilize a neighborhood. An earlier study explored the relationship of religious buildings and neighborhood stability (Kinney and Winter, 2006).

FIGURE 3.9 New Bethel A.M.E. Church dreams of expanding their ministry.

The results might surprise some: when compared with freestanding churches and non-church establishments, storefront churches were surrounded (in a 125-foot radius) by the lowest levels of vacant land and the shortest duration of vacant buildings. The researchers concluded that

> storefront churches should not be overlooked as quiet but significant partners in neighborhood stability.... In localities where urban blight and decay threaten to overshadow efforts to create community, the mere presence of a religious place of worship may provide limited but notable relief from disinvestment and declining property values.

Well-maintained houses of worship, however humble or grand, can anchor a commercial district and attract businesses. These faith communities support businesses in tangible ways as well. As noted, congregations are likely to hire local contractors and skilled workers when engaging in renovations. Beyond that, congregations are consumers of services and all sampled on Germantown Avenue listed the local businesses they patronized: florists, bakeries, caterers, hardware stores, banks, rental supply companies, grocers, and the like. In addition, members gathered at local establishments after services and meetings for food and drink. One Baptist minister was such a regular at a local barbecue restaurant that he had worked it into his sermons and was proud to say that his picture was on the wall!

As they were out and about in the neighborhoods where the congregations were located, most informants (76%) felt that the property values around the house of worship had increased. Considering the neighborhood overall, 41% felt it had improved, compared to 24% who perceived it as deteriorating. Further, a greater proportion felt that crime had decreased (41%) than thought it had gotten worse. More also reported that they had seen an increase in construction around their house of worship in recent years (47%). These perceptions did not always correspond to what data would show, but they indicate that congregation members have a positive sense of their context.

Those with more space let the community in as well, making space available (for free or at a discounted rate) to outside groups for events, meetings, and educational and cultural programs. Smaller spaces are used by congregations for their own social programs but larger churches host as many as 12 to 15 groups regularly. Mega-churches are at an advantage here, since they are often in new, large buildings. Up the Avenue in Mt. Airy, New Covenant is located on the sweeping campus of the old Pennsylvania School for the Deaf.

The real estate held by the church is impressive: there are 16 buildings on the pastoral, 42-acre campus. This enables them to house four schools (a public charter school, a pre-school, Waldorf school, as well as their own parochial

FIGURE 3.10 New Covenant's sanctuary space at the back of its expansive campus.

school, Covenant Academy). Together with the state Department of Aging, they developed a 56-unit senior housing facility. They provide space for the Business Center, which they consider a ministry of the church, as well as other non-profit tenants. Besides the church, which draws 2,000 participants each week from around the region, New Covenant has three other incorporated entities under its umbrella—a CDC (Community Development Corporation), an educational organization, and the land management corporation. Relations with the near neighbors became rocky when they considered developing a shelter for homeless families. After an energetic public meeting at the Lutheran Seminary across the street, they did back away from that endeavor. However, New Covenant continues to have community-wide events including health fairs, 4th of July celebrations (with fireworks), and outdoor concerts, and provides space for youth sports. A middle-aged woman who has been a member for more than 20 years described their relationship with "the great lawn." "When we first came to this campus, we couldn't believe it. Look what God has done! And we have to give back, we have to share it with the community."

FIGURE 3.11 Bishop Grannum dedicates a baby at New Covenant Church.

Whether a house of worship makes space available for a single Alcoholics Anonymous group or community meeting, or becomes a major provider of space, it can come to function as a community center—this adds value to the neighborhood but it also adds wear and tear to what can be a well-worn building to begin with.[32]

Beyond contributing to the local economy by spending dollars and offering space, congregations have been creative about their support of business development. Several congregations directly invest in local small businesses. This is particularly true of the Germantown Masjid. Muslims at the Germantown mosque developed a strategy for improving the local economy in their immediate context. Sitting in his small office in the used car dealership he owns, Brother Saadiq of the Germantown Masjid explained how the mosque had approached the development of the neighborhood:

Once you put a stake in the ground you need to secure the perimeter. So you have to look at the area where you're at. You need to look at existing conditions of the area and then you have to look at quality of life and ask what would be the things that would add to the quality of life? What would be the things that would take away from the quality of life for the people who live in that environment? We talk about revitalization…in conjunction with safety and security. So we had a program called The Nine Block Radius. We looked at the components that needed to be there for daily life…like food, Halal food. Then we needed a barber shop. And we needed places where we could buy clothing…. The masjid invested in these businesses…but when you look at these things, like the senior housing, it's not just for Muslims. Its quality of life issues are to uplift everyone. One thing we have to be very clear about is that the majority of people [impacted] are not Muslims. But they are from our tribe. They are our mothers, our aunts, our uncles, our nieces, our neighbors…at the end of the day there has to be love and compassion.

This sense of responsibility for a defined geographic area is reminiscent of the Catholic parish or the way some Protestant churches discuss contributing to a healthy neighborhood through "wholistic ministry." But here the mosques are engaging the local ecology not just by providing ministries of compassion (such as the provision of food, clothing, or shelter) but also by enabling business startups. In so doing, they are not only making important services available and improving the quality of life in a neighborhood; the new commercial ventures contribute to the local economy. Starting a small business is risky for an entrepreneur. But in a development strategy like "The Nine Block Radius" there are a number of built-in advantages when generated by a community of faith. Like a multiple-service mega-church, which can offer a variety of needed services in one location, the members of Germantown Masjid can come to prayers, pick up food for dinner, get a haircut, or shop for clothing in one locale. Their membership increasingly comes in from outside the neighborhood, but such businesses help members to cultivate an attachment to a particular place. In addition, successful businesses provide financial support for the mosque. And (as shown in Chapter 6) everyone in the radius benefits.

A similar strategy of faith-based entrepreneurship has been pursued by Triumph Baptist Church, one of the mega-churches on the Avenue. They developed a grocery store in the 1990s in their neighborhood of Hunting Park. The neighborhood was one of the "food deserts" in the city in which food was primarily available to residents through corner "Mom and Pops." Without a grocery store, food prices were high and selection was limited. Pastor James Hall followed the legacy of the Reverend Leon Sullivan of Zion Baptist Church on Broad Street. Often referred to as "the Lion of Zion," the Reverend Sullivan was well known for deploying economic development strategies by and for the African American community in the 1960s. Sullivan's list of accomplishments is long and his impact reached far beyond Philadelphia as he worked to improve the uneven playing field for people of African descent in both the United States and on the African continent. Locally, Philadelphians associate Sullivan with Progress Plaza, the first black-owned shopping center in the country, dedicated in 1968. Sullivan was able to leverage financing through the modest but faithful investments by Zion members. Progress Plaza was anchored by a grocery store and surrounded by 16 specialty shops. It created jobs and entrepreneurial opportunities for the beleaguered neighborhood of North Philadelphia, and continues to do so almost 50 years later. Reverend Sullivan died in 2001 but his legacy continues to inspire entrepreneurship among black clergy in Philadelphia.

The Reverend Hall was organizing Triumph Baptist Church not far from Zion as Progress Plaza was being developed in the late 1960s. His background in the civil rights movement had given him an understanding of both the political and economic inequality that challenged African Americans, in addition to a deep appreciation for the capacity of the faith community to effect change. As well as developing a vibrant congregation grounded in the black Baptist tradition, Reverend Hall has always incorporated economic development into his ministry.

Like Sullivan, Hall recognized the largely unacknowledged economic potential of the African American community, even in poor neighborhoods and facing an uneven playing field. Perhaps his most important contribution was to start the Triumph Baptist Federal Credit Union, which was chartered in 1974 to educate members about financial management, to enable them to save, and then to provide loans. There are currently 500 members saving through a variety of plans, including 120 accounts for teens and for children under 12. The credit union is able to make loans for those with low credit scores who would be denied by banks. For those who do not qualify for a loan even through the Triumph Credit Union, the organization sponsors a six-week "credit building" course. At the end, participants are given a small loan of $500 with a plan for repayment to build their credit score. With assets after the recession hovering around $635,000, the Triumph Baptist Credit Union is able to maintain over 100 loans at one time for cars, home repairs, credit consolidation, and other purposes. Director Sharon Saulters sighed when describing the recession:

> It really hit us hard. A lot of our members lost their jobs and had to take money out of savings just to pay the bills. We tried to work with our members, adjusting loan payments, but it had a really negative effect. I think people are just now getting readjusted.

The familiar greeting at Triumph, whether in worship or when answering the phone, is "Victory!" This is a consistent reminder of hope, but folks at Triumph, like Sharon Saulters, know that their victory requires a lot of commitment and hard work.

In 2011, Triumph began moving into development, building 55 units of senior housing on a parcel of land close by. Like the shopping plaza and grocery store it also owns, the housing development is a for-profit venture. Both the Germantown Masjid and Triumph Baptist Church have focused investment in the neighborhoods of Germantown and Hunting Park as a way of bringing much-needed services to residents and as sources of revenue for the congregations. By participating in the local economy, they are indeed able to "do good and do well," or in the words of the Prophet Jeremiah, to find their own welfare through seeking the welfare, or shalom, of the city.

Spirit and Business

Walking into the Divine Beauty School of Esther at the corner of Germantown and West Armat, one is immersed in the color purple. A friendly woman staffs the front reception area. Behind her is the familiar furniture of a beauty shop—chairs, sinks, and mirrors—and several young women at work with shampoo and scissors. The owner/founder/director is an attractive woman whose smile precedes her outstretched hand. Although she looks as if she's spent her life in this context, she explains that for many years she worked in a large aeronautic corporation as an engineer. Then, while at a spiritual retreat with her church, she had a vision—a literal vision, she says—of starting a program for women who are making the transition from prison or rehab into a new life. For minimal tuition, women enroll for training in cosmetology skills, with some wisdom thrown in about success on the job and in life. Ms. Jones explains how the whole program is based on the vision she received: "The Lord gave me the name of the school and even the color purple!" She was able to start this business during the recession of 2008 and to persevere because of prayer and the support of her faith community. Across the street is Divine Toddler, a day care center with several locations, named because of the faith of the owner, who attends Impacting Your World, which is right next door. Up the street, the owner of God's Given Gift Salon attributes the name and success of her business to God's leading and sustenance, especially as mediated through her congregation.

Congregations large and small contribute to the local economy indirectly but vitally through support and encouragement to entrepreneurs within their fellowships. Opening a small business is an act of faith, especially in the rocky economy of recent years. These three businesses have stayed open and viable throughout the course of my study, even as so many other commercial properties on the Avenue have turned over, including a number in the tony shopping district in Chestnut Hill. Even without investing hard capital, the "spiritual

FIGURE 3.12 A beauty school inspired by prayer.

capital" that communities of faith provide gives these small business owners invaluable resources to take risks, work hard, and to create and sustain vision.

In 1999, a member of New Covenant, Pamela Rich-Wheeler, saw the need for a more formalized resource for the development of small businesses. The church became a partner and physical "incubator" for the new non-profit, the Business Center for Entrepreneurship and Social Enterprise. The Business Center itself developed into a small-business incubation program, dedicated to helping individuals design, develop, and sustain small businesses. It became an independent non-profit organization (501(c)3) but is still based at New Covenant. Programs are offered throughout the community, but the church considers it part of its mission in the city. Individuals bring their dreams into Business Center's "communiversity," to test the viability of their ideas and to design a business plan. Ongoing coaching is available to new business owners through the "virtual incubation" plan, which matches them with mentors who are established businesspeople. The Business Center particularly targets youth, women, and minorities as untapped sources of entrepreneurship. Each year they have a youth entrepreneurship after-school program, which attracts

150 to 300 children from underserved areas. They also have a summer day camp program, which brings in 15 to 35 children from a broad economic spectrum: private school students work alongside kids from economically disadvantaged homes in writing business plans for everything from designer baseball bats to remarketed sneakers. In 2012 they worked with PNC Bank to open a bank in Germantown High School. The program includes a curriculum for students to learn about personal finance, entrepreneurship, and banking practices. The Center's annual "Enterprising Women Business Plan Competition" was lauded by the city council in 2011—the Center's 10th year—for inspiring its 60 winners to create businesses.[33] Working together with leaders from the business, political, and non-profit communities in Mt. Airy the Center has made a significant contribution to "building community, one entrepreneur at a time." By 2012, it had trained 454 people and had provided $225,000 in startup loans for businesses, which have created 448 jobs in the city.

At a more basic level, in congregations of all sizes and traditions, religious adherents are instructed in the meanings of work and wealth, and values around money and enterprise are formed and reinforced. In recent years a lot of attention has been given to the so-called Prosperity Gospel. In churches that embrace this paradigm, the central message is that God intends believers to have abundance. Through faithful acts—prayer, living an upright life, attending church, and tithing (giving at least 10% of personal income to the church)—one will be rewarded by God with wealth and the accoutrements of the good life, such as good health, big houses, nice cars, and lucrative jobs. Although the Prosperity Gospel has made a resurgence in recent years, it is not a recent phenomenon. Preachers such as Oral Roberts, Reverend Ike, and Jimmy and Tammy Faye Bakker had emphasized a reciprocal relationship between a believer and God: contributing to their ministries was an investment, since God would give material blessings in return. Currently, the Prosperity Gospel is associated with well-known preachers such as Joel Osteen and T. D. Jakes, who have created uber-churches of over 30,000 members as well as impressive business empires. The leaders within the Prosperity Gospel movement have become conspicuous models of how faithfulness pays off in health and wealth leading one critic, himself a minister, to note, "The fact that the people most likely to do well in the prosperity gospel movement are the people at the top suggests that it is all an ecclesiastical pyramid scheme."[34] Although some African American leaders and theologians are concerned about the widespread exploitation of the black community through the propagation of such magical thinking to those whose economic hardship is perpetuated by structural injustice, the Prosperity Gospel is not strongly represented among the congregations on Germantown Avenue. To be sure, values about personal finances are a theme of sermons and educational events up and down the Avenue, but perspectives and meanings vary.

The one pure-form Prosperity Gospel church on the Avenue was Impacting Your World Christian Center (IYWCC). Pastors Ray and Tracey Barnard acquired the old Market Square Presbyterian Church in Germantown, where George Whitfield had preached and George Washington had occasionally worshipped. In 2009, they expanded to another location in Cherry Hill, New Jersey. Ray Barnard studied at Oral Roberts University after feeling a call to preach a gospel of abundance and has been influenced by another high-profile proponent of the Prosperity Gospel, Kenneth Copeland (also from Oral Roberts University). Entrepreneurial in his own right, Copeland's organization provides training resources for local churches.

In the antique sanctuary of Impacting Your World, filled with worshippers in dark-wood pews, Reverend Barnard preached between two cardboard thermometers measuring the progress of contributions during the height of the recession. "My job is to lead you to your inheritance…" he explained in his sermon on a Sunday in July 2009. Earlier in the service the congregation was led in the litany of "A Thousand-Fold Blessings" repeating such scriptures as "The Lord shall increase you more and more, you and your children." Barnard exhorts his flock to be disciplined, work hard, study the Bible, pray, and give more to the church. He and his wife have been faithful tithers who now donate 27% of their income to the church. They used to have a Honda but now they can afford a Mercedes. The church was $115,000 away from the $1 million goal, he reported in this service; if everyone just gave an extra $75, they could close the gap. As the worship service came to a close, he and an entourage were whisked away in two waiting luxury cars for Cherry Hill— rolling testimonies of the abundant reward God will bestow on those who are faithful.

Members experienced the ministry of IYWCC as a resource that would enable them to live up to their potential, not in the sweet by and by but in the here and now. The church sponsored a plethora of retreats and seminars, all focused on self-improvement, especially financial. A thriving youth program carried the same message of the benefits of education, discipline, and faithfulness to God and the church to young people who respond to the energetic pastor, a former football player at Temple University. Material success does not randomly appear but is a predictable manifestation of a transactional relationship between the human and the divine, leading one researcher to observe that how the Prosperity Gospel works is "part hard work, part miracle" (Rosin, 2009). Rosin's analysis, which appeared in the *Atlantic*, linked prosperity preaching to the greed among lenders in the 1990s and early 2000s in creating a perfect storm for the development of the housing bubble, as prosperity preachers and their followers identified big new houses with God's blessing and easy access to mortgages as miracles. Hard work was part of the equation leading to prosperity but was unrealistically deemphasized as necessary to achieve and sustain the material blessings. Rosin argued that the Prosperity Gospel masked the exploitation that was taking place as lenders unscrupulously targeted the same audiences as prosperity preachers, especially Latinos and African Americans. In some cases, Rosin found, bankers and preachers worked in collusion.

Whether or not prosperity preaching ultimately caused the crash, members of Impacting Your World found in the preaching here that personal faith is not a theological abstraction but is grounded in material existence in tangible ways. One single mother of three children was typical of the loyal members, "I give God all the glory for the things he has done in my life and for this church that really cares about people and is interested in increasing the capacity in a person's life to become what God wants them to be." Through the teaching and support of IYWCC she had been encouraged to complete a college degree. For her, self-betterment was more about hard work than miracle; the community gave her the support she needed, not magic.

The prosperity teachings have been tempered recently at IYWCC. The message has broadened to focus on developing a faithful lifestyle beyond just the expectation of wealth. It is not clear whether this came in response to outside critics, the realities of the recession—which made promises of abundance increasingly at odds with economic reality—or rumored pushback from adherents locally as well as nationally. If the Prosperity Gospel was, in fact, related to the housing boom, even tangentially, when that bubble burst it challenged the supporting religious rationale as well.

At Impacting Your World Christian Center, human agency is seen in individual terms—it is up to the individual, in relationship with God, to "impact your world." Such individualism led Professor Eddie Glaude of

Princeton University to generate heated debate and much soul-searching within African American churches when he declared, "The Black Church, as we've known it or imagined it, is dead."[35] Glaude argued that African American churches have abdicated their "prophetic" stance, which had led to public critique of racial injustice and to mobilization for social change. The lack of outrage at economic disparities has been replaced by worship that is entertaining and edifying to individuals, but not focused on social transformation of the very conditions that create the hardship. The debate is not new. Since the 1960s, scholars of African American religion have discussed whether the Black Church is an accommodationist or transformational institution—or a combination of both. The individualized prosperity message is a limited voice on Germantown Avenue and it is less prominent in the second decade of the millennium. In fact, there are some congregations that are overtly anti-prosperity.

Pastor Hall stood at the pulpit at Triumph Baptist Church, not looking the 80 years that he marked on this day. After a service in celebration of his birthday, complete with an eye-popping liturgical dance worthy of Alvin Ailey, he turned to his text, Psalm 73, which addresses the problem of the wicked prospering while injustice is visited on the righteous, "who can hardly make ends meet." He exhorted the large congregation not to be envious of prosperity but to know that God is on the side of the righteous, and that is enough. The faithful should thank God for what they do have. There is a lot of celebration at Triumph—other Baptists might be surprised at how much social dancing there is. It does not give the impression of scarcity and yearning, but of commitment and joy. Although there are two offerings (one for tithers), the appeal to contribute is relatively understated. Yet there is a pledge repeated by the congregation that essentially commits one's finances to God and asks for deliverance from all temptations that would undermine one's budget.

Pastor Jackie Morrow, who leads the much smaller Jesus Is the Way Church, tells her flock that the Christian life is no guarantee that troubles will not visit the believer. In fact, things can get worse as the trials mount. This is in contradiction to the promises of prosperity preached elsewhere, and she has extended pastoral care to some refugees from those churches. "They come here and they need healing. They think there's something wrong with them, that they're not getting all these blessings." Pastor Jackie assures them that God loves them whether they are rich or poor, employed or not.

FIGURE 3.13 Pastor James Hall leading worship at Triumph Baptist Church, one of three mega-churches on the Avenue.

FIGURE 3.14 Pastor Jackie Morrow preaching at Jesus Is the Way Church.

With the rich variety of expressions of African American religion on the Avenue, clearly there is not a single dynamic at work, accommodationist or transformational, although these congregations help their congregants to construct meanings as they navigate through a difficult social and economic milieu.

Congregations do contribute to individual agency as well as having their own agency as institutions. Whether individual or institutional, each can either contribute to enabling people to accommodate, or adapt to, existing social conditions, or to critique and seek to effect systemic change. Communities of faith play an important role in forming perspectives on the social realities that their adherents encounter on a daily basis. They frame meanings of wealth and poverty that have consequences for individual action or agency in the world; they encourage individuals to acknowledge and pursue their potential and construct meanings and opportunities for engagement with their surroundings. When acting as institutions offering basic human services, providing job training, economic development, or access to health care, faith congregations are vital participants in urban ecologies. They are responding to the conditions of their context. But their ability to act on and change those conditions is also present on the Avenue, as we will see.

4 POUND FOR POUND: THE SOCIAL IMPACT OF SMALL CHURCHES

A horse-drawn carriage filled with wide-eyed children slowly clopped through Fair Hill Burial Ground, past rows of low head-stones marking the old Quaker graves. At the end of its oval route, the young passengers climbed out and others took their places, most of their faces painted with spectacular butterflies and super-heroes. And so went the afternoon. Normally, the Burial Ground, a green oasis in the densely populated neighborhood of Fairhill, is still and tranquil. But on this summer afternoon, its brick walkways echoed not only with the horses' hoof beats but also with musical beats of hip-hop and salsa music. Neighbors and visitors sampled the barbecued chicken, beans, and rice prepared by a member of Chestnut Hill Friends Meeting and a Puerto Rican chef from the neighborhood. As salsa gave way to gospel, the crowd gathered around liturgical dancers from Mt. Calvary Church of God in Christ in the street just outside the cemetery gates. Three African American women in long black-and-gold dresses, gracefully and emotionally interpreted the music, and entranced the Latinos and white Quakers in this unusually mixed crowd. Dwayne Grannum, the music director from Father's House of Prayer Mission Baptist Church, who had recruited the disk jockeys and performers, remarked, "We forget that a lot of people have never seen this, and it's so familiar for us." Next, the Reverend Jomo Johnson took the microphone, in baggy jeans and a dark cap. Johnson, a co-founder of Philly Open Air, a nearby storefront church that opened in the fall of 2010, yelled into the microphone, "Who here loves Tupac? Who loves Jesus?" He then launched into an intricate and impres-sive rap about Jesus and his "awesome God." The Latino and white Quaker members of the crowd, for whom Christian rap was another new genre, listened with curiosity.

This chapter was co-written with Beth Stroud who conducted the ethnographic research presented in New Bethany Holiness Church and Father's House of Prayer Mission Baptist Church.

FIGURE 4.1 Carriage rides are a highlight of the annual fair in the burial ground for neighborhood children.

FIGURE 4.2 Open fire hydrants keep children cool and entertained.

Children played in an open fire hydrant on the corner. A Quaker lawyer from Chestnut Hill joined a group of Puerto Rican men drinking beer and playing dominoes on a lacquered table. As people of different backgrounds and languages strolled with plates of food and chatted, a volunteer from the National Association for the Advancement of Colored People (NAACP) registered voters for the upcoming presidential election. Three red-tailed hawks that are raising a family high in the pin oak tree circled overhead, taking in the scene.

Although block parties and neighborhood fairs happen all over Philadelphia on summer Saturdays, there was much that was remarkable about this one. With the lowest average income level in the city in 2009 ($17,754), Fairhill also had the highest percentage of people living in poverty—63% (U.S. Census Bureau, American Communities Survey). One might think,

FIGURE 4.3 Liturgical dancers perform at the fair, a new art form to many in the neighborhood.

given the economic hardship, that there is not a lot to celebrate here. While the neighborhood is diverse and has a growing Latino presence (the highest concentration of Latinos in the city at 82% in 2010), there is not a great deal of interracial mixing. Racial and religious isolation are especially visible in the congregations of this crowded religious ecology. In the four blocks of Germantown Avenue between Lehigh and Glenwood Avenues, which form the boundaries of Fairhill, 14 congregations occupied small buildings in 2011. While the several independent Baptist congregations, all African American, sometimes held joint services, there was scarcely any interaction between Baptists and Pentecostals, between African American and Puerto Rican congregations, or even between the two Puerto Rican Pentecostal congregations.

At this festival, however, African American Baptists and Pentecostals were not only chatting and laughing with their Latino Catholic and Pentecostal neighbors, but also with white Quakers from Germantown, Mt. Airy, Chestnut Hill, and Center City.

William Penn gave the 4.5 acres of the present-day burial ground to George Fox, the founder of the Society of Friends, in 1691. A meetinghouse was first built there in 1703 and it became a way station on the day-long journey between Philadelphia and Germantown. It also played a role in the Revolutionary War, as the triumphant British soldiers took over the meeting-house after routing the Americans at the Battle of Germantown. The Quakers, committed to equality and non-violence, buried both British and American

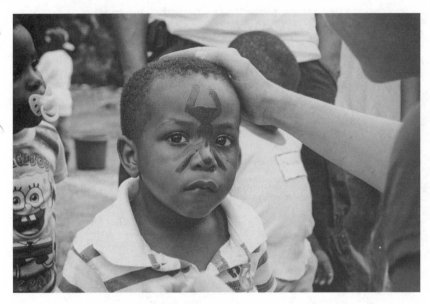

FIGURE 4.4 Face painting at the fair.

Born in Relation (Centre City (early))

soldiers at Fair Hill. Later, the burial ground figured into the racial history of the new country as it became the final resting place for abolitionists Robert Purvis (an African American businessman who became the "President of the Underground Railroad") and Lucretia and James Mott. Lucretia's comrades in the suffrage movement, Mary Ann and Thomas M'Clintock, are also buried there.

The neighborhood around the burial ground became more urbanized as waves of immigrants arrived from Europe. For much of the early 20th century, there was a vibrant German community clustered around the now-crumbling St. Bonaventure Catholic Church, which looms over the former meetinghouse. During the 1960s, as deindustrialization undermined local neighborhood economies in Philadelphia, Fairhill gradually became predominantly African American. The Quaker meeting dwindled to a membership in the single digits, and in 1984 the Quakers sold the meetinghouse to a Baptist congregation, with the stipulation and endowment to maintain the burial ground. However, the covenant was not honored, perhaps because of the magnitude of the task and the slender resources of a small congregation. The burial ground was soon neglected and became overgrown with weeds, garbage, and worse. Everything from dead animals to tires and refrigerators was thrown over the iron fence, piling head-high. The burial ground became a center for drug activity as the crack epidemic spread through many sections of the city, disrupting and redefining community life. This was the once-peaceful neighborhood the police and media dubbed "The Badlands" in the 1980's.

Historian Margaret Hope Bacon, biographer of Lucretia Mott, said that "If Lucretia had awakened from her grave and seen what was going on in Fair Hill Burial Ground, I'm positive she would have gotten to work because that's her style of being."[1] In 1992, Bacon and other Friends decided to form a non-profit to reclaim the sacred ground, and in 1993 they re-purchased it. Over the next decade, volunteers came on weekends to clear and clean the property. The massive restoration and gardening effort brought the historic green space back to horticultural life, and the non-profit chose to take an active role in the embattled neighborhood as a center for education and urban gardening. The Quaker stewards of the burial ground also partnered with neighborhood leaders, who were becoming engaged in their own reclamation project.

Sitting in her immaculate living room, surrounded by her large collection of candles, community leader Peaches Ramos remembered how bad it had gotten at the Burial Ground and in Fairhill:

> The trash was everywhere. In fact, we didn't see anyone come around so everyone thought it was a pet cemetery, for dogs and cats. There was drugs everywhere. You could see the drug dealers in the corners, 24 hours a day, seven days a week.... I had 5 children of my own and it was hard raising them here and there was shooting, shooting.... We got used to it, but I was getting tired. Every time I turned around, someone was getting killed.

A friend of her daughter's was shot one night in a dispute over earrings, and that was when she had had enough. Ramos and her neighbors organized a block watch and stood on the corners, making eye contact with dealers and their customers. The neighborhood watchers and those cleaning up the Burial Ground encouraged and inspired each other. The police soon became partners and Ramos urged neighbors to extend hospitality instead of hostility to them. In an unusual thawing of mutual suspicion, the neighbors even held barbecues for the police, who would sometimes stop and shoot hoops with the kids. The Reverend Beatrice Streeter, who was passionate about youth ministry, bought the old meetinghouse from the previous church and started a congregation. She and the members of St. Mark's Outreach Church joined with the neighbors. "They've got our back," she acknowledged. Ramos also hounded Philadelphia's Mural Arts Program until they came and began adding art to the walls of buildings surrounding the burial ground. Today there are a number of colorful murals in Fairhill, most of them incorporating the faces of those who have been involved in the struggle for the neighborhood and one honoring Harriet Tubman and the conductors of the Underground Railroad.

There is still crime in the neighborhood, to be sure. But residents agree that it is far safer than it was a few decades ago. Today the Burial Ground has an active urban gardening program both inside and outside the fence. It also operates gardens at a recovery house for women and in a public school's schoolyard. The green space itself is a magnet for children, who come to ride their bikes, run, and play in a safe environment. Staff members provide natural science programs for the public schools in the area, which have little science in the curriculum. In the spring of 2012, for example, over 400 children came to Fair Hill to participate in their four-session curriculum. For many children, it was their first experience touching a worm, learning where vegetables come from, or watching the fledgling hawks in the tree. Twice a year the non-profit organization Historic Fair Hill sponsors "Astronomy Night," where children can discover the night sky with real telescopes. Every winter, when the gardens are dormant, the organization sponsors an essay contest and awards ceremony for 5th and 6th graders, who write about slavery, the Underground Railroad, and the historic figures buried there. There is an award ceremony for the young scholars. For adults in Fairhill, the burial ground serves as a park where they can sit on a bench and listen to the birds. Maria Santiago, a deacon at St. Mark's and a longtime Fairhill resident, enjoys sitting on her front stoop facing the burial ground on summer afternoons just listening to the cicadas, and she is quick to notify someone from Historic Fair Hill if she notices so much as a fallen tree branch. "It's amazing what you can accomplish with faith and determination," she says.

The congregations along the Avenue here have been slow to engage the neighborhood revitalization process. Except for St. Mark Outreach, which bought the old meetinghouse, and Universal Hagar, the Spiritualist congregation that has met in a former heating and air conditioning business on the corner of Germantown and Indiana since 1967, none joined in the coalition of neighbors, non-profits, and police. This reflects what Sampson found in Chicago: that while the presence of non-profit organizations is correlated with collective action in neighborhoods, a density of churches has the opposite effect and is negatively related to collective efficacy. He concluded: "In the black communities with the most churches per capita trust is lowest.... Trust in one's fellow man is apparently not enhanced by the church."[2] However, he does not pursue from an ecological perspective why this might be. He cites Omar McRoberts's finding that black churches in dense "religious districts" with members commuting in for worship are not as engaged in the neighborhood.[3] But there are other neighborhood effects as well. Oftentimes, churches are overlooked as being potential partners in collective action. For example, in 2010–2012, the city of Philadelphia conducted a strategic planning process to develop an economic development plan for the Fairhill commercial district. For two years they did research, including interviewing all the business owners on the Avenue—but did not talk with any of the 14 or 15 congregations. As their plans were unveiled to the community, no representatives from these faith communities were invited, though they were located on the Avenue and would be affected by the proposed renovation. Such an oversight is unconscious and cannot be entirely blamed on city officials; the invisibility of these congregations is a social construction. All of these churches are small, with 50 or fewer in attendance on a typical Sunday, and they keep a low profile in the neighborhood. The participation of the liturgical dancers and the rapping minister months later represented the first steps into the public square for two of these congregations. Still, the Germantown Avenue congregations are a presence in the urban ecology in Fairhill, though perhaps a subtle one. They bring between 400 and 600 worshippers to the Avenue each week, and usually have more than one event weekly.

Two small African American congregations, one in the Fairhill section and one quite nearby in Hunting Park, did not want to be low profile and essentially nominated themselves for intensive ethnographic research during our study. As described earlier, it was often difficult to make contact with small churches to schedule interviews. Members of Father's House of Prayer Mission Baptist Church in Fairhill and New Bethany Holiness Church a few blocks north in Hunting Park, however, engaged our researchers in conversation on the street. While waiting for the 23 bus on a freezing cold Sunday afternoon, a member of Father's House gave an enthusiastic account of her church's food programs. On another, warmer day, members of New Bethany

FIGURE 4.5 The low headstones in the burial ground contributed to an urban myth that this was a pet cemetery before Quakers reclaimed and restored it.

were outside their church handing out fliers about an upcoming fundraiser, a sale of chicken and fish dinners called "Straight Out the Pot." Encouraged by these encounters, a researcher visited each of these congregations. The pastors, Reverend Edmund Jackson of Father's House and Reverend Hazel M. Mack of New Bethany, each generously gave permission for a researcher to participate as a member of their congregations for several months, taking notes on worship services, participating in congregational events, and interviewing as many members of the congregation as possible. Neither congregation had a formal church directory or membership roll, but they provided the names and addresses, or at least the zip codes, of all the regular attenders.[4] Both congregations referred to our researcher, and still do, in their occasional text messages and emails, as "Sister Beth."

These two churches, Father's House and New Bethany, represent the single most common type of congregation on Germantown Avenue. Like some 30% of the churches in our study, they are independent black congregations, meeting in former commercial buildings, with 50 or fewer attendees on a typical Sunday morning. These congregations are scattered along most of the Avenue, but they are heavily concentrated along its poorest stretches (and there are none in affluent Chestnut Hill). Both Father's House and New Bethany are located along the poorest stretch of Germantown Avenue in North Philadelphia. New Bethany, in the shadow of Temple University Hospital and just a few blocks south of the busy Broad and Erie intersection, has some active shops and restaurants in its immediate vicinity. Around Father's House, nothing ever seems to be open save a dozen churches and a single bar.

FIGURE 4.6 Today, the burial ground is a welcome green space for this impoverished neighborhood.

In raw numbers, Father's House, New Bethany, and other small congregations reach few people. However, they make important contributions to urban life in at least three areas. Located in the second-hungriest congressional district in the United States, both Father's House and New Bethany are engaged in anti-hunger programs. In a city where school and neighborhood arts programs have undergone deep cuts, they both provide ample opportunities for artistic expression and production. Finally, in an uncertain economy, they help their members find and keep meaningful paid work.

In light of their small size, their impact can be considered remarkable. Dwayne Grannum, the music director from Father's House, grew up at New Covenant Church in Mt. Airy, one of the Avenue's three mega-churches, where his mother and father are still the pastors. New Covenant is known for its many community programs as described in the previous chapter. By comparison to New Covenant, Father's House is a humble place indeed. Yet, as Grannum mused about the number of Thanksgiving food baskets Father's House had distributed in 2009, he couldn't help comparing it favorably with New Covenant: "Pound for pound, for the number of people, Father's House does more," he said. "I think that they are exponentially more benevolent."

FIGURE 4.7 Father's House of Prayer housed in a former restaurant supply store.

Neither of these congregations is among the smallest in the study. Each draws between 30 and 50 people to a typical Sunday morning worship service, and each has a critical mass of young adults. Father's House and New Bethany are also among the older and more stable of the small congregations: Father's House was founded in 1984 and moved to its present location in 1996. New Bethany, to our knowledge the oldest independent black Protestant church on Germantown Avenue, was founded in 1954 and moved to its present building in 1974.

Because Father's House and New Bethany were more forthcoming, they may be more engaged with their community than other small independent churches, some of whom were more reticent to speak with outsiders. Our intuitive sense was that these two congregations are indeed special, but not entirely unique. While we certainly made important connections at Father's House and New Bethany, we also witnessed and experienced profound moments of vitality and service in at least a dozen other small congregations. At one small Baptist congregation in Fairhill, about a block south of Father's House, we met young women who served breakfast and lunch to neighborhood children every single day, all summer long. At a Pentecostal church in a former bank, also in Fairhill, the pastor explained how hard he was working to purchase an adjacent empty lot and clean it up.

This is not to say that every small congregation on Germantown Avenue is equally effective in contributing to a vibrant urban life. But Father's House and New Bethany represent the modest, often unrecognized ways that small churches engage and impact their local contexts. Pound for pound, their contributions are indeed significant.

Father's House of Prayer

Welcome into this place, welcome into this place
Welcome into this broken vessel.

—"Welcome into This Place," by Orlando Jaurez, a favorite opening song at Father's House

Father's House, which meets in a former restaurant supply store with vacant lots on either side, is unprepossessing from the outside. The old display windows have been covered with white stucco, and except for two glass-block crosses built into the front wall, simple black block letters spelling out the name of the church, and a door with blinds, which are covered by a metal grate on weekdays when the church is closed, the building is unadorned.

Even on Sundays, although the metal grate is pulled up, it is not always immediately apparent that the church is active. Inside, however, typically 30 to 35 people, including six or seven children and young teenagers, meet in the nicely furnished red, white, and gold sanctuary with dark wooden pews. Large red and black lettering painted on the left-hand wall reads, "This is my commandment, that ye love one another, as I have loved you. Eddie P. Wood II 1984–2002," 1984 being not his birth year, but the year he founded the church. His family still makes up more than half of the active members, and his grandson is an assistant pastor. In more ways than one, this is their father's house.

The current pastor, a middle-aged man named Edmund Jackson, seemed enthusiastic yet slightly intimidated to meet a researcher. "I went to seminary for two years, but I couldn't keep it up," he says. "The Greek! I believe in Jesus and I believe in being born again, and I just try to do my best. You can pray for me, and for all of us." He introduced the researcher, and took a moment before starting the service to write down his name, telephone numbers, and e-mail address for her.

The well-dressed, very tall man at the keyboard, who turned out to be Dwayne Grannum, sang "Faith of Our Fathers" in a slow, almost melancholy cadence with just a hint of jazzy syncopation. His baritone voice was velvety:

Faith of our fathers, living still, in spite of dungeon, fire, and sword,
Oh how our hearts beat high with joy whene'er we hear that glorious Word!
Faith of our fathers, holy faith, we will be true to thee till death.

In this unassuming building in an economically struggling neighborhood, the professional quality of music seemed out of context. However, as we came to learn, such fine music was very much a part of the everyday context of Father's House.

Pastor Jackson retired from a job with the postal service in 2009 to serve Father's House full time. He had been a deacon at a church in South Philadelphia, but his pastor asked him to come preach for six weeks in place of Pastor Wood. When the six weeks were up, Pastor Wood asked him to preach for two more weeks, and then Pastor Wood died. Jackson thought the church would get a new pastor, but says, "They told me, 'Don't you know we want you to be our pastor?'" He was quickly ordained at his home church, and has been at Father's House ever since.

Jackson's predecessor, Eddie P. Wood Jr., was born in Franklin, Virginia, in 1924. He and his wife, the former Teresa Hatter of Bayboro, North Carolina, settled in Philadelphia after Wood was discharged from the Army in 1946. He owned a small auto body and fender repair shop on Fountain Street in North Philadelphia, but his primary calling was as a pastor. While his children were growing up, he served as an assistant pastor at the Temple of Divine Love also in North Philadelphia. Later, he served as pastor of a small Baptist church in Germantown. In 1984, as he neared retirement, he opened his own church, in a small space above his shop—Father's House of Prayer.

When the Reverend Wood decided to move the church to lower Germantown Avenue, even his family wasn't sure what to think. His youngest daughter says that when her father first showed them the building, he said, "I see the pulpit here...and the pastor's study here..." and everyone thought he was crazy. She says the place was a mess. Today, the front door opens to a traditional-looking sanctuary with shining wooden pews, red carpets and pew cushions, and an imposing wooden pulpit. A small door behind the chancel leads to the pastor's study. A flight of stairs along an inside wall leads to a second-floor banquet hall with a new linoleum floor, a sparkling kitchen, and restrooms.

The founder's youngest daughter, Helen Wood, a middle-school math teacher, often leads the singing, sometimes with her sister Michelle Armstrong or with Tiffany Cook, a seminary student who is also related by marriage to the family. The opening songs are often repeated week after week; Orlando Jaurez's "Welcome" is one of their favorites.

Even as Sunday worship at Father's House is in full swing, the atmosphere remains decorous and restrained. A meticulously prepared bulletin includes the full name and title of every church officer and every person who participates in the service: even an eight-year-old child is listed with an honorific title—"Sister Trinity Trueblood" ("Sister" and "Brother" are the default titles for anyone who does not hold a particular office designated by a title such as "Pastor," "Minister," or "Deacon"). The ushers wear white gloves and collect the offering in gleaming silver plates. Worship leaders pay attention to unwritten rules of conduct, such as never crossing in front of the pulpit. The music and preaching are spirited, and sometimes a few congregants will shake a tambourine or stand up and wave their arms during a musical selection, or murmur "That's right" or "Amen" during the sermon. The more exuberant displays of religious emotion seen in other congregations along the Avenue, however, are rare here.

Only 15% of the regular attenders at Father's House live within 10 blocks of the church. Some members travel long distances across the city to worship here, with a few commuting in from the suburbs and New Jersey. With a few exceptions, they became connected to the church through networks of friends and family members, not because they lived nearby. Twenty-five percent of the congregation, including most of the founder's family and some of their friends who have joined the church, live in a single middle-class neighborhood, East Oak Lane. A majority of the members work in service and trade occupations or are retired, but a substantial number work in professional occupations. A few are on disability, and even fewer are unemployed.

Betty Smith, a former home health aide who now subsists on disability, manages the cornerstone of neighborhood mission work at Father's House: a modest food pantry that receives food from a citywide program called Self-Help and Resource Exchange, or SHARE. Father's House is one of hundreds of small organizations that distribute SHARE food throughout

Philadelphia to about 20,000 people. SHARE provides basic food at a discount in exchange for volunteer service, but people with extremely low incomes may be exempted from the service requirement as well as the discounted cost. In principle, the food pantry is open every other Friday, but in fact it operates on a flexible and slightly irregular schedule, depending on Sister Smith's availability. She can't always get to the church on time to open the food pantry at the stated hour, but she is always willing to make arrangements with regular clients who call to find out if they can pick up their food at a different time to accommodate their work schedules or medical appointments.

On a typical Friday afternoon when the food pantry was open, there was an easy familiarity between neighborhood residents, mostly men picking up food for their families, and the church. They called the chair of the mission board "Betty" or "Miss Smith," instead of "Sister Smith." They looked over the clothing on the tables and selected a few items they could use. Some pitched in to help pack groceries or to double up grocery bags. One joked about how much red tape you have to go through to get a Thanksgiving turkey from the state senator's office, and Sister Smith responded by saying, "You just come here for your turkey! You know we won't put you through all that." Another man, a 40-year resident of a nearby block, joined in a conversation about the neighborhood, saying, "This neighborhood is just a neighborhood trying to stay together. It's not a bad neighborhood." The boundary between church and neighborhood was fluid and relaxed.

Father's House also serves free breakfast, snack, and lunch at summer Vacation Bible School, a week-long children's program run by Sister Smith and her sister, Sister Johnson, a school custodian. The Archdiocese of Philadelphia provides the food for Vacation Bible School, as part of their summer feeding effort. Father's House is one of a substantial number of congregations up and down Germantown Avenue that offer free meals during summer children's programs, often through the same archdiocesan feeding program (even though there is no Catholic church on the Avenue, the church's presence is felt). In addition, Father's House distributes about 15 food baskets at Thanksgiving, and another 15 at Christmas, funded by the church. Finally, every year, a group from the church participates in the citywide Walk against Hunger, a fundraising walk organized by the Greater Philadelphia Coalition against Hunger, earmarking the money they raise for the church food pantry.

Sister Smith said that since Pastor Wood knew she had volunteered at a food pantry before, he asked her to start one at Father's House. Because large hunger organizations were well organized to collaborate with very small neighborhood institutions like Father's House, the critical resources were available, and the leaders of the congregation had the capacity to access them. Such activation of social capital challenges perceptions of small inner-city congregations as being isolated and without agency or resources.

As the music minister noted, Father's House distributes a lot of food, especially relative to its small size: if 50 people per month receive enough groceries for five meals, and 10 children receive breakfast and lunch every day for a week during Vacation Bible School, then this congregation with about 35 active members is helping provide more than 3,100 meals a year. Even without calculating funds raised through the Walk against Hunger, each member is providing 88 meals for others per year—a significant contribution to those who are "food insecure" in their neighborhood. "Pound for pound," this is impressive.

Father's House also addresses another kind of hunger: hunger for the arts. The congregation provides many opportunities to make music and learn new musical skills, offering young people a distinctive musical education with regular opportunities to dance, sing, and play instruments in public. In the School District of Philadelphia, funding for arts education is becoming ever scarcer: in 2006, 67 of the 267 Philadelphia public schools (25%) had no music teacher, 55 (20%) had no art teacher, and 66 (25%) had neither a music nor an art teacher (Philadelphia Citizens for Children and Youth, 2011). Today, arts education is even more scarce in the public schools. In Fairhill, the local elementary school is fortunate to have some instrumental instruction twice a week, "for a selected number of students." For the children at Father's House, the opportunities for self-expression through the arts provide important avenues for them to explore their talent and to gain the self-confidence that comes with performance

A congregation's small size may be seen as an advantage for any individual looking to discover his or her musical gifts. In virtually all small congregations, every member usually has at least one role to play in church life, and many of those roles are musical. Even in the smallest gatherings of worshippers, someone often plays the keyboard, another plays the drums, and still others (often a small ensemble of three or four voices) lead the singing. In addition to Grannum, who plays the keyboards, sings, and directs the choir, Father's House has a second paid keyboardist, an eight-member choir, a drummer, and a nine-member praise dance and mime group that includes many of the children.

FIGURE 4.8 At Father's House, artistic expression is nurtured.

Children and teenagers are encouraged to take up instruments and to express themselves artistically in worship, sometimes side-by-side with a parent. At Father's House, one of the most beloved praise dancers is an elementary-aged girl who leaps around the sanctuary with exuberance; her mother, also a praise dancer, has taught her to dance. Even very young artists learn to express themselves confidently in front of the familiar congregation.

Father's House sponsors an annual "outreach" event that resembles nothing so much as a day-long talent show. On a Sunday afternoon in the fall of 2010, singers, dancers, poets, mimes, and a drill team from Father's House and neighboring churches and community organizations took turns performing for over three hours. It was planned as an outdoor service in the vacant lot next door, but due to a few clouds and a prediction of rain, it was moved inside. The performers included young children, families, and people of all ages. Plates of hamburgers and macaroni and cheese were passed from table to table, and long tables on the side of the room were piled with used clothing and school supplies that members had donated for the community. "Outreach" might be a misnomer, since virtually all who attended were either church members or guest performers from other congregations, but bonds were built and all the artists were warmly affirmed for their contributions. The afternoon culminated in a sermon by a guest preacher.

Grannum, who has had classical music training and holds a law degree, described the role that this small church had played in his own spiritual and musical development. He first came to Father's House through the vast network of personal and informal relationships that ties black churches together. His sister, who directs a singing group, was a friend of one of the daughters of the late founding pastor and had brought her group to sing at Father's House from time to time. She also used to teach the Father's House choir occasionally. When Grannum first returned to the area after a three-year sojourn in England, he began coming along to help out. Eventually, that led to his becoming the music director. It was his first continuous paid musical gig.

"At first, I thought I was doing them a favor," he said. The church was so small, and their need was so great. But he now says that he has received as much as he has given. Initially, he was comfortable on the keyboard but shy about singing in public, or singing or playing unfamiliar music on the spot. Leading the music at Father's House has made him a more versatile musician, he believes. He is better able to improvise and to try something new if the spirit moves him. He notes that the well-known singer and songwriter John Legend was the music director at Bethel A.M.E. church in Scranton, Pennsylvania, for nine years before he became famous. Then he grins: "Not that I'm comparing myself to John Legend."

FIGURE 4.9. Dwayne Grannum, music director at Father's House of Prayer.

Although Father's House is small, its musicians are exposed to a citywide audience through a network of churches that regularly visit one another. Like many small black congregations, Father's House hosts other churches for afternoon services once or twice a month, and visits other churches in the afternoons as well. Speakers, choirs, musicians, and congregants travel from church to church. Personal relationships lead to congregational ones: sometimes a friendship or a relationship with a co-worker leads to a connection between two churches. The churches' social impact often radiates through the resulting networks beyond Germantown Avenue, and nowhere is this more evident than in the production of music and audiences for music. Tiffany Cook, a member, produced her own Christian rap album and began distributing it online and at church services. Her potential market included not only the small Father's House family but the broader audience Father's House had opened up for her through its network.

The recession exacerbated the existing economic distress in Fairhill. The percentage of individuals below the poverty level rose from 59% to a staggering 73% by 2009—three times the rate for the city of Philadelphia. Congregations in Fairhill are confronted with the reality of poverty every day, not only in paying their own bills as offerings decrease but also in responding to the hardship faced by their members. Again, measuring this response is difficult, since there is no organized job placement program or other economic relief strategy. However, Sunday after Sunday, members reported that the service helped them feel refreshed after a difficult week at work, and strengthened them to face the week ahead. Father's House was not reflective of Fairhill in that few were unemployed, which raises the question of causality: does religious affiliation help individuals to be more successful in the job market, or do congregations inadvertently seem socially inaccessible for the unemployed?

Father's House is one of the congregations on the Avenue that preaches against the so-called prosperity gospel—the teaching that faithfulness leads to economic success. Pastor Jackson, his assistant pastors, and visiting preachers alike criticize the notion of God's financial blessing on the faithful as superstitious and unbiblical. The simplicity of the church and its building stands as a reproach to the large, flashy churches with their high visibility on television and in popular culture. Pastor Jackson forwarded an e-mail to the entire congregation entitled "Concerns about the Teaching of T. D. Jakes." The critique of the famed Texas preacher raised questions about the orthodoxy of Jakes's theology and zeroed in on his belief that God guarantees health and wealth:

> Prosperity teachings stand out more than other Word of Faith teachings in T. D. Jakes's ministry. Jakes is a very wealthy man and enjoys it. The 19 November 1998 *People* magazine describes his $1.7 million Dallas home, his blue BMW convertible, and his colorful expensive clothing. (He also drives a Mercedes.) He feels his financial success is a sign of growing economic empowerment for African-Americans....
>
> It's not disturbing that Jakes is wealthy and has this lifestyle, but it's very disturbing that he portrays Jesus as being rich in order to justify his wealth. He describes Jesus as having been rich in order to support His disciples and their families during His ministry. Jakes says the myth of the poor Jesus has to be destroyed because it's holding people back.[5]

By rejecting the prosperity gospel, Father's House members assert that God's blessing does not necessarily result in worldly success. Anyone can lose a job; anyone can struggle economically despite working faithfully at a steady position for many years, as does Sister Smith, who worked as long as she could but now gets by on disability. Father's House helps its members assert a sense of personal worth that cannot be measured in dollars and cents, or in nice cars and houses. Ironically, their members do not reflect the poverty rate in the neighborhood.

New Bethany Holiness Church

New Bethany Holiness Church is housed in a small storefront building with brilliant red doors, white trim, and a row of painted yellow crosses in its windows. Above the door, a sign in neat blue letters announces "GOD'S NOT THROUGH BLESSING." A schedule of services posted next to the door bears the slogan "The Church where Everybody is Somebody, Jesus is Lord and our Signature is Praise." With its brilliant colors and bold messages to passersby, New Bethany seems to communicate life and energy, even on a weekday afternoon when no one is there. On Sunday mornings, typical attendance is around 40 people, including three or four infants and young children.

New Bethany, like Father's House, is a product of the Great Migration of African Americans moving north. The founding pastors, Jonah and Mary Lee, moved to Philadelphia from Suffolk, Virginia, in 1948, in search of a better education for their children. One of their adult daughters was pregnant and was determined not to give birth to her child in the South. In Philadelphia, the Lees attended a Pentecostal church called Lily of the Valley Bibleway Church before founding New Bethany in 1954. Establishing new churches ran in the family: Mary's grandfather had established the largest Baptist church in Suffolk, and her brother had established the first Pentecostal church in that town.

The Lees held services in four different rented buildings before purchasing 3440 Germantown Avenue in 1974. A number of New Bethany members answer the question "How long have you been a member?" by saying "I was born here." They quickly clarify that they don't mean their mothers literally gave birth at the church but rather that they grew up in the congregation. Sylvia Britton, the daughter of the founding pastors and the fourth pastor of the church, recalls, "Mom had a philosophy that you grow up, you go to school, you get a job, you contribute to the household and you help build the church. All your time, all your free time, all your fun time went to the church.

FIGURE 4.10 New Bethany Holiness Church.

And you tithe." Some of the Lee family members remember living upstairs over the church as children. Hazel Mack, Britton's niece who has pastored the church since 2004, recalls, "They carried us up when we fell asleep, and when we woke up, they carried us back down."

When you walk through the front door and enter the tiny vestibule with a coat rack, you can hear the sounds of passionate singing and prayer coming from the sanctuary. One morning after a storm, a man thanked God for deliverance from the wind and rain of the previous night: "God, we thank you that you didn't let the roof blow off the house!"

Continuing into the sanctuary, one might be surprised to see only 12 to 15 people at the front of the church, given the volume. The small number of people pray in a variety of postures: one kneeling at a chair, some facing the walls, and some dancing, bent over as if in pain or ecstasy while their feet move in rapid, intricate steps. Several leaders take turns praying into the microphone, but almost everyone prays out loud and at the same time: one person leads without dominating. One prayed, "Give us a new idea, God. Give us new ministries." Most are very physical in their prayers—dancing, swaying, tapping their feet, waving their arms.

This is the prayer and praise time that precedes the official opening of the service. A young woman in a white nurse's uniform over jeans quietly greets newcomers, shows them to seats, and gives first-time visitors folders with information about the church. The sanctuary at New Bethany is long, narrow, and windowless, with rows of folding chairs. Against the far wall, a pulpit stands at the front of a large, square platform, with heavy, ornate chairs along two sides. A Hammond organ, drum kit, and large speakers dominate the space in front of the platform, although there is also plenty of open space between the platform and the first row of chairs. The floor is parquet, and resembles a banquet-hall dance floor, which will be put to good use.

The praying is followed by singing, preaching, an offertory, and ritual acts such as anointing sick members with oil for healing. Preaching responsibilities rotate between Pastor Mack and a number of assisting ministers. Pastor Mack encourages members of the congregation to pray for each other, especially for anyone who comes forward for special healing prayers. One Sunday, she explained that while she didn't want the church to be a nosy church (it sounded more like "noozy," a typical Philadelphia pronunciation)—no one but her needed to know about people's problems—she wanted them to pray for each other even if they didn't know the exact situation.

Outside of worship, Pastor Mack comes across as mild-mannered and efficient, and has a pleasant smile. She works full-time as the payroll manager at the major performing arts center in Philadelphia. She is often tired, she says, but nevertheless is always welcoming. When leading worship her demeanor changes: she takes on a stern expression and projects a commanding, authoritative presence.

Mack's immediate predecessor, Sylvia Britton, holds the title "Bishop"; Mack's younger brother also plays an important role in leading the congregation and holds the title "Prophet." Bishop Britton, who is in her 60s, holds significant symbolic power in the congregation—if she has even a few words to say, everyone hushes to listen—but it is Pastor Mack who provides the day-to-day leadership. Members of the congregation often speak about how wise it was, and how unusual, for Bishop to designate a successor while she was still in good health.

Ecstatic dance is central to worship at New Bethany. Pastor Mack says New Bethany has a reputation as a church where "you can always get a praise." Prophet says, "I don't mind those quiet churches every once in a while, but I want to go to church where people lose their minds." At New Bethany,

FIGURE 4.11 Praising God at New Bethany Holiness.

the loss of conscious control over one's bodily movements is understood as a way of offering honor and gratitude to God. One Sunday when the dancing seemed slow to start, Pastor Mack urged the congregation on, saying, "If He's still meeting needs for you, then you owe Him praise." Another Sunday, when no one was playing the Hammond organ, a loud banging, like gunshots, began, although no one seemed surprised. It was the sound of one of the saints stomping her feet ecstatically, without any music to drown it out.

Once a month, on "Pack the Pew Sunday" (when members are encouraged to bring friends and neighbors to church), the whole congregation circulates through the sanctuary and each member personally shakes hands with each visitor, while singing their rendition of the theme from *Cheers*:

> I want to go where people know that people are all the same.
> I want to go where everybody knows my name.

The members of the congregation laugh as they sing: the irony of using a song from a TV show about a bar in a distant city is not lost on them. Some might find it irreverent, but the song communicates their view that the church is a site of the authentic and down-to-earth community that some people might seek in a neighborhood pub. Even when there are few visitors, the song reinforces the joyous sense of belonging that New Bethany's members find in their church, a place "where everybody knows your name."

North Philadelphia East, where New Bethany is located, had a poverty rate of 27.3% in 2009, much lower than that of Fairhill a few blocks away, but higher than that of the city (25%), the state (12.5%), and the country (14.3%). Like Father's House, New Bethany draws a socioeconomically and geographically diverse congregation. About 25% of the regular attendees live within 10 blocks of the church; this is a higher percentage than at Father's House, but still only a fraction of the congregation. New Bethany, like Father's House, even draws a few people from the suburbs and other states. The pastor estimates that nearly 50% of church members are either professionals or business owners. Few are unemployed. A substantial number of members are related to the founding family and have attended New Bethany most of their lives; others learned about the church through colleagues.

New Bethany addresses the problem of urban hunger differently from Father's House. While they do not distribute food at the church, every other month the entire congregation travels to a neighborhood about three miles south of their church to help serve a hot meal at a large Christian feeding ministry called "Chosen 300." Chosen 300, like SHARE, works with many small churches and organizations, but whereas SHARE distributes food throughout the city, Chosen 300 brings in volunteers to central locations to feed as many as possible in a single sitting. In 2012, Chosen 300 was the focus of controversy in Philadelphia for its open-air feedings on the Benjamin Franklin Parkway and in a park near City Hall, dividing homeless advocates, religious groups, and civil libertarians. These feedings have drawn large crowds of the hungry to highly visible tourist locations but were banned by Mayor Michael Nutter in April 2012. Chosen 300, like several other religious groups, defied the ban and fed the crowds anyway (Slobodzian, 2012).

On one sweltering June evening, about a dozen members of New Bethany gathered at the Chosen 300 storefront on Spring Garden Street, just a few blocks north of Center City. A line of hungry people already stretched down the block. The church members found their way in through the back door on Ridge Avenue, past a small kitchen where large trays of chicken were baking in a convection oven. The little corridor opened onto a large multipurpose room, already filled with over 100 people packed efficiently around folding tables and chairs.

On a small stage at the front, Sister Stephanie and Elder Evans, not the usual church musicians, sang "Ain't Nobody Do Me Like Jesus," and Prophet preached a short sermon from the book of Job. Many of the dinner guests looked bored and hungry, but a few appeared to be receiving his message enthusiastically. Then somehow the volunteers all found places along a long serving table and were handed large spoons or tongs. Others began carrying hot trays of food in from the kitchen. The volunteers created plates of food assembly-line style: in addition to the baked chicken, there were mashed potatoes, greens, corn, salad, rolls, and cake. There was a short break for the volunteers as people got up from the tables. Then a second seating began and the plate production started over again.

At the end of the night, the New Bethany folks helped to clear and wipe down the tables, fold and put away the tables and the chairs, and clean the floor. The leaders from Chosen 300 called all the volunteers together in a circle and asked them to say what they had seen and experienced. They announced that 285 meals had just been served, and then offered a prayer.

New Bethany serves a meal at Chosen 300 every other month. When they volunteer, it is a bonding experience for the whole congregation. Like Father's

House, they do not actually provide the food, but they provide the volunteer labor to distribute it. In very rough terms, if 285 people eat at Chosen 300 each time, then New Bethany helps serve just over 1,700 meals per year.

Music is as significant a ministry at New Bethany as it is at Father's House, although this congregation has a different constellation of musical talents. There is no choir, but Prophet is very gifted on the Hammond organ. A praise team of four voices leads the singing, and on a few special occasions, Bishop sings (her rendition of "Calvary" is an annual highlight of the Good Friday service). The music may be of uneven quality if the most gifted musicians are absent, but no talent, however hidden, will be overlooked for long.

New Bethany also demonstrates how the dense network connecting small churches results in broader exposure for artists. Congregations visit one another for afternoon and evening services three or four times a month. New Bethany members make music at other congregations they visit, and visiting preachers and evangelists for New Bethany's monthly "Sunday Night Power" service (the last Sunday night of the month) are often celebrated as much for their musical gifts as for their preaching. The joint evening services can be two or three times the size of the morning services, or larger. This means that a musician or choir from a small church like New Bethany, with fewer than 50 in attendance on an average Sunday, may perform in front of 150 people on a Sunday evening, or more than 1,000 people over the course of a year. A talented musician can quickly gain a citywide following. The musical economy of the small independent churches, moreover, is connected to the larger cultural life of the city. In the churches, musicians make contacts and develop relationships that help them find opportunities and audiences beyond their own congregation.

One hot June evening, New Bethany Holiness Church was celebrating their Bishop with a special worship service. Several other churches had been invited, and the small space was packed. Worshippers responded to the music and the preaching with dancing and shouting. One of the elders announced that for Bishop's special day, they had arranged a surprise: a local singing group they must have heard elsewhere. As a trio of women made their way up the crowded aisle, Bishop Britton exclaimed audibly, "Oh, my God, it's that singing girl!"

They began to sing, and the lead singer did indeed have a powerful voice. Their rendition of "Angels Watching over Me" brought the congregation to a frenzy. After they sat down, Pastor Mack came to the microphone and said,

"I want you to know that I work at the Kimmel Center, and they asked me to be on a committee to help choose local groups for a gospel festival. I want you to know that I am going to give them your name." This was a striking example of Pastor Mack affirming local talent, and using bridging social capital to help religious musicians find success in a secular venue.

Poverty is not as grinding in the area around New Bethany as it is in Fairhill. Nevertheless, people struggle to make ends meet. New Bethany helped its members navigate a troubled economy during and after the recession. Church members not only referred one another for jobs, but supported one another in maintaining habits, behaviors, and attitudes they believe will lead to economic success. As W.E.B. Du Bois argued in *The Philadelphia Negro* more than a century ago, black churches have performed this service for generations, beginning in a time when there were no employment agencies to which free blacks could turn.[6] The "Christian life" to which New Bethany members commit themselves is not simply spiritual but encompasses a strong commitment to education and hard work along with modest dress, sexual restraint, and avoidance of drugs and alcohol. This commitment even includes care with 21st-century behaviors that could affect employability: Pastor Mack is always reminding the "saints" to practice good judgment in their use of social media such as Facebook. At New Bethany, the "Christian life" also includes entrepreneurial risk-taking: members who decide to quit secure jobs and start their own businesses are encouraged. These behaviors are not merely seen as expressions of moral and spiritual commitment but as the tools that will enable individuals to avoid or escape poverty as well. With apologies to Max Weber, one might speak of a *Pentecostal* ethic and the spirit of capitalism.

Alice Johns is a quiet, serious young adult who completed her bachelor's degree online while working full-time as a member of the support staff at a law firm. For Alice, New Bethany provided a surrogate family that encouraged her to pursue education and a career. She did not grow up at New Bethany but came to the church on her own as a teenager. She says that she grew up "in the projects," and describes her parents as unmotivated to work. "I've always been a person that came in the house and did my homework," she says. When she first began attending New Bethany, she says, her mother was jealous of Pastor Mack because of Alice's special relationship with her.

When Alice speaks about what the congregation means to her, she says, "It changed my whole outlook. My dream is to graduate and to move beyond the family stigma of always staying at home. My dad gives me a lot of motivation because I don't want to be like him." Alice is also a cancer survivor: at 19, she had surgery and radiation to treat a tumor. "I can't imagine going through it without God in my life," she says. The church did not create Alice's drive for success, but it constantly reinforces her determination to thrive physically, educationally, and economically.

Some aspects of the so-called prosperity gospel loom large in the collective consciousness at New Bethany. Like some high-profile prosperity pastors, Prophet often urges the congregation to become financial "partners" in the ministry, predicting that if they give generously, they will be rewarded with fine houses, clothes, and cars. However, at New Bethany, this prosperity gospel is combined with a deep commitment to the Protestant work ethic— a hybrid approach to religious economics. Members of New Bethany openly desire luxury and material comfort, and they use that desire to motivate spiritual discipline and hard work. "God can make us wealthy and calls us to be," says Pastor Mack. Her sister, who operates a day care center and is the chief financial officer for the church, quickly adds, "Wealth is not always money. It's your health. It's having your family still with you. It's having an education."

Leaders at New Bethany believe that God has singled out their church for a particular blessing, which is constantly being revealed to the leaders in dreams, visions, and signifying events. Sometime during the cold winter months of 2010, Pastor Mack experienced an inspiration about a verse from Hebrew Scripture, and shared it with the congregation. The verse, which recalls the institution of the Passover, reads, "This month shall mark for you the beginning of months; it shall be the first month of the year for you."[7] Pastor Mack interpreted the verse as a message heralding a season of success and blessing for the congregation. She continued to preach about "the beginning of months," and often transmuted "the beginning of months" to "the month of months," telling the congregation, "It shall be a *month of months* for you." "Month of months" does not appear to be a phrase from the Bible, but was a common 19th-century expression for a particularly lovely, prosperous, or busy month.[8] For Pastor Mack, describing the present as "the beginning of months" or "the month of months" locates the congregation in a sacred time of prosperity and blessing that transcends the calendar: it may be three, six, or twelve months since she began using the phrase, but it is still "the beginning of months" and "the month of months." This frames the promise of abundance, if not prosperity, as hope.

Pastor Mack and the church leaders believe that the blessing will touch not only those who belong to the church and give generously to its mission but will rain down on anyone who walks through the door. During one service that our researcher attended, Prophet "prophesied" over her and her work, saying, "Sister Beth, you might not be able to dance like we dance. You might not be able to shout like we shout.... But people gonna *read* what you write. People gonna *buy* it!"

Frequently, events appear to confirm this belief in a particular, generous blessing. One Sunday morning after the offering, Pastor Mack and other worship leaders called for a two-minute "praise break" of rhythmic clapping and dancing because the church had just received an unexpected donation of $1,000. At Pastor Mack's pastoral anniversary, one woman stammered out in a tear-choked voice that a time of personal financial struggle had finally ended, saying, "Since I been here, the month of the month of the month of the months—*they started happening for me.*"

The idea that God will bless the faithful with financial success is central to the congregation's identity, but hard work is a significant element of faithfulness. There is a clear expectation of financial miracles at New Bethany, but also a hard-edged practicality. God helps those who help themselves. "It's not going to fall out of the sky like Henny Penny," says Bishop Britton. "The Bible also says they that don't work, don't eat."

Gender matters at New Bethany: the most visible leaders, both women, are aware that women face different obstacles to economic and personal success than men. Pastor Mack encourages the young women in the congregation to finish their education and get a job, so they won't ever have to depend on a man. She urges them to use the church as an excuse to keep themselves out of bad company. "When I was in school, people would say, 'No point even talking to her—she's a church girl," she will say. "There is nothing wrong with being a church girl." Bishop Young preaches about taking her granddaughter to fancy dinners and giving her nice jewelry. "I don't want her to be impressed if a man does that for her," she says.

New Bethany members make no apologies for desiring material things in this world. Little luxury items are even visible sometimes in worship, as when Pastor Mack presented each of the female preachers who spoke at her pastoral anniversary with a small box of Godiva chocolates.

New Bethany dreams of leaving Germantown Avenue for a nicer building elsewhere. Because their building is adjacent to the ever-expanding property of Temple University, it is possible they could indeed one day sell their building at a substantial profit. But their dream of greatness includes social outreach along with material comfort. Pastor Mack and Prophet's sister, Danielle, who now pastors a church in Virginia, articulated the dream in a sermon at Pastor Mack's anniversary:

> Prophet, you ain't danced your best dance yet. James, you ain't shuffled your best shuffle yet." [The congregation laughed—Prophet *is* the best dancer, and James *does* shuffle.] "When I was in the praise team you used to skip. You ain't even begun to skip yet. Keisha, you think you singing now. Just wait for the opening night and the red carpet.

> You ain't seen nothin' yet. You're going to see a *better you*.
> Don't get robbed of the soup kitchen. I see a ministry where you will feed the hungry and preach the word. Pastor gonna preach until it comes to pass. I see about thirty people.... Pastor, the passion, vision, determination is in your heart, is in your mouth. Find it!

Father's House and New Bethany are connected to some of the nearby institutions in their community, but are not even aware of others. New Bethany is intensely aware of its neighbor Temple University: tearful family members of patients at the university hospital are often welcomed to evening services with compassionate prayers and open arms. New Bethany is as likely to "fellowship" with a congregation from Delaware, however, as with a Pentecostal congregation a few blocks away.

New Bethany Holiness and Father's House of Prayer are profoundly connected to a broad network of churches and institutions that spans the city, the region, and beyond. They provide important services in the areas of hunger relief, the arts, and employment, among others. However, they are not necessarily well connected to their most immediate neighbors—to the other congregations, the small businesses, the schools, and the community organizations that may have the greatest impact on daily life on their particular blocks. But how much do small independent churches really differ, in this, from larger denominational churches—are larger churches actually any better connected on their blocks and in their neighborhoods? What difference do the cultural and social connections make, or could they make, to local communities?

5 PENTECOSTAL LATINAS: ENGENDERING SELVES IN STOREFRONT CONGREGATIONS

For me, the person I was becoming when we left was erased, and
another one was created.

—ESMERALDA SANTIAGO, *"When I Was Puerto Rican"*

There are two small storefront Latino/a Pentecostal churches in
Fairhill, across the street from each other on the same block as the
Burial Ground. They are so unassuming that pedestrians would not
know that they are houses of worship. They blend in with the other
buildings on the block—the façade of one is plain stucco; the other,
brick. Those attending worship in the congregations pass each other
on the sidewalk on Sundays and prayer meeting nights. Although
there is a lot that they share culturally, they barely interact. They are
as different as two congregations in the same tradition can be.

Entering Iglesia Pentecostal Maranatha's glass doors, one is
immediately struck by the brightness of the interior: gold trimmings adorn the altar, a grand chandelier hangs right above the pulpit and sparkles from the blinding florescent light. Beige benches
span the nave and four royal chairs grace the altar, along with
the American and Christian flags. On the side walls are identical
framed prints—one in English and the other in Spanish. There are
two gold Victorian-style mirrors on the walls as well that reflect the
light even more. On each side a small mantel holds three decorative
candles and banners advertising the women's and children's societies. There is also a framed poem. The prints are of the well-known
"Footprints" poem about being carried by God and the smaller
poem encourages the believer, "Don't Quit."

On any given Sunday the church is in active prayer 10 minutes
before the service begins, "warming up" for worship. On one Sunday
five women were assigned as "prayer warriors" in the front, facing the
congregation, holding hands in prayer on behalf of the congregation.[1]

This chapter was co-written with Leila Ortiz who conducted the
ethnographic research presented.

The pastor, Eduardo Maldonado, a Puerto Rican man in his early 50s, is leading the collective prayer from the altar.[2] His bright red suit, white patent-leather shoes, and gold jewelry seem to amplify his already grand and authoritative voice. Some congregants are kneeling at their seats or at the altar, others stand to pray, all verbally respond to the pastor as he fervently prays for church growth, the youth of the congregation, and the community. He prays for God to bring an associate pastor, that God will surround addicts and drug dealers in the neighborhood, that the church family might be strengthened, and that the worship service be a good one: "God, work in each person here, so that they will not leave the way they came." As Pastor Maldonado says "Amen," all stand prepared for worship and ready to be changed. (Later, Maranatha would move farther down the Avenue to a new location in a former theater.)

Across the street at Iglesia Pentecostal Esperanza, beyond the slim tin door and a hanging display of evangelistic booklets with titles like "How to be saved and know it," "The Romans Road Map," and "The Grace that Saves," is the narrow and humble nave. The benches have been recently painted a glossy chocolate brown, the walls hold baskets flowing with bright faux flowers, and on either side of the altar are two columns emblazoned with the words "santidad" (holiness) on the one and "a Jehova" (to Jehova) on the other. The people at Esperanza are praying as passionately as, if somewhat differently from, their Pentecostal neighbors across the street.

Julio Eduardo Torres, the pastor, a slender Puerto Rican man in his mid-30s, has invited all to stand and pray together as the official service is about to begin. He wears dark slacks and a light button-down shirt, but no tie or jacket—the air conditioning system is temperamental. Pastor Torres invites the church to pray with him for all that is in their hearts. He has specific petitions, or requests, for God: healing for the sick and the depressed, strength for the minds of the people, help for the community, and a change of heart for those not converted (or "saved"). He also prays for the liberation from the spirit of division—apparently the church is in the midst of conflict and it is the Devil that is fueling it, not the individuals involved:

> We are at war! The devil is attacking us, attacking this church, and we cannot give him the victory. Lift up your voices in praise! Cry to the Lord! We need deliverance! We are at war, church! We do not know what time we will be leaving this place [the world]. It does not matter. What matters is "que le hagamos guerra al Diablo," that we declare/ have war with the devil!

The congregation clamors, "we rebuke you [the devil] in the name of Jesus!" over and over again. After this time of "spiritual warfare" Pastor Torres reads a portion of the sacred text and hands the microphone over to Mario, his right-hand man who will be leading the next section of the service.

The differences between these storefront Latino Pentecostal churches are aesthetic, doctrinal, and generational. At Esperanza, the young pastor asks his first-generation Puerto Rican seniors to decorate the sanctuary. This sacred space is reminiscent of a humble home back on the island—with faux flowers and simple trimmings. In this space piety equates to holiness, alienation from "the world" assures salvation, and modest dress reflects purity. This congregation is consistently proclaiming the "final days" when the world will end with judgment, and the need to repent and be prepared. Once a month the women take turns evangelizing at Temple University Hospital two blocks away. They walk the streets in their long, flowy skirts, hair in a bun, no makeup, and plenty of tracts (religious brochures). They go to the psychiatric ward and "rebuke" demons—driving out the foreign spirits they believe are responsible for mental illness. They then move to pediatrics and pray with children and their parents, and finally roam the other floors in the hospital to pray for the elderly, sick, and lonely. The men also go out once a month and "hit the street corners" to evangelize to the local drug dealers, addicts, and homeless. Together, the men and women live out their conservative faith and work for the transformation of the community, one soul at a time. A couple who has responded positively to the evangelistic outreach comes on Tuesday nights and sits in the second-to-last pew. At 9:30 pm sharp Pastor Torres interrupts his sermon and announces to the congregation "Sonia and Paul are heading out now," and addresses the couple, "Be safe. See you next week" as the congregation blesses them as they go on their way. Paul had been a drug dealer and was now under house arrest with a "grillete" (ankle bracelet). One of the church ladies is the couple's neighbor and has made the necessary arrangements for them to come to the church once a week to hear the Word of God, with the hope that they might be "librados de una vida en cautividad"—liberated from a life in captivity.

At Maranatha, in contrast, you find a young congregation that is very much oriented to living in American culture. Though they share the same fundamentalist doctrines as Esperanza, the members of Maranatha differ in how they embody and express their faith. Their sanctuary is loud and bold. The older women wear makeup and earrings, dye their hair, and are fashionably dressed, albeit in loose-fitting clothing. The teenage and young-adult women wear pants and/or more fitted attire. The pastor preaches that "God sees the heart, not the shell." Here aesthetic piety does not equate to holiness or modest dress to purity. Instead, Pastor Maldonado will also assert, "Women are always going to be tempting to men. I mean, they're Puerto Rican! Doesn't matter what they wear—they're beautiful. Besides, we are sons and daughters of a King! We should adorn ourselves as such.... Christian women don't have to look pale and lifeless. That's depressing."

This "adorned" Pentecostal congregation also tries to live out their faith and serve the community. As at Esperanza, they evangelize on the Avenue and visit the sick at Temple University Hospital. They have built relationships with the local drug dealers who share a wall with them, and they make Thanksgiving and Christmas baskets for the poorer families in the neighborhood. Maranatha has also developed a three-year-long Bible Institute that welcomes fellow Christians who are recommended and supported by local pastors.

These neighboring Pentecostal churches intentionally engage the community, sometimes in inconspicuous ways and at other times abrasively.

FIGURE 5.1 By 2012 Maranatha had moved to a higher profile building—a former theater on Germantown Avenue.

However, they do not engage each other. Though they share a block on Germantown Avenue, they do not share understandings regarding holiness, piety, and women's dress. They blatantly avoid confrontation and separately go about their ministries. The pastors primarily dictate this non-interaction. However, faith is not all that informs these opposing religious views. Lived experience, culture, and social location also provide insight into how two Pentecostal congregations can share urban space, doctrine, and a culture, and still part ways as to the embodiment of their faith.

Nostalgia Puertoriqueña: Puerto Rican Nostalgia

Upon entering either Iglesia Maranatha or Esperanza, one is likely to be greeted by the *faith-full* Latina who testifies of how she was abandoned at the age of 11 in the slums of Puerto Rico, and "rescued by God through the church." You are sure to meet the Latina who denies herself rest and freedom in order to please God, take care of her "familia carnal" (blood family), and serve her "familia iglesia" (church family). You may even enter in conversation with the intellectual Latina who, though "firme en la palabra" (firm in the Word), is a selective reader of the sacred text and is skeptical of oppressive interpretations of the Bible that are commonly taught in Latino congregations. These women are representative of the diversity of personality and experience found in small Latino congregations along the Avenue; they embody the tensions that Latinas struggle with when negotiating complex sociocultural, political, and ecclesial infrastructures in a foreign land they now call home.

For over a year, ethnographic research was conducted in Esperanza and Maranatha. As well as participating in worship regularly, the researcher interviewed men and women in the congregations, in both formal interviews as well as in rich informal conversation. It was clear that a central dynamic in the congregations revolved around gender—the meanings and expressions of gender roles and the power that reinforced them.

The Pentecostal members interviewed were all Puerto Rican and shared a common story of emigration to the United States. Pastora Sandra (Pastor Torres's wife), Beatrice (Esperanza's drummer), and Luis (Maranatha's Sunday School teacher) each had personal narratives of their parents leaving the island in search of better opportunities for their families. Carmen (Maranatha's church secretary) could recall and describe moving first to

New York, and later Philadelphia, to find community among other Latinos/as. Both congregations had members who spoke of how they encountered racism and discrimination daily that pushed them to the margins of their new society. They also reminisced and told of growing up with a sense of pride in being Puerto Rican as well as of having political status as citizens of the US commonwealth. They would become nostalgic as they remembered the stories their parents would tell, and the experiences they also had, of living on "la isla del encanto"—the island of enchantment; how the land was disarmingly beautiful, how neighbors were like family, and daily life revolved around music, food, and laughter. They also remembered in vivid detail how hard it was to find well-paying jobs and how they struggled to provide. These memories and present reality coexist for Puertoriqueños/as. They live a hyphenated existence with "two places, and no place on which to stand."[3] "Here I'm not American enough because I'm Puerto Rican, and when I visit the island I'm not Puerto Rican enough because I'm 'Americanizada'—Americanized," says Ana, a one-and-a-half generation Puerto Rican woman who has lived in Philadelphia for over 30 years.[4] Ana, and all the Puerto Rican participants in this study, are passionately bound to the island "que les vio nacer"—that saw them come to life, *and* have circumstantially assimilated to the land "que mana leche y miel"—flowing with milk and honey, or so has been claimed.[5] Clara E. Rodriquez paints a historical picture of how Puerto Rican men and women arrived to this "Promised Land," the United States, and can now call it home.

Puerto Rican Migration Stateside: The Development of a Hyphenated Existence

Rodriguez recounts how during the first wave of immigration, 1900–1945, the pioneers established themselves in New York City. During this period, contracted industrial and agricultural jobs were available to the new migrants.[6] Economic opportunities provided the base for many of the Puerto Rican communities outside of New York City as well, including Philadelphia. The second phase, 1946–1964, is known as the "Great Hispanic Migration," which overlapped with the second wave of the Great Migration north for African Americans. Rodriguez notes how during this period the already established Puerto Rican communities in New York City further increased their numbers and expanded their borders. Data show that while communities in new areas of New York, New Jersey, Connecticut, Illinois, and other parts of the country emerged and developed, the majority of the Puerto Rican population still remained in New York. By 1960, the census showed that there were 600,000 Puerto Ricans in New York alone. By 1964, the Puerto Rican community made up 9.3% of the total population of New York. The final stage of migration from the island began in 1965 and has continued to the present. In this stage there is a different dynamic at work—"the revolving-door migration." Puerto Ricans have not just permanently landed on the continent, or even just in New York. Rather, there has been dispersion to many other cities as well as mobility back and forth to the island.

By 2000, there were 128,928 Latinos in Philadelphia, accounting for 8% of the population. But the first decade of the century saw dramatic growth in the Latino community, which swelled to 187,611, or 12% of the city's population--the Latino community in Philadelphia had grown by 46%. Although this includes Mexican and South American immigrants, Puerto Ricans constitute the largest proportion of Latinos by far; Philadelphia remains the third largest Puerto Rican community in the continental United States. The Latino population has remained proportionally stable in the Fairhill section along Germantown Avenue, where these two congregations are located. In 2000, there were 8,006 Latinos living there, making up 44.4% of the population. By 2010, Latinos made up 48.3% of the neighborhood.

The data only provide a superficial profile of the lived experience of Puerto Ricans in Philadelphia—their struggle to find community away from home and the longed-for prosperity even as they navigate the experience of being "strangers in a strange land" that they did not think would feel so strange. Those who come to the States, and to Philadelphia in particular, come largely because of the push factors of socioeconomic realities back home. They come with dreams of a better life, ambitions, and the expectation that things will be different. They also come with religious faith. They often encounter a difficult and confusing reality as they encounter racism and exclusion that is foreign to their experience, and marginalization as they try to break into the job market and into society.

> I didn't believe racism would be so in your face the way it was when I first got here—and I was bilingual! I remember going to work at the factory and making sure to find "la pastora"—the pastor's wife—during lunch

personalization

so that she wouldn't eat alone. She didn't speak English and didn't have many friends. I loved getting to talk to her in Spanish.... It was like getting away from the all the racism and zoning into what came natural to me—my language. The people who sat around us would taunt us and murmur, "You're in America, speak English," "We no speaky Spanish here. Only English," "Go home if you can't speak the language. You're not welcome here."... One day I got SO mad. I looked up at la pastora and said "That's it!" I turned to the two who were saying all that garbage and said "You know what? I don't know why you're always talking so much about us because you're bilingual too! You speak English and whole lotta bullshit too!" I'm sorry. I know I cursed but you know, it gets to be too much!... I turned back around just hoping to God they wouldn't do anything and apologized to the pastora, cuz I knew she understood that last word.... The whole room was in shock. But that was it. They never bothered us again.

Anthropologist Samuel Sullivan has noted that Latinos in the United States understand their struggle as being rooted in American racism; the politics of exclusion and discrimination are thwarting their dreams. Latin Americans outside the United States, on the other hand, understand their oppression to be rooted in the structures of poverty.[7] Encountering the bitter experience of racism stateside, Puerto Ricans seek sanctuary in community.

If there is an experience that unites Hispanic/Latinos in the United States, it is a hyphenated existence of belonging, yet not belonging. Historian Justo Gonzalez describes this experience as *mestizaje*. The term *mestizaje* cannot be easily translated into English. In fact, it cannot be properly defined. At best we can simply describe its origin and the possibilities within it. The category of mestizaje was first applied by Father Virgilio Elizondo to the Mexican American experience, and it was then employed as a tool for sociological, psychological, and theological analysis.[8] Elizondo noted how in colonial times, in what is today Latin America, a *mestizo* or *mestiza* (feminine) was a person born of a Spanish and Native union. This union created a "new thing"; an unexpected, unknown and ultimately, uncomfortable reality. Elizondo makes the following claim: "Biologically speaking, mestizaje appears to be quite easy and natural, but culturally it is usually feared and threatening. It is so feared that laws and taboos try to prevent it from taking place" (Elizondo, 1995). The irony lies in the fact of history; the massive mestizaje that gives rise to a new people is the result of force—usually through conquest and colonization. As such we find that in many ways "the ideas, the logic, the wisdom, the art, the customs, the language and even the religion of the powerful are forced into the life of the conquered."[9] The newness that resulted from this forced union— a hyphenated identity— had, ironically, a sense of integration. The *mestizo/a* was Spanish *and* Native, even if that identity resulted from colonization.

The Puerto Rican migrant experiences the same complexity; their land was also conquered; they too are a "new people" who rise out of Spanish, Native, and African parentage. The identity that results from being Puerto Rican and "Americanized" is ambiguous; they have many, but not all, the privileges of US citizenship. Their sense of identity is further complicated by their new, chosen mobility. Feeling marginalized by the new country and no longer at home on the island, many Puerto Ricans cling to their communities of faith as places where they can safely navigate the construction and recon-struction of their social and individual identities.

From "Newcomer" to "Local": Puerto Rican Families in Transition

As a *mestizo* people, Puerto Ricans come to Philadelphia for myriad rea-sons: seeking employment, health care, education, or to join family are the most common. In search of that which is familiar (like all immigrant groups), they find their way to a community of faith to discover a taste of home and the experience of belonging. Here they will not need to negotiate difference or social stigmas but can find accompaniment and solidarity. Those who have recently arrived stateside do not hesitate to seek assistance and mentorship within the church. There is a cultural expectation of help from those who understand the journey and have somewhat mastered the system. New arrivals look to more established people for guidance and networking, and perhaps, at first, food and shelter. The only requirement is connection to the island. Flora (Maranatha's treasurer) did not know anyone when she moved to Philadelphia. She had come with her husband and four children because he had found a job here. She described the role of community in making the transition:

> Oh, it was fine. You know how we are. Once we see, or meet, some-one from the island we're quick to connect and help each other out.

> It so happened that my neighbor was from Santurce! Like us!...We became good friends; she showed me around, helped me with getting the kids in school...translating and making sure they had what they needed....She was also there when my husband abandoned us and I was left to provide for my 4 kids alone....She was the one who invited me here! I was Catholic but I decided to come anyway. It was such a difficult time.

Flora and her children have been members of Maranatha since 1976. Like her friend, she has now become mentor, and mother, to many newcomers throughout the years. She has also found comfort in the teachings and rituals of the Pentecostal church, despite spousal abandonment and the sudden loss of her 24-year-old son to a ruptured aneurysm. Each time she talks about him, her voice cracks and she needs time to gather herself. Yet she easily talked about how her faith, and the church, had helped her make sense of the tragedy:

> At first I questioned God and was disappointed that God had taken my son away before he could repent, but I soon came to terms with the *fact* that all children are God's children and they are but "prestados"—lent—for a season. I was never mad but always very sad. I look back and I'm sorry I asked. God has always been my comforter, but it's not easy [crying]. These wounds are always bleeding, but God has never failed me....My son has passed, my other son died of Hepatitis C in his forties, but he was right with God, and my youngest can barely breathe or talk—he has a tracheotomy [She explains that her daughter, thankfully, is in good health]. It's so hard to be happy with everyone else when my family is either gone or struggling.

Scholars have long seen the relationship between economic hardship and spiritual experience. For Marx, religion functioned to reinforce economic disparities by providing a rationale justifying the maldistribution of resources, as well as a coping mechanism for those who are poor. Other-worldly religion promises reward in the next life and the opportunity for catharsis in the sufferings of this life. Later analysts of Pentecostalism affirm that people facing deprivation and abandonment "enter, through the Spirit, into another realm. They find themselves in another world, an open world, in which the gates

FIGURE 5.2 Small congregations provide a refuge for Latinas who carry heavy burdens in an often hostile context.

of their prison have been unlocked. It is a world in which the sick are being healed, broken families restored, broken lives put together again, and desperate economic situations often changed" (Shaull and Cesar, 2000). Flora is in constant pain, yet she feels that she can deal with it because she believes "God is always my comforter" and "has never failed me yet." This is why she can cry and lead, question and teach, suffer and preach. In this space, migrant members of these congregations can safely live in the tension between temporal heartache and faithful hope for a better (literal and heavenly) tomorrow. They can do so because they are not alone on the journey. Everyone has become vulnerable in this space; everyone knows the other's stories, and for the most part, all are welcome. This space and community provide stability, security, and family when the world seems fickle and erratic. Members are no longer merely newcomers in a strange land; they have become locals and experts who have found a "home" in these small storefront churches.

Despite the generational differences we find in Maranatha and Esperanza, assimilation to the North American context requires struggle for all the newly arrived. Members of both congregations suffer the social injustices that come with being a Latino stateside. Both communities find solace in a space they can call their own; a space where the powerful in society have no authority over their dealings. The sacred spaces they create are controlled by the people within them; systems are developed, change is authorized, and identities are formed. This safe space, where vulnerability is encouraged, also empowers its members to use the skills acquired as people living on the hyphen. To live on the hyphen requires the ability to balance two realities (Puerto Rican and North American), the need to be savvy, the ability to manipulate your environment and to survive its injustices. The church becomes the arena where its members use these skills to explore their social and religious identities. It is also where gender roles are contested through the practices of lived religion—the reading of the Scriptures, sharing in corporate prayer, and participation in cultural expectations and religious tradition.

Becoming a Mestiza Woman of God

The Latina women in Iglesias Esperanza and Maranatha are in a constant process of putting together various pieces of an identity puzzle. Beyond challenges of negotiating the hyphenated identities of self and group that are borne by all Latinos/as, women are engaged in a particular process of constructing their gender identities. Anthropologist Marcela Lagarde describes this unique process for Latinas:

> Feminism cannot only be identified by public mobilization, protests and demands, with women with fists up in the air, with the burning of brassieres, or with women dressed in black as in mourning in light of genocide. *Feminism also happens in solitude.* It does not only take place in public struggles, but also in new forms of human sharing and everyday life. It happens around coal stoves and kitchen tables, in the market place, the hospitals and in the churches.... To associate only a few prominent feminists with the totality of the cause makes invisible the millions of other feminists.[10]

Though the Puerto Rican Pentecostal women in these congregations would not consider themselves feminists, they process, "in solitude," what it means to be a woman in multiple contexts—in the Puerto Rican diasporic community as well as in the workplace and marketplace; in their familiar communities of faith and in secular American society where they encounter gender models of independent and self-defining women. As described, they live in tension, holding their need to accommodate to and to resist the oppressive social structures they encounter, all the while maintaining their place in the community. This *mestizo* dynamic places them in what cultural theorist Gloria Anzaldúa (2000) argues are "liminal spaces, transitional periods in identity formation." Anzaldúa believes this is a liberating location, since in it there is the possibility of transformation. Building on this idea, historian Daisy Machado argues that to live in these liminal spaces "is to want to remember who we are.…It is to not compromise their identity by crossing the boundary of total assimilation."[11] That idealized interpretation does not always capture the lived experience of conflicting identity claims for the women interviewed. Balancing the impulse to assimilate as well as to resist that which is oppressive, to respond to a new context and to remain loyal to familiar traditions, can be paralyzing. All of these simultaneous claims come with different role expectations and personal agency. The easier route is to submit to prescribed identities allotted by church and culture; contesting identity can be confusing and exhausting. The voices of the women from Iglesias Esperanza and Maranatha illustrate these complex dynamics as Puerto Rican migrants struggle to embody social expectations in their faith communities, social groups, and the urban context that is now home.

Ana: Tough and Fragile

The worship service was just beginning at Maranatha one Sunday morning and Pastor Maldonado was criticizing the women of the congregation from the pulpit. A woman from the church had been in the hospital the previous week and, to his knowledge, none of the church ladies had gone to visit her, as was their expected role. For an uncomfortable 20-plus minutes the pastor expressed his extreme disappointment. He accused the women of not living out their call to serve God and neighbor. Though the pastor was addressing all the women, at one point he specifically addressed Ana. He yelled, "Where is the love sisters?! I don't want to hear any excuses!" He continued, "None of you, not even Ana, the president of the women's society, had the courtesy to visit sister Mayra!"[12] At this statement, Ana jumped out of her pew, "Oh yes

I did! I was with her all day Wednesday!" Everyone looked over at her as she dared to confront the pastor. She stood with determination, expecting retaliation. There was none. At that unusual moment, Ana stood up to the pastor, essentially challenging his authority, in order to protect her sisters from further harassment. Although Ana may not consider herself a feminist, her urgent willingness to defend herself and "liberate" her sisters from her pastor's patriarchal suppression reflected feminist principles of self-determination and individual agency.

The pastor attempted to enforce his priestly authority, and his authority as a man, over the women. His genuine interest in the hospitalized member was overshadowed by his *machista* (sexism) approach, an approach that is supported by his ecclesial infrastructure and his reading of the biblical texts.[13] [14] In his teaching and preaching the pastor has employed fundamentalist and literalistic interpretations of the biblical texts traditionally invoked to keep women "silent."[15] As a man in the Puerto Rican culture, and the pastor of the congregation, he is considered the authority through whom all things concerning this church are mediated. In this particular encounter the pastor, though well intentioned, used his priestly authority to shame the women, demonstrating both his fundamentalist doctrinal beliefs and his *machista* attitudes.

Ana's courage in correcting his mistake challenged the authority rooted in her religion and culture, and allowed for the harassment to cease, at least that day. In a year of observation at Maranatha, this was the only time Ana was willing to publicly resist unwarranted and humiliating criticisms from the pulpit. On every other occasion she simply accepted the indictments by looking down, occupying herself with her three-year-old granddaughter, or going to the restroom to cry. She later disclosed in conversation that she did not counter his verbal attacks because of a deep sense of shame. If the pastor accused her of shirking her duty as a Christian, she could resist as she did in the service, but when charged with bad parenting or reprehensible sin, she retreated into a sense of guilt and was silent.

> Do you know how many times he has humiliated me from the front and I can't defend myself. When I'm alone I think of what I want to say, but when I'm in front of him I just shut down.

Ana "shuts down" because she has been taught to believe and affirm the oft-cited injunction from the Bible about obedience to leaders: "Obey your leaders and submit to them, for they are keeping watch over your souls and will give an account. Let them do this with joy and not with sighing—for that would be harmful to you."[16]

The source of Ana's shame is that she was a victim of repeated sexual abuse as a child. A relative convinced her that if she allowed him to "do with her what he wanted" he would not touch her sisters. As an adult she learned that he molested each of her four sisters under the same pretenses. Her own powerlessness has been a complex, lifelong issue for Ana, whose story, regrettably, is not uncommon among women. Ana seeks to have power in relationships with men but it is a struggle. Her ambivalence toward a male pastor who can publicly humiliate her is evident: "I never had a father figure. All the men in my life abused me. I have trouble hearing any man tell me what I gotta do. I've gotten better.... He's a good pastor. He wants to lead me the right way."

This is how Ana justifies her willingness to submit to male authority and oppressive infrastructures: he is the pastor. This is not an ordinary man; he is ordained by God to lead her into eternal salvation. He is, according to Ana, the mediator between her and God. As such, his perspective is divine and his admonishments "must be" well deserved.

Unfortunately, Ana believes she deserves to be punished. As a single mother who went through a string of severely traumatic relationships, she suffers from tremendous guilt. She has a past full of sexual, verbal, and psychological abuse. She told me that, after her conversion, she became intimately involved with a woman who had a drug addiction. As a result, she lost her home and her children were estranged. Ana believes her past warrants her present suffering at the hands of her religious leader. She is willing to stay under these conditions because "God hasn't opened doors for me to move from this church.... I think by this time I should be at a level with God that my faith is higher, but it's not. I take advice. I take the punishment, I take the verbal abuse, I take it all. What else? I mean I do what I can." It is important to note that Ana is not submissive to other men (in or outside of the church) but because her pastor represents God she is easily disarmed and left defenseless. This might seem like an extreme and unusual situation. But Ana's experience highlights what is a difficult choice for many Latinas: to suffer in silence or leave a congregation, cutting oneself off from the community, which gives a sense of place. As difficult as the situation seems to outsiders, consider Ana's negotiation of safe space: the small, familiar congregation is still safer than life outside of the protection of the community, even if this space is defined by *machismo*.

Other scholars have argued that Pentecostal women feel empowered in the church. They describe how Pentecostal women can be authorized by a Spirit that transcends even church authority to preach, teach, and to find their voice within their communities (Adams, 2002; Lorentzen, 2009).[17] They are also happier than they were when "in the world" because their husbands are no longer drinking or abusive. This is not the reality at Iglesias Maranatha and Esperanza. Most of the women there are single mothers: widowed, divorced, or abandoned. That said, this does not keep them from being empowered by their experience of the Spirit to be agents of liberation in their communities. They have suffered, but they are also teachers, preachers, evangelists, and prophets.

Adams and Lorentzen illumine how Puerto Rican Pentecostal women can be empowered by their church participation and how they can also be subjugated within the church. As they move in broader society they can appeal to a divine source for their identity. They bring conflicting models of gender identity into their congregations where gender roles remain complex and selectively accommodated. There is a hyphenation of gendered religious identity as women are free, but not free; with agency, but submissive. As we see in Ana, three significant factors determine when male authority is accepted and subservience enacted: the woman's unwillingness to break solidarity and challenge *machista* attitudes and behaviors; the adoption of an ascribed state of irrevocable sinfulness and the immobilizing shame it creates; and a belief that the pastor has responsibility for her soul. Though the pastor is the more theologically progressive of the congregations in this study, Pastor Maldonado's *machista* inclinations are reinforced by his theological reading of the sacred text. This causes Ana to consistently negotiate her salvation and subdue her instincts to resist.

Philosopher Ivone Gebara speaks in more theoretical terms of the cultural constructs of gender affirmed and intensified by the church which are the lived experience of women like Ana. To be specific, she addresses how *machista* attitudes are supported by religious infrastructures that apply a literal reading of biblical passages such as 1 Timothy 2:11–15:

> Let a woman learn in silence with full submission. I permit no woman
> to teach or to have authority over a man; she is to keep silent. For
> Adam was formed first, then Eve; and Adam was not deceived, but the

woman was deceived and became a transgressor. Yet she will be saved through childbearing, provided they continue in faith and love and holiness, with modesty.

To read and internalize this text, as a *machista* Puerto Rican male, is to confirm what his culture has considered a given—the dominance of men. He is able to use the biblical text to justify female subjugation and keep women in "their place." To read and internalize this text as a Puerto Rican woman, who accepts *machismo* as a natural part of the male role, is to also accept an oppressive social arrangement as her "cross to bear," since according to the literal reading of the Bible she is the embodiment of sin itself.

In the Pentecostal doctrine, salvation is conditional upon one's behavior and faithfulness. If one is committing a sinful act at the time of one's death he or she is considered eternally damned. For this reason it is common to hear that one "has to be ready at all times." The Pentecostal congregant understands that salvation is dependent on obedience to the biblical commandments, which include honoring their pastor. To disobey and challenge the priestly order is to sin and, therefore, to do so threatens one's acceptance by God. As such, when deciding whether or not to refute an unjust accusation from the pulpit, the woman is indeed negotiating her eternal salvation as well as her identity.

Ultimately, how women internalize their own sin and guilt is highly significant when considering whether to act according to the gender roles established in the culture and the church. In fact, a mental map of what it is to be male and female becomes fused with "God the Father" for Latina women. It is remarkable that Ana's identity negotiation in her moment of contestation was in a public space. This was not "in solitude," nor behind closed doors in a private conversation. The community of faith becomes an arena in which identities are formed, contested, and perhaps changed.

Ana continues to struggle with her identity as a woman, a Latina, and a member of this Pentecostal congregation. The pastor continues to criticize her and she continues to wrestle in the moment with who she is and how she should respond.

I stayed thinking…I don't deserve to be treated this way. God forgave my past. I don't need to be reminded all the time that I failed God and that

> I wasn't a good mother to my kids. I'm a good Christian woman now. My
> kids forgave me. We love each other and we're good....So the other day,
> I did it! I was able to say what I was thinking when the pastor went there
> again from the pulpit. He was preaching about how sin makes us sick and
> brings division to our families. He looked over at me said, "Right Ana?"
> I stood up to him and said, "Yes, sin makes us sick and brings division,
> but God forgave me and threw my sins to the bottom of the ocean. He
> restored my family and I am a new person. To God be the glory!"

For her, this was a small moment when she rescued a positive sense of her
own strength from the pastor's attempt to again define her as a failure. Ana
is still in the congregation and has found resources within it to help her get
ahead. Recently she relinquished her position as president of the women in
the congregation, and graduated from Maranatha's three-year Bible Institute.

Nydia and Deborah: Church Mothers

Nydia has a strong leadership role in Maranatha, as church deacon, singer, and
teacher. She identifies herself not by her roles in the congregation but by her
relationships with the children within it. "I am 'Lucilla' and 'David's' mother,"
she said. She is recognized as a woman devoted to God and church, but she
identifies herself as a mother. Like Flora, the single mother at Maranatha
who had lost two of her three children, Nydia had a failed marriage and had
devoted her life to her children; "Son la luz de mis ojos"—they are the light of
my eyes. Nydia has translated her passion and care for her children to her role
as deacon. She advocates with love, honor, and respect for the sacred space
and for all those who take part in the ministry. Nydia is not interested in
being liked, but insists upon reverence and fairness in the congregation.

> I keep order in the church. There is not talking, or eating, or chewing
> gum. One time I went over to a woman who had a habit of chewing
> gum in the church and I took a napkin and went right over to her and
> put my hand to her chin; "Spit it out." She refused so I told her like
> it is, "that is disrespectful to God and the preacher! Don't you know
> that everyone that stands up there deserves respect, even if it's a child?
> Don't chew gum in here! Either hand it over or throw it out." She got

up and threw it out. [The pastor] asked me to be a deaconess because he knows I don't play. I keep order while the service is going on.

Though this may seem insignificant, respect in this sacred space is imperative in Nydia's theological understanding and she enforces it in the congregation. As such, the authority with which she confronts those with "a lack of consideration" and even her approach to the situation is telling of her self-identity as mother and disciplinarian. To be a mother in Puerto Rican culture is to embody a constant support system that provides nourishment to body, mind, and soul. The mother is revered as sacred, "all knowing," wise, spiritual, and holy. To be a mother in this context is to be respected and honored. To fall from this elevated pedestal is to draw dishonor and shame, as we have seen in Ana. Nydia, however has lived up to the cultural expectations and wears her role proudly. So much so that as caretaker she is willing to be perceived

FIGURE 5.3 Pentecostal religion is an ambiguous but important component for Latinas in the construction of gender identity.

as the "bad guy" to ensure a healthy and respectful dynamic in the congregation. She insists that everyone is to be treated with respect and is prepared to confront whoever disrupts that possibility within the congregation. This unwavering stance is common among the women at Maranatha.

In conversation with Pastor Maldonado, he humbly tells of his experience with Deborah:

> If you only knew the things I've done. I've been a pastor now 33 years and the things I've done, the people I've hurt and the souls I may have caused to be lost....About 12 years ago I was serving in another church and we had a very active member there. She was married to a man who was not a Christian and had a baby. One day she came to church with the baby and I noticed that the baby had pierced ears. After the service I told Deborah she needed to take those earrings off of the baby. She began to explain that her mother-in-law gave them to her and if she took them off she would have problems with her husband. I told her that there are some battles we must be willing to fight in obedience to God. She began to cry and tell me she couldn't and wouldn't. She didn't want to have problems with her family. So I told her that if she didn't take those earrings off of her baby she could no longer be an active member in my church. She was an anointed and great woman of God! I can't believe I did that....I never saw her again and now I can't even apologize....It's about the heart. I know that now.

Despite the fact that Deborah may have agreed with the pastor and recognized that pierced ears were considered a sin in her denomination, she opted for family and culture against her church and denomination. Not even her faith would impede her effort to maintain a healthy marriage, and so she abandoned her leadership in the congregation.

Deborah, like Nydia, is fully invested in her sociocultural identity as a mother. Nydia carries the additional weight of being a single parent; she takes her parenting very seriously, to the point of translating it into an official role in the congregation, and in so doing finds social affirmation. She defends the "holy place" and "holy people" and feels they are hers to care for and protect. This devotion to others in both the "familia carnal" and the "familia iglesia" sustains them as the church is again the arena for identity construction.

FIGURE 5.4 Family is of central importance among Latino immigrants, and especially in congregations.

Raquel, Maria, and Sandra: Testify

What we hear from Latinas on any given night during worship at Esperanza is a public declaration of their devotion. As they testify, the congregation yells words of affirmation, "Amen!" "Si, Aleluya," "Dios es bueno!"— God is good! Their delivery is powerful enough that they become catalysts for others to find their voices. The scene at a typical worship service in Esperanza might seem to the visitor to be chaotic and cacophonous. Participants might cry, run to the pulpit, kneel with hands up in the air clamoring for deliverance or in complete surrender to the spirit in the room. And this is just the time of testimonies. The women at Esperanza testify how they will seek change in their home, in their finances, in their emotional life, or even in their body.

Pastora Sandra, Pastor Torres's wife, immediately began to share what she believed were miracles in the congregation. She testified that she had been healed from cancer three times and had the papers to prove it. With great satisfaction and joy Sandra explained how the doctors didn't know what to say about her condition but could simply state that she was healed. She then affirmed this account by stating how that morning there had been a prayer vigil. She arrived to the vigil hurting from arthritis in her hip; "I prayed and prayed then I asked the church to pray for me as well. They did and now I feel no pain! I'm healed!" she says. "Este es el Dios que nosotros servimos; el que cuida de sus siervos y los libra de toda enfermedad. Amen? Amen!" ("That's the God we serve; the God who cares for his servants and liberates them from all illness. Amen? Amen!")…God knows I can't afford health insurance. He always makes a way…"

On another day, during a congregational fast, Nancy, a member of Esperanza, unashamedly declared

> I know you've heard this before, but I have to testify!…I was abandoned when I was eleven years old. I was raised by the streets. I prostituted myself. Became a drug addict. Had illegitimate children. Attempted suicide countless times. I was lost. Hopeless. And alone. I believe I delayed God's work because I didn't come to him sooner.…But I am a child of God now. Amen? Amen! Sometimes God allows tragedy in our lives to demonstrate His glory! Today I can give testimony of his glory because I am alive!

The congregation had heard this testimony several times before, but it didn't keep them from clinging to her every word. They yelled in affirmation, nodded their heads in agreement, and applauded every statement that gave credit to God for her miraculous rescue from the street life. Her sense of agency and the inner strength it took to turn her life around was not part of her oral narrative, nor was it the primary concern of the congregation. Exalting God always takes precedence.

Maria, another woman in the congregation, followed:

> Sister, Glory, Glory, Glory!…I was tormented by demons. Imprisoned and later institutionalized. I went crazy and could no longer raise my children. Oh Jesus.…One night on leave from the psych ward I couldn't take it anymore and begged my sister to take me to a church. Yes, Lord…It was past 10 pm during a snowstorm here in Philly and we drove and drove looking for an open church. Thank you Jesus.…I couldn't give up. I knew that if I didn't come to Christ that night I would die. Holy, Holy…Can you believe that after midnight

we found an open Baptist church?! Glory to God! They were having some sort of vigil and it was packed. I went straight to the altar and cried and cried and cried [Maria begins to cry]. I was delivered that night. Those demons left me and I have new life....Halleluiah!

Sandra, Nancy, and Maria each had a story to tell. They each praised a God who healed and rescued them just in time. They persisted and dared to convince their hearers that despite very serious obstacles, "God will make a way." They proclaimed that they were healed, alive, made new—and gave God the credit. In public their testimonies are dramatic and unashamed. In their narratives they reduced themselves to unworthy, broken beings who would be incapable of contributing to the world were it not for God's rescue. In private they are proud and eager to share tales of their direct connection to the divine, but did not acknowledge their own agency. These stories demonstrate public constructions of individual identity. All three women described surmounting incredible obstacles of physical and mental illness, addiction, and the extreme measures it takes to survive on the streets and to leave them. Yet in the narrative, they do not ascribe any strength or capacity for change to themselves. They have a voice, but chose to highlight their spirituality instead of an innate, or acquired, transformative agency. "God picked me up when I was lowest of the low." Giving God all the credit speaks to their humility, which, within this context, is a virtue. To announce every move, decision, strategy, or tactic used to come out of "the lowest of the low" is counterproductive. This community recognizes absolute surrender to God as holiness. These women seek holiness and surrender it all with the faithful expectation of being heard by God as humble servants.

In a private conversation with Pastor Torres's family, Pastora Sandra tells of how she met her husband during a visit to Puerto Rico. "I went to Puerto Rico for a spiritual retreat led by our council. I saw him during worship....I was smitten by his devotion and leadership....I remember I began to pray and asked God to keep me on his [Torres's] mind." Pastor Torres then recounts; "I woke up one night and she was all I could think about, but I was confused. I started praying and telling God how she didn't even know I existed. I asked why she was on my mind." He went back to sleep but the next day nothing had changed; he couldn't stop thinking of her. He saw her the next day and dared to confess his inability to stop thinking about her. They chuckled as Laura told him how she had "prayed believing" he was her future husband

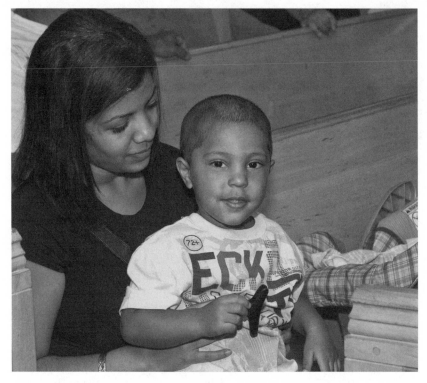

FIGURE 5.5 Many women in the congregations studied had dramatic back stories of transformation.

and that "God had answered the prayer of the faithful." Pastor Torres affirms, "She is a holy woman of God. God really did listen to her prayer.... That's what happens when you surrender your life to God. God listens and answers our prayers."

These migrant Puerto Rican women at Esperanza and Maranatha in Fairhill are consistently defying, and submitting to, cultural and ecclesial norms. They live on the hyphen between Puerto Rican and American culture, between personal defeat and spiritual victory, between surrender here on Earth and favor up in heaven. They are selective enforcers of their agency who act depending on the circumstance and the projected outcome. If they seek corporate affirmation they praise God and return to their pews exalted for their humility. If they seek change they speak out and confront their accuser, the disrespectful gum-chewer, and anyone who might interrupt collective

FIGURE 5.6 Faith and culture are passed on as Latina mothers struggle to make church a safe cultural space for themselves and their children.

harmony; and if they seek to remain part of the community, however dysfunctional, they are not afraid to stay and endure the tensions.

Conclusion

Describing the Puerto Rican Pentecostal experience found in two neighboring storefront churches is complicated by the many factors that inform the socioreligious dynamic. The churches are located in a neighborhood where the Latino population is growing, and more than half live in poverty. Sociocultural and economic realities, experience, and ecclesial expectations often dictate individual and collective interactions. Those who live within this reality constantly have to construct, and reconstruct, their social and individual identities. Coming from a patriarchal society, they find themselves in a context where women are allowed to speak out and encouraged in their own agency. And yet, that new context can be hostile to newcomers. The church becomes an arena in which these constructions take place, sometimes publicly, sometimes in solitude. The church is where social and religious identity is explored and where gender roles are contested through the practices of lived religion. Despite, and also because of, these complex dynamics, Iglesias Maranatha and Esperanza play an active role in the Latino/a community by embracing newcomers to the United States and offering a "home away from home": a sense of belonging in this new and strange land. As part of the Latino community they encircle, shelter, and help mend those on the margins: the family with no health insurance, the addicted, tormented, suicidal, and imprisoned. As such, these inconspicuous small storefront churches contribute to life on the Avenue by providing a social and psychological safety net for those who find themselves without one.

6 MUSLIMS ON THE BLOCK: NAVIGATING THE URBAN ECOLOGY

O mankind! We created you from a single (pair) of a male and a
female and made you into nations and tribes that ye may know each
other (not that ye may despise each other).

—Qur'an 49:13

A crowd gathers at Al Aqsa Islamic Center on Germantown
Avenue to begin the Interfaith Peace Walk, as they have every year
since 2003. It is a walk, not a march, organizers insist. There are no
signs or chants, just a sea of white clothing, signifying peace and
unity among the wide diversity of faith traditions represented—
Muslim, Jewish, Buddhist, Sikh, Christian, Quaker, Hindu, Native
American (Lenapi), and others. After Muslim prayers they walk
for several hours to various sacred sites—a synagogue, a church, a
mosque, and, one year, the Liberty Bell—for short prayer services
from a variety of faith traditions. On a Sunday afternoon each May,
500 to 1,000 people join in this "walking dialogue," encountering
those from different traditions, often for the first time. Here they
can share their beliefs and ask questions in a safe context.

"Why do you identify yourself as a Jew if you don't go to
synagogue?"
"Because I would be Jewish enough for Hitler."

"Why do you choose to wear a veil?"
"It is a sign of modesty...and I am proud to be identified as a
Muslim."

"Does your church teach peace or support the wars?"
"That's complicated..."

The annual event is a 21st-century expression of William Penn's
Holy Experiment—the designation of space as a safe haven for
those escaping religious persecution, "where lion and lamb could

FIGURE 6.1 The annual Interfaith Peace Walk.

lie together" in a diverse and tolerant community. Could Penn have imagined the religious diversity of this group walking down Germantown Avenue? After all, his utopian vision stopped short when it came to true egalitarianism— only Protestants were allowed to vote and hold office in early Pennsylvania.

The Interfaith Peace Walk is but one example of the increasing visibility of faith groups, particularly Muslims, in Philadelphia and on the Avenue. The American Muslim community has experienced exponential growth in the first decade of the century. The number of mosques increased by 74% between 2000 and 2011, from 1,209 to 2,106 (U.S. Mosque Study, 2011). Pennsylvania ranked seventh among states with 99 mosques; the Philadelphia area has the fourth-largest number of mosques among US metropolitan areas. In the city itself, there are 40 mosques. It is estimated that 2.6% of the city's population (39,540 people) is Muslim—and that number is growing (ARDA, 2010). Not long ago Muslims were seldom seen on some parts of Germantown Avenue, particularly in Chestnut Hill and Mt. Airy. That has changed in the last decade.

There are two mosques on the Avenue, which are quite distinct from one another. [1] Yet both are Sunni, both have acquired and adapted former commercial properties, and both are relative newcomers in the religious ecology and have had to learn to navigate it carefully.

Masjid as Sunnatun-Nabawiyyah
("The Germantown Masjid")

The neat red awnings of the Germantown Masjid, a former furniture store, designate the separate entrances for men and women. Prayer is offered five times daily, but it is on Fridays, at the Jum'ah, that the largest crowds gather. After the prayers, a throng spills out onto the Avenue where vendors sell wares—oils, books, foods—creating a festive atmosphere that lingers into the afternoon. National data show that the average attendance at Jum'ah has increased from 150 in 1994 to 353 in 2011. Almost two thirds of American mosques reported an increase of 10% or more in Jum'ah attendance, according to the U.S. Mosque Study (2011). "Membership" is defined in the study as the total number of mosque participants, which has also grown—from 485 in 1994 to 1,248 in 2011. The median membership per mosque is 400. The Germantown Masjid has experienced growth as well. In 2004, it reported that 300 people were associated with the mosque. By 2012, according to Brother Saadiq, a leader in the mosque, there were 1,000 participants, which is about average for the city's mosques. The growth does not surprise Brother Saadiq. "It's one of the fastest growing mosques in the area.... It galvanizes people into a community."

Brother Saadiq is representative of those who gather at the mosque: he is African American and was raised in a Christian church, as were all the mosque participants interviewed for this study at the Germantown Masjid. His beard is long and tinted with red at the end, and just barely touches his long ivory tunic. A large photograph of Mecca dominates the wall beside him and he refers to it often. Although he struggles with Arabic, he has made the hajj, the pilgrimage to Mecca, 15 times.[2] The sense of community he finds in Mecca, a dense gathering of people from all parts of the globe who are able to communicate and to get along, is holy to him and shapes his vision for community back home.

The men from the Germantown Masjid were always polite and open to talking with us. While Christianity had not been satisfying for them personally, they were not critical of it. But they were eager to share their Islamic beliefs. One of the men in the shop near the mosque, who was selling books and tapes about the faith, came closest to a criticism of another faith. The young man explained why he had left the church: "Why would I worship a God who let his son be killed?" Islam, he felt, provided more structure and

FIGURE 6.2 The Germantown Masjid.

safety, and a stronger deity. The streets of Philadelphia claim the lives of too many African American men each year; seeking a strong, protective God makes sense.

Founded in 1993, the Germantown Masjid is middle-aged among American mosques, more than a quarter of which have been founded since 2000. The attacks of September 11, 2001 did not have a chilling effect on the spread of Islam in the United States despite the spike in hate crimes against Muslims.[3] Only 3% of mosques have only one racial or ethnic group, making Islam more diverse than other American religions. Predominantly African American mosques, which represent a small fraction of mosques in the United States, are more dependent on conversions than those that attract immigrants from South Asian or Arab countries. And they are better at recruitment: African American mosques average 20.3 conversions a year compared to 15.3 for other mosques (U.S. Mosque Study, 2011). As in other faiths, sharing one's own story of salvation can be compelling. The men of the Germantown Masjid engage in theological conversation easily and unselfconsciously. They explain their faith in passionate and sincere language.

The women are more guarded in conversation. They often have children in tow and are segregated not only in the mosque but elsewhere. The local Halal Pizzeria has separate booths for "sisters and children." Gender roles are clearly delineated at the masjid. Women who are completely covered by their *hijab* and veil, and stay covered outside the mosque, are referred to as the *muhajjabah*. The covering is intended to preserve their modesty and prevent them from being enticing to any man except their husbands. Most, but not all, of the sisters were *muhajjabah*. Watching these women walking down the street in the dark clothing on an August day in Philadelphia makes one wonder why African American women who had not been raised as Muslims would choose to affiliate with such a religious community. (After all, Catholic nuns gave up their distinctive but heavy "habits" and veils in favor of modest clothing that affords more comfort and freedom of movement.) The social relations at the Germantown Masjid are patriarchal in structure, compounding the curiosity of outsiders. Men may marry up to four wives and can have wives from the other Abrahamic faiths (Christianity and Judaism), whereas intermarriage is forbidden for Muslim women. This question of the conversion of African American Muslim women is the subject of an excellent ethnography by Carolyn Moxley Rouse (2004), who was able to tease out the nuances and complexity to address the question of converting into a patriarchal community, which seems to work against the interest of women. Or does it?

On Germantown Avenue, Fadwa, a woman in her late 20s with eyes that pierced through the narrow slot in her veil, identified her motivation in pragmatic terms. She had encountered what sociologists have identified since the 1980s as the "shrinking pool of marriageable males" in urban African American communities (Wilson, 1987). The streets and the prison system have taken a huge toll (Alexander, 2010). Those men still in the community are disproportionately unemployed and under-educated. Many are self-medicating with various substances. For Fadwa, the mosque offered a structured community with strong, disciplined men who are part of a system of accountability. Donning the hijab was a small price to pay to be able to fill out a marriage application and find a good man.

Rouse was able to explore the complexity in the lives of the muhajjabah and found that the hijab enabled the women to "use their bodies as sites of resistance" to racism, the exploitation of women, and economic disparity. "Before their conversions, most lacked the language to express their anger and resentment at a racist and sexist social system. . . . Islam gave them a language and methodology for challenging those systems of oppression" (Rouse, 217). Rouse found varying levels of ambivalence about the faith and about social relations among the women—the very act of questioning in itself signified individual agency.

Although more African American men convert to Islam, the proportion of women coming into the faith is increasing. By 2011 women accounted for 41% of all converts (U.S. Mosque Study, 2011). The reasons for any religious conversion are complex. But in the case of African American women making such a dramatic conversion, certainly the search for a partner and co-parent, as well as the attraction to a community that lives in resistance to social systems that oppress, moves toward an understanding of the gender dynamics around affiliation.

The Germantown Masjid can be seen as countercultural and embodying a discourse of resistance to the dominant culture. Adherents are forbidden to vote or enter the military, for example. The cluster of shops around the mosque has created an economic and cultural enclave. The discourse of resistance is also verbalized in critiques of the dominant culture and its institutions. This too is reflective of African American Muslims nationally, who are much more likely than other Muslims to agree with the statement that "America is an immoral society." Overall, the proportion of all Muslims who agreed fell from 56% in 2000 to 24% in 2011, but African American Muslims stayed near the 50% mark (U.S. Mosque Study, 2011). It might first appear that the participants in the Germantown mosque are constructing a moral community in opposition to the dominant society, and are in spatial and cultural withdrawal from it. For example, sermons can focus on the immorality of pornography, the need to keep the fast during Ramadan, and calls to remember that Islam is the one true religion.

However, the principles of Islam, as they interpret them, lead members of the masjid to transcend their particularity, even as their identity as African American Muslims is reinforced. Brother Saadiq is not only involved as a co-chair with the interfaith health fair in Germantown but also serves as a commissioner with the city Human Rights Commission. When he first joined the commission, he went to a retreat where members were asked to bring an artifact that represented their motivation for serving. Brother Saadiq brought his Qur'an because his impulse to work for the whole community is rooted in his faith. "You want to do things that benefit people and get you your reward from the Lord. I like those types of things and sometimes they're not just for

Muslims…but for humanity. Because the real message of the Prophet (may the peace of blessings of Allah be upon him) was for humanity, it wasn't just for Muslims."[4] Consequently, Brother Saadiq said that he works with public officials for programs and policies that will bring "safety and security for the whole environment, not just for Muslims." Creating a sense of safety and security is a recurring theme for him and for the masjid. Two years earlier, a student at the Germantown High School had attacked a teacher, breaking the teacher's neck. Despite the presence of security officers and metal detectors in the school, it remained a dangerous place for those who came to teach and learn. Brother Saadiq then organized a cadre of 24 brothers from the mosque, which is a mile down the Avenue from the high school. They came in and stayed for two and a half months, providing discipline and security, acting with firmness but not physical force. They were able to stop a lot of drug dealing and harassment, restoring safety by the end of the school year.

The Germantown Masjid has been increasingly engaged in venturing outside of the "9-block radius" (the geographical area for which they feel primarily responsible) whether celebrating the end of Ramadan by holding their their *Eid al Fitr* prayers in the nearby public park or participating in the health fair. This higher public profile and engagement follows national trends for American Muslims. Almost all mosque leaders (98%) agreed in 2011 that "Muslims should be involved in American institutions." Ninety-one percent

FIGURE 6.3 Women set up small kiosks outside the masjid.

agreed that they should participate in the political process as well. Both percentages had increased slightly since 2000. Although African American leaders showed somewhat lower support for political participation, there was still strong support for engaging the political system—84% (U.S. Mosque Study, 2011). Even if not through the electoral process, African American Muslims, like Brother Saadiq, are able to engage the system and improve the quality of life in communities.

The Germantown Masjid is located in a crowded religious district. Across the street is the New Redeem Apostolic Church, a congregation of 300 that was founded in 1865 and is housed in a former Episcopal church. On the other corner across the Avenue from the mosque is the New Jerusalem Church of God in Christ, also well established. Down the street is Victory Baptist, with a spiffy new banner outside. Right beside Germantown Masjid is Overcoming Church of Jesus Christ, with the smallest congregation on the block. The founder, Reverend Enwright, left New Redeem over a theological dispute. He firmly believes churches compromise their integrity when they become involved in "buying and selling," which includes most fundraising. If clergy are dependent on the offerings of others, they will cease to preach the truth, he feels. Therefore, to prevent hypocrisy, he is self-supporting, although his small congregation does contribute several thousand dollars during a year, which helps offset his expenses in the house/church.

All four of these churches are within a few steps of the mosque and have their own histories, cultures, and faith commitments. Like their Muslim neighbors, these faith communities have core beliefs and make strong, if not exclusive, truth claims. Sharing limited urban space, passing on sidewalks, hearing the music, and seeing the dress of people of other faiths requires a daily negotiation for all of these true believers. Rhys Williams, in a review of writings of urban religion, observed that faith groups in densely populated urban neighborhoods cannot avoid confronting religious pluralism: "And no matter how sealed one's theology—how bright the line between the saved and the damned—one must see the nonelect every day and decide on a practical response to them (even if not a theologized response)."[5]

The potential for conflict in such close quarters was great—there is no avoiding the "nonelect." Reverend Enwright in particular was privately critical of the habits of his neighbors next door ("too messy"). All the congregations had a number of services and meetings during the week and parking was limited. All believed in evangelism—that is, presenting their faith claims to others, including strangers, in the hope of conversion to their understanding of truth. And yet the only real conflicts anyone could remember were about trash after Friday prayers and a dispute over parking when the mosque first moved in. Apparently the priority of clergy parking conflicted with the need for the street space after Jum'ah, which became framed as a lack of reciprocal respect. The parking authority was called in and the conflict was resolved.

Since then there has been a kind of religious "code of the street" (Anderson, 1999), which has allowed the five religious groups to negotiate the sharing of urban space. In his ethnographic research on Germantown Avenue, when crack dominated some local economies and redefined neighborhood life, Elijah Anderson was looking particularly at social "codes," which he defined as "a set of informal rules governing interpersonal public behavior."[6] "At the heart of the code," he wrote, "is the issue of respect."[7]

On these blocks on Germantown, crack is not the currency, but it could be said that truth is. Communities of faith are organized around their understandings of ultimate truth. Rather than "deal," they meet, and urban space is negotiated through (usually) non-verbal codes that signify mutual respect. After the parking dust-up, which was very much about perceptions of respect, communication in this local ecology has been encoded. Scheduled times for worship services, prayer meetings, and Bible studies are staggered throughout the week to allow each congregation to have access to parking and sidewalk space. Fridays belong to the mosque. There is even a spatial differentiation of evangelism turf, with the Christian congregations going in different directions for "witnessing," and the Muslims relying on the self-selection of those who are interested in discussing the faith to approach them on the Avenue. Individuals of all the congregations share their faith in conversation with those they meet in everyday life, but there is no apparent competition for converts on the Avenue that they share. While the relationship among the congregations falls short of the engaged, even celebratory, pluralism of the Interfaith Peace Walk, there is a detente negotiated through a religious "code of the street," which enables each group to focus on its own congregational life.

The accommodation of others does not come from a passive resignation to realities beyond one congregation's control—that is, "They're here, like it or not. Let's just live with it." There is an active mental engagement in creating space—physical and theological—for others. Three themes emerged in conversations with the believers on the block, both Christian and Muslim. First of all, there was a respect for the "other" faith, particularly in terms of

FIGURE 6.4 In this crowded religious district, five faith communities share one block.

racial politics. In conversations throughout the project, the Muslims avoided criticizing other religious groups, both within and outside Islam. Even though most had left their Christian upbringing, they respected, for example, the role of black churches in the civil rights movement. Similarly, church members did not dismiss Islam out of hand, particularly as they observed it being practiced on their block. They did not agree with many of the practices and theology, but they did respect the strength and clarity of the African American Muslims in their clear witness against the dominant culture. They appreciated the role that Islamic chaplains played in the prisons and the role of mosques in enabling men to re-enter society with a supportive community to help in the transition.

Second, almost everyone had members in their family from the other faith tradition. They had had practice in trying to understand the other faith, to negotiate holidays and marriages, and to accept the members nevertheless as family. Robert Putnam and David E. Campbell documented the social impact of the increasing religious diversification of extended families (Putnam and Campbell, 2010). They found that two thirds of Americans have at least one extended-family member of another religion.[8] The presence of an "Aunt Susan" can create a cognitive dissonance for a Christian believer:

> We call it the "Aunt Susan Principle." We all have an Aunt Susan in our lives, the sort of person who epitomizes what it means to be a saint, but whose religious background is different from our own.... But whatever her religious background (or lack thereof), you know that Aunt Susan is destined for heaven. And if she is going to heaven, what does that say about other people who share her religion or lack of religion? Maybe they can go to heaven too.[9]

In fact, they did find that such cognitive dissonance did result in a change in one's thinking. Almost two thirds of African American Protestants (62%) agreed with the statement, "People not of my faith, including non-Christians, can go to heaven." Such an inclusive theological perspective would have been unthinkable in previous generations. The theology espoused at the Germantown Masjid is more inclusive of the other Abrahamic faiths; Jesus is acknowledged as a prophet for Muslims in a way that Mohammed is not for Christians. The church folk are traveling a long theological distance to be able to bridge a short physical space on Germantown Avenue. But bridges also need to be built between the Christian churches. Interfaith understanding and cooperation is desired by the Muslims, even though the lack of unity among Christians surprises them. Brother Saadiq was caught off guard by this:

> Everybody has their congregations. One of the things that amazed me the most when I started getting involved (in the health fair) was...I was under the impression that there was more connection among the Christian churches. But then when I started working on the inside I started seeing that it's the same thing. Everyone still just represents and does what they do in their respective areas and the other people do what they do over there—it's sort of their business and we're not doing that. Forget about Muslims. It's that church there and that church over there.... You start learning that there's still some human healing that needs to happen.

Certainly, part of the lack of conflict among the Pentecostals, Baptists, and Muslims can be attributed to insularity—the focus on maintaining their own congregations. But besides a mutual respect for the other, and learning habits of interfaith tolerance within families, the Christians interviewed were conscious of another reality, which made them even more appreciative of their Muslim neighbors: these residents of this section of Lower Germantown had all benefited from the presence of the Germantown Masjid. However exotic the Muslims might have seemed when they came in 1993, it became apparent over the years that "all boats had risen," all had benefitted from their presence: the streets were safer and cleaner. Their establishment of some businesses encouraged others to open. This was just a nicer neighborhood to live in or come to, to worship or shop. The numbers bear this out.

Mapping out an approximate nine-block radius around the mosque, there are some hopeful signs of a neighborhood coming back to life. Between 1998 and 2006, the overall number of crimes, both against persons and property, decreased in this area by 26.5%.[10] The crime index for the city as a whole was also falling during this time, but only by 9.8%. Although not every crime category in the area around the mosque declined, there were positive indicators in robberies, for example, which were down by 18%, and car theft, which decreased by 43%. Prostitution saw a dramatic decline, dropping 86% during this time period, and there was a 30% increase in drug arrests (which could be due to increased drug activity or improved policing). Burglaries were down 28%—particularly in commercial establishments. Aggravated assaults with guns saw a slight decline of 5%. The neighborhood was getting safer.

As new businesses opened—a fashion shop, two Halal pizzerias, a deli, and a book shop among them—home sales started increasing as well. The number of home sales more than doubled from 1998 to 2006. Arsons were down (by 24%) as were the numbers of vacant properties. Physically, the area around the masjid improved, which is remarkable since poverty increased from around 29% in 2000 to 42% by 2009.[11] One longtime resident of the area looked down the Avenue toward the Germantown Masjid and exclaimed, "You could eat off these sidewalks now!"—not something often heard in Philadelphia.

Al Aqsa Islamic Center

Moving down Germantown Avenue for more than 30 blocks, through two commercial districts, passing blocks that are blighted and blocks showing signs of improvement, a distinctive building appears—a welcome display of color amid the drabness of crumbling brick, boarded-up row houses and weedy lots. Al Aqsa Mosque commands a block with its gleaming building, school, store, parking lot, and playground. On any given day, its true color, though, is the buzz of human activity.

Al Aqsa began as a mosque serving Palestinian immigrants in Center City Philadelphia in 1991. At first hosted by an Albanian mosque, it soon relocated on the edge between struggling South Kensington and the longtime up-and-coming Northern Liberties neighborhood. The mosque moved into a former furniture warehouse—a large, nondescript red brick box without any indication that it was a house of worship. When I began this project, 500 people came to prayers each week. The school on the upper floors had an enrollment of 300 students. For a largely immigrant Muslim congregation, the industrial exterior enabled them to maintain a low profile, lending a sense of security. And yet Al Aqsa was well known in the Muslim and Arab communities. Many were drawn to it because of its Academy (Pre-K through 12), and because the mosque offered services such as marriage and funeral rituals in the Sunni tradition. It maintains its own cemetery as well. The membership, as well as the leadership, became much more multinational—immigrants from northern Africa and throughout the Middle East were drawn to the mosque, while it maintained its base of Palestinians. Since its inception, Al Aqsa has grown exponentially. By 2012 there were 3,000 families participating in the mosque, with 1,500 coming to Friday prayers. Many come from throughout the region, including New Jersey, but 100 families live close enough to walk to it.

The student body of the Al Aqsa Islamic Academy reflects the same diversity. Sixth graders enthusiastically described their school as a "United Nations," with children coming from 12 different countries and cultures, not all of them Arab. Almost half of the students are African American Muslims, whose cultural experience here is different from that of students in the academy at the Germantown Masjid. Interestingly, the principal at Al Aqsa, Abdur Rahman, is from the more mystical branch of Islam, Sufism—and is also a former Lutheran pastor.

The ethnic variety of the student body reflects a diversity of practices and, to a certain degree, beliefs. Girls wear a variety of headscarves of different styles and colors, but all expose their faces and reflect a rainbow of fabrics and complexions. One girl, from a bi-cultural family, wears a blue denim veil that she takes off when she goes back to her Latino neighborhood. Another sports a Phillies cap on top of her veil. Rather than eschewing attention, these girls mug for the camera, draping their arms over each other or striking a more sophisticated pose in their long skirts.

The school buzzes with the energy of any middle school in an urban area—lockers slam, there is laughter in the halls and on the playground, and students put their heads together, working intently on a shared assignment. The policy is that girls and boys are to be kept separated in the school (to the degree that that is possible) but there is a lot of interaction nonetheless.

Farah, a 17-year-old senior, reflected on putting together her identity as both a Muslim woman of Palestinian descent and an American. Beneath the hem of her hijab, blue jeans and fashionable shoes signify the hyphenated identity. Her sleeves do extend to her wrists, but her nails are neatly painted. Farah wants to attend nearby Temple University. She explains, "Ladies need the weapon of a degree because you never know what will happen." She wants to study public speaking and have a career in real estate. Marriage is also on her horizon. She and her family do not believe in forced marriages, but there will be a pre-nuptial agreement with an education clause so that she can pursue advanced degrees, if she chooses, as a married woman. In the meantime, she prepares for college but takes time to go to movies or to stay in touch with friends on Facebook.

Farah feels comfortable in her identity and safe in the world. Once, a drunken man on a bus asked her, "So are you going to bomb us now?" The driver immediately kicked him off the bus, and she did not really feel threatened, then or now. The constant interaction across cultures within the school prepared her for crossing boundaries outside of it. Every year she participates in the citywide Day of Service on Martin Luther King Day, along with her classmates. During her upper school years she participated in an interfaith youth group, Walking the Walk.[12] In the program, youth from clusters of churches, mosques, synagogues, and temples meet regularly for sacred text study and a service project. Farah believes that by participating in Walking the Walk, "I have fulfilled one of my duties as a Muslim woman to give dawah.[13] Hopefully I can touch others, like when I explained why we don't eat pork." But others had also touched her. In a discussion of homelessness, Farah was particularly moved and inspired by the "loving response of a Jewish girl" who identified the humanity of a person on the street whom other students had found scary. It was kind of an epiphany for her to see such "noble values" in someone of another faith. She began to see the commonality of beliefs and ideals, such as the call to charity.

At Al Aqsa—both the school and the mosque—there is a culture of crossing boundaries. Al Aqsa's diversity gives members daily opportunities to transcend the particularities of race/ethnicity, language, national background, and gender. Certainly, for the many immigrants at Al Aqsa settling into American society, this is a valuable skill.

In the mosque, there is the traditional separation of prayer space by gender. However, the independence demonstrated by Farah is true of many of the adult women in the mosque. In fact, women maintain leadership roles in the administration of the mosque and in community organizations they participate in. Although the *imam* (an Ethiopian) does not shake hands with women, all of the men of the mosque interviewed for this study did. (The imam does greet women with a warm, wide smile.) There is flexibility in the construction of gender roles and interaction between the sexes.

Al Aqsa has worked pro-actively on developing good relationships with the neighborhood of Kensington rather than becoming an ethnic or religious enclave. By 1997, members of the mosque organized an Arab-American Community Development Corporation. Its purpose is to "to empower the Arab-American community in the Philadelphia metropolitan area, promote its economic development, and combat racial, ethnic, and religious discrimination."[14] The community development corporation (CDC) began as many CDCs do—developing some of the abandoned land in the neighborhood.

At Al Aqsa, 9/11 (the date of the terrorist attacks on New York and Washington in 2001) hit hard. Despite the fact that they had a mosque culture that enabled participants and students to develop relationships across the boundaries of nationality, gender, and religion, all of this social capital did not prevent them from feeling a sense of vulnerability. Part of the outcome from 9/11 was the social reconstruction of Muslim as "other," as evidenced by the increase of hate crimes and hate speech at this time, like that directed at Farah. Of course, what became known as Islamaphobia was not universal in the United States—media and leaders of the dominant culture also demonstrated fairness, equality, and an individualistic perspective that tempers stereotyping. Still, it was hard for members of Al Aqsa to feel entirely safe. Marwan Kreidie, a leader at Al Aqsa and the CDC, said that they had been involved in more traditional development projects, "And then 9/11 happened," forcing them to redirect their efforts toward taking care of Arab Americans, many of whom were new to the United States. For the next decade, they focused on food distribution, English as a second language (ESL) classes, "citizen training," legal services, and a benefit bank that gets people connected with needed public services. Only by 2012 were they able to move toward developing low-income housing across the street from Al Aqsa. This will provide 40 to 54 units of housing for low income families, regardless of religion or national origin. Part of giving immigrants from Arab countries a sense of safety has also meant cultivating bridging social capital —those connections with people or agencies outside one's community.[15] Administrator Chukri Khorchid, who had come from Syria, has worked on developing good relations with civic authorities—the Federal Bureau of Investigation (FBI), the police, and the city government. The mosque serves as a neighborhood polling place. A picture of the staff with Mayor Nutter is featured on their website's home page.

In these first few years after 9/11, Al Aqsa continued building social capital, both among its multinational membership (bonding) and with institutions outside its walls (bridging).[16] Al Aqsa is not surrounded by the density of communities of faith as is the Germantown Masjid. There are two independent storefront churches a block and a half away, and a COGIC congregation and a Catholic parish are located off the Avenue, three blocks in either direction. Interfaith relationships in the immediate vicinity are unproblematic. But because of its public profile, Al Aqsa was known in the wider interfaith community. After 9/11, clergy from Christian and Jewish congregations contacted Al Aqsa to offer support. The mosque responded, engaging the broader religious ecology, a process that relies on social trust.

Members of the mosque soon began to talk more seriously with their friends from other traditions about building up the interfaith community at this moment when Muslims in the United States, including those coming to prayers in Lower Kensington, were feeling especially vulnerable. One of their first actions was to organize a commemorative interfaith service on the first anniversary of the 9/11 attacks.

During the course of those early conversations, Jewish and Christian members pointed out that Al Aqsa did not look very mosque-like on the outside, so together they imagined a "beautification" project. In 2003, through the initiative of the Arts and Spirituality Center (now called Artwell), an interfaith collaboration was developed that soon brought new partners into the venture, including Philadelphia's Mural Arts Program. The participants from Al Aqsa were eager to strengthen their relationships with their neighborhood and to have a building that would reflect the beauty of their faith.

The renovation became an exercise in cross-cultural relationship-building. Two women emerged as primary organizers of the effort: Adab Ibrahim of Al Aqsa and the Reverend Susan Teegan-Case, director of Arts and Spirituality. Joe Brenman, an artist and longtime resident of the neighborhood, as well as a member of the Mishkan Shalom Synagogue, joined the effort and eventually oversaw the artistic installation. Sitting in his row home two blocks from Al Aqsa, Joe remembered those early conversations. "Everone wanted to have it look like their mosque back home in Pakistan, or Palestine, or Egypt." Surrounded by his sculptures—many of which are variations of Jacob wrestling with the angel—Joe admitted that he did not even realize that there was a mosque was in the old, familiar furniture warehouse he had walked by so many times. Cathleen Hughes, a Catholic artist with Mural Arts, was brought into the project and together, for over a year, they worked with members of the mosque, researching Islamic architecture and graphic design. Joe even took a course in Islamic art.

Then a transformation began, both architectural and social. Volunteers from Joe's synagogue and from St. Vincent's Catholic Church worked first on stuccoing and painting the facade. Later, members of St. Michael's Catholic Church became involved. This was particularly poignant for them since their church had been torched by anti-Catholic mobs in the mid-19th century. Joe started to work with a multifaith cadre of children from public and parochial schools, local churches and synagogues, to design tiles depicting their ideas of peace. For most of the non-Muslim children who created the tiles, it was the first time they had entered a mosque. The tiles were incorporated into the design, framing "doorways to peace" along the side of the building. A Muslim artist, Fadwah Kashkash, designed and produced more tiles representing the "99 Names of Allah." Joe created a glass mosaic of Mecca, which was installed over the front entrance. Neighbors strolled over every day throughout the summer of 2004 to watch the unlikely collection of volunteers on the scaffolding gradually transform the furniture warehouse into a colorful mosque. Finally it was dedicated on Eid al Fitr, November 14, 2004.

Along the way important relationships were built. Joe and Adab became close friends. "Her family treated me like a brother. She even came to Mishkan (Shalom Synagogue) and participated in the High Holy Day services.... Toward the end of the project, I was working with three Palestinians on some tiles. They asked me why Israelis treated Palestinians the way they did. We could not have had that dialogue if we had not worked together for months on this project." This narrative—of individuals from groups isolated from one another, engaging an entrenched and divided social dynamic—continues to inform the identities of the participants. The story of the transformation of the mosque is described prominently on Al Aqsa's website:

> The disparate groups overcame their initial wariness to make the Al-Aqsa Islamic Society building into a living symbol of interfaith community and cooperation, humanizing the Muslim community and forging lasting relationships in the process.[17]

The renovation was completed in 2004 and remains unviolated by graffiti, an indicator of sacred space in many urban neighborhoods like Kensington. Al Aqsa has continued as a center for interfaith dialogue. The Interfaith Peace Walk was launched the following spring. Each year since 2005, the Walk begins with prayers at Al Aqsa. The mosque hosts the monthly planning meetings year round which are, in themselves, occasions of interfaith dialogue.

FIGURE 6.5 Al Aqsa Mosque, in a former furniture warehouse, before its transformation.

FIGURE 6.6 Designers Kathleen Hughes and Joe Brenman observing the colorful painting in the summer of 2004.

FIGURE 6.7 Joe Brenman, an artist in the neighborhood and active member of his synagogue, oversaw the production of the project.

FIGURE 6.8 Artist Fadwah Kashkash produced tiles reflecting the 99 names of Allah.

FIGURE 6.9 Volunteers, including children and those from many faith communities, helped design and create tiles for the exterior.

Layers of Navigation

Germantown Masjid and Al Aqsa share a street and are separated by only 34 blocks, but they represent two very different sets of social and religious dynamics. They reproduce meanings about their place in the world, and participate in the urban ecology differently. Each has to balance the construction

FIGURE 6.10 Al Aqsa is now the aesthetic focus of its neighborhood, and a symbol of interfaith collaboration.

of its own group identity with the need to make connections outside their walls in the neighborhood, city, nation, and, in fact, world. Although it can be argued that all communities of faith are engaged in similar processes, it becomes especially complex for Muslims, whose presence in American society has been regarded with suspicion and, at times, hostility. How do they cease being the "other" while maintaining a clear sense of religious identity? How do Muslims locate themselves within their social contexts—engaging the ecology and maintaining their integrity?

As with the neighborhood around the Germantown Masjid, nothing does more for building positive neighborhood relations like contributing to the quality of life for everyone. In the years between 1999 and 2006, the neighborhood around Al Aqsa stabilized. Despite the hulking shell of the former Gretz beer brewery across the street, there were indicators the neighborhood was holding its own, perhaps even looking up a bit. The Kensington neighborhood as a whole was not in great shape: there was a slight decline in population (2.8%) and property values had declined a bit (5%).[18] Kensington maintained a poverty rate of 41% in 2009—well above the 25% rate citywide.

But in the census tract around the mosque, the poverty rate had dropped from 34% to 30% (U.S. Census, American Communities Survey, 2009). Real estate sales multiplied during this time and lien sales for properties with delinquent taxes dropped by more than two thirds.[19] Fires and arson fell from 15 to 0 during that time period.[20] Although there are many variables in play, the aesthetic transformation of Al Aqsa no doubt had an effect on the immediate context. The neighborhood still faces big challenges but the social capital generated locally is something to build on in the future. In the process of the renovation, the mosque built connections with schools and congregations in the neighborhood and beyond. As the CDC moves forward into developing low income housing, Al Aqsa will be even more firmly rooted in the local ecology.

Al Aqsa reflects the Islamic principle of *ummah,* which encourages the transcendence of parochial and kinship networks—particularism—to cultivate links with other peoples in a universal Islamic community. Scholar Aminah Beverly McCloud explains the principle:

> The *ummah* (larger community) is composed of many particular groups who can put aside their individual identities and mutual suspicions in order to uphold what is right, forbid injustice, and worship Allah in congregation. Ummah is thus a general concept…unifying Muslims across specific national, ethnic and cultural boundaries. [21]

At Al Aqsa, the conscious and ongoing crossing of boundaries in identifying with the global Muslim community spills into social relationships outside the faith. The lay leader of the mosque described the basis for such movement: "Islam is a faith of openness.…It is important that the tribes know one another.…Mohammed also instructed us *to speak to all people* in the best way." Ummah undergirds their bridging activities. There is still occasional reticence on the part of some members to collaborate with those of other traditions, particularly Jews. However, that fear and distrust becomes fodder for interfaith conversations. Those interviewed believed that the openness to interfaith relationships has defused potential suspicion and aggression against the mosque and its members. The spike in hate crimes against the Muslim community nationwide after 9/11 was not reflected in Philadelphia—a reality that baffles yet relieves the Human Relations Commission. There was a whispered concern about whether the new high profile façade of Al Aqsa might attract hate-based vandalism but it has not. Ummah, as practiced within this multinational mosque, and outside in deep connections with other faith traditions, has contributed to creating social trust and finally to security for Al Aqsa. Indeed, there has been an astonishing increase in the sense of comfort Muslims feel in this country: in 2000, prior to 9/11, 56% of Mosque leaders agreed with the statement that American society is hostile to Islam. By 2011, that number had dropped by more than half, with only 25% of Muslims agreeing.[22]

African American Muslims face a different social reality. There is a tension between ummah and another Islamic principle, 'asibiya, which refers to the central importance of social solidarity within the tribe, or congregation. McCloud argues that 'asibiya was, particularly in the first half of the 20th century, the predominant organizing principle for African American Muslims, who needed to create community identity apart from the dominant culture. McCloud asserts that "the history of African American Islam can be viewed as a history of a people attempting to create 'asabiya in a hostile environment." Through 'asibiya, they could construct an identity that, in the words of another faith, is "in the world but not of it." African American Islam allows believers to craft their own identities, apart from those ascribed to them by the history and legacy of slavery. Yet, since many slaves were Muslim when they were forcibly brought to America, the reemergence of the faith has also been a way to claim their African origins.[23]

This same impulse has led to the development of other religious groups whose Afro-centric organizations are marked by narratives of resistance and self-definition. There are four such groups on Germantown Avenue, all unique, which contribute in interesting ways to the mix of faith groups. For example, Universal Hagar Church sits on a corner across from the Fair Hill Burial Ground. It is part of the spiritualist sect known as the *Hurleyites*, founded by Father George Hurley in 1923. During the 1960s there were 41 Universal Hagar Temples in 11 different states, with the heaviest concentrations in Michigan and New York.[24] This spiritualist movement is an amalgam of religious sources, incorporating elements of Catholicism and Protestantism, as well as borrowings from Masonic rites and the spiritualist and black nationalist movements of the early 20th century. Father Hurley, who died in 1943, eventually claimed to be the messiah; his picture is on the altar in the modest sanctuary on Germantown Avenue. He taught that Africans (Ethiopians) were the original peoples and connected Jews to that heritage as well. White Christianity, he argued, had corrupted the African people, creating slavery and Jim Crow. He wrote that the "black man at one time reigned supreme and is bound to reign again."[25] Although Father Hurley opposed intermarriage, he did not call on his flock to go back to Africa, but to claim a rightful stake in the American political economy. His rhetoric was highly political in its public critique of religious institutions and racism.

Hurleyites retain their own holidays, dietary regulations, and version of the Ten Commandments, but the political language has been tamped down. A small congregation gathers each week at Universal Hagar across from Fair Hill Burial Ground. It is largely made up of women and is led by a woman, reflective of Hurley's legacy of elevating women to positions of authority. Donning white and black robes, members sing tunes that would be familiar in African American churches, but substituting the name of Christ Hurley for the deity. There is a time of silent meditation, as in a Quaker meeting, accompanied by chanting "peace, peace, peace." A sermon emphasizes God's presence and mercy; prayers are offered for strength and healing, "in the name of Christ Hurley." Although spiritual mediums have been part of the movement, today a brochure stresses the potential of the inner soul: "We believe that whatsoever good we need is within us at all times. We believe that when we have realized Christ we can draw all good from within us." The congregation is in tune with the Quaker values represented by the burial ground across the street and is excited about the transformation of that space and what it has meant for their neighborhood. Ironically, the few drug dealers seen on this block, which was once an open-air market, often hang out on the steps of Universal Hagar.

Although they are very different from the Hurleyites, there are three other groups on the Avenue that combine racial consciousness and connection to Africa with elements of Judaism and Islam.

A modest sign in the window of a row house in the Mt. Airy section incorporates a Star of David and a crescent and star, identifying the space with the *Islamic Hebrews*. Brother Kenyatta is the priest of this small group, which has Sabbath service each Saturday afternoon. The connection with Africa is through lineage: his great–great- grandfather, from a royal family in Ethiopia, was brought to this country as a slave but died as a free man at 99 years old, and was the first black man to vote in his county in Virginia. He had come from the Ashanti people, who are from the tribe of Judah. Brother Kenyatta's Islamic Hebrews do believe in Jesus, "just like the Old Testament says and just like the New Testament says." But the emphasis on the ancestral origins locates their religion in Africa and Israel, putting a distinctive spin on black Christianity. The Islamic Hebrews believe a fusion of the Abrahamic faiths is the authentic religion for all diasporic Africans.[26]

Farther down the Avenue in Germantown is the Beth Hephizibah Philadelphia Extension of the Kingdom of Yah, which is part of the *African Hebrew Israelite* community. Its members believe that the original Hebrew Israelites were displaced by the oppression of Rome. Many of those who scattered to Africa were then brought to America as slaves. In the 1960s a group of 400 African Americans, led by Ben Ammi ben-Israel, Messianic Leader of the Kingdom of God, returned to the continent, also claiming a connection to the Ashanti tribes and Israel. After spending two years in Liberia, attempting to purge themselves of negative thoughts, they moved to Israel, where a community of 2,000 now lives in three communes, fulfilling, they believe, the dream of Martin Luther King to get to the Promised Land.[27] By adopting a vegan diet, observing an environmentally conscious lifestyle, and following Jewish customs based on the ancient texts of the Hebrew scriptures, they believe they can be vehicles of change in a world that is corrupted and ecologically endangered. In Philadelphia, a small congregation holds Shabbat services on Saturday and maintains a vegan catering service called "East of Eden." Through this they carry the message of vegan eating through menu offerings that are both tasty and affordable (such as their scrambled tofu for $2.00).

The most distinctive, and most closed, of the syncretist groups on the Avenue is the *Ha Yasharahla Kanas.* Based on their reading of the Bible (both Old and New Testaments), they believe that Christ was a dark-skinned man; that slavery was predicted in the Bible because of disobedience to God; and that the chosen people of God are the Afro-Carribbean peoples, who are each identified as one of the 12 tribes of Israel. As such they are to live in strict accordance with the biblical laws. They do not consider modern Jews to be authentic people of God, but this sect does observe traditional Jewish practices, such as beginning the sabbath at sundown on Friday through sundown Saturday. The Ha Yasharahla Kanas further distinguish themselves from the dominant culture through elaborate dress incorporating detailed color symbolism. We were not able to interview in this community: numerous messages were not returned and no one appeared for classes and worship at the times advertised although the space was clearly in use, so most information was gleaned from their website and YouTube postings. One of the members of the African Hebrew Israelites offered his evaluation: "Those are some angry brothers."

All four of these groups are different from one another. In fact, they would probably be insulted to be considered together. But there are common threads. In different ways all are engaged in self-definition, particularly as African Americans. As such they resist identities ascribed to them by a racist society and by religious groups, which they see as extensions of oppressive power. In constructing their own religious identities, African origins become prominent. Like African American Muslims they are able to appropriate a cultural identity not dependent on slavery. Their narrative of resistance also affirms their sense of chosen-ness in the world, as mediated through spiritual leadership. In the scholarship on African American religion, a continuum stretching from accommodationism to protest is often used as an analytical tool. In that vein, it might be said that the Universal Hagar church now has a more therapeutic approach that enables its adherents to cope with, or adapt to, a racist society, which is accommodationist. Those such as Ha Yasharahla Kanas—and, to a lesser degree, the African Hebrew Israelites and the Islamic Hebrews—have utopian goals and create places where religion enables the development of an ideology of protest and ongoing resistance to the dominant culture. But it is not always so clear-cut. A scholar of African American religion, Hans Baer concludes, for example, that the Hurleyites can be seen in both lights.[28] Any group that establishes an independent identity as separate from the predominant social norms can be seen as having agency in opposition to the wider culture, even if they are not trying to change that culture but create a separate space within it.

The principles of ummah and 'asibiya do not perfectly align with the poles of accommodation and protest. But they do identify an internal tension for all Muslims, particularly those who are African American. There are competing incentives at work: first to build up the social solidarity of the group ('asibiyah) as a distinct racial group. In this sense Muslims share the same impulse as the other Afro-centric groups on the Avenue, which are appropriating their own religious identity. But the principle of ummah also pulls Muslims to build connections with the broader family of Islam and to expand moral agency outside the faith. The Germantown Masjid has been increasingly drawn into engagement with the wider communities of Islam as well as other faith traditions. An important public indication of this came in 2008, when the mosque was asked by a family to have the funeral of their son, a Muslim, who had killed a police officer with a semi-automatic weapon. The managing director of the Germantown Masjid said in a public statement, "No, we will not bury him at Germantown Masjid. We don't want one slight scintilla hinting that we condone his behavior."[29] Public response was positive—the mosque had chosen to identify with all Philadelphians, who were grieved and angered by the murder of the police officer.

The Germantown Masjid and Al Aqsa are very different mosques, particularly in how they have navigated their presence within the urban ecology. These differing dynamics should not be attributed to theological commitments alone without considering social location—particularly race and class in the United States. The strong identity construction at Germantown Masjid—'asabiya—echoes other Afro-centric strains in the history of African American religion. Strict adherence to Islam provides resistance to the dominant culture from a position of strength rather than marginalization. Yet as that identity is secured, the congregation is able to broaden its vision and develop relationships outside of the mosque, including partners from other faiths, in working toward shared goals of improving the quality of life for the whole community.

Muslims who have immigrated here, such as many at Al Aqsa, are seeking to establish a home in American society while maintaining their ethnic and Muslim identity. Given the diverse makeup of both the congregation of Al Aqsa and its academy, members and students cross boundaries of language and nationality every day. Their community life depends on the cultivation of a lived pluralism, rooted in ummah. Indeed, during a period in which they felt vulnerable, they found their safety and security in being part of broader networks, both within global Islam and in the region, as part of an interfaith community.

As religious communities participate in the pluralistic faithscape, theological beliefs become less important than public practices in establishing religious identity. Exclusivist convictions might reinforce congregational bonding, but they fade in prominence; it is religious practice that has currency in establishing distinctive identity in the urban ecology, and in building connections across social boundaries to work for a common good.

7 URBAN FLUX: MOBILITY, CHANGE, AND COMMUNITIES OF FAITH

When I came here I wasn't sure whether this was the promised land, the waste land or fertile ground.

—PASTOR MELANIE DEBOUSE, *Evangel Chapel*

There is much that is constant about Germantown Avenue. From its earliest days as a well-worn trail for the Lenni Lanape native peoples, this route has served generations of Philadelphians. The historical sites and old meetinghouses, churches, and cemeteries, date back to the birth of the country, giving the street a sense of permanence. And yet it is constantly changing. You can see it on each trip up or down the Avenue—a small storefront is closed, another has opened; a tired-looking church is spruced up with new banners; a restaurant has appeared; a different language is heard on the street; new apartments are being built. During my research there have been dramatic changes in which sections of the Avenue and the surrounding areas have been redefined physically, economically, and socially. Like a biological ecosystem the urban ecology examined here is living, adapting, and changing. Communities of faith are very much part of that.

Clearly there have been demographic shifts in the first decade of the millennium. Philadelphia had been losing population for years, as jobs moved out of the city and workers relocated. After hitting a low point of 1.4 million residents in 1999, population gradually started to increase. By 2011, it stood at 1.54 million people, its growth largely due to immigration. While the proportion of African Americans remained relatively constant at 42%, the non-Hispanic white population fell by 13% to 37%. The real growth was in the Asian and Latino communities, which grew by 42% and 46%, respectively. Today, almost 1 in 5 Philadelphians is new to the city (Pew, 2012).

Stories of people coming to Philadelphia seeking better lives have been part of the city's history since its inception as a "Holy

Experiment" in religious and cultural pluralism. From those early days, when mixing Mennonites and Lutherans constituted the epitome of radical diversity, communities of faith have played a central role in the settlement of immigrant communities and in their negotiations in sharing urban space. As Europeans came to Philadelphia, the city became dotted with the spires of Catholic churches, claiming neighborhood space for ethnic communities. Protestants organized congregations to serve arriving immigrants as well. The Presbytery of Philadelphia, for example, opened a Hungarian church (Magyar Presbyterian Church) in a building they acquired from the Moravian Church just off the Avenue. They also organized a Czech congregation on Germantown Avenue (Jan Hus Presbyterian Church) right next door to another Protestant church (Hammonds, 1993). But it was the Catholic churches that dominated the ethnic neighborhoods. On Germantown, the parishes of St. Bonaventure, St. Ladislaus, and St. Edward the Confessor were the cultural and spiritual centers for German, Polish, and Irish immigrants. Those congregations have all closed now.

St. Bonaventure casts an ominous shadow over a street of row houses in Fairhill. The large Gothic structure was built in 1894 and served its German congregations until the parish was closed by the archdiocese in 1993. It was sold it to a small Christian ministry that cannot maintain such an enormous building. Friends from Historic Fair Hill, as well as city officials and those in the preservation community, are trying to save the building—or at least have it demolished before it becomes more of a safety hazard. Unfortunately, St. Bonaventure is one of many sacred spaces built around the same time that have become unsustainable for congregations and a source of blight in neighborhoods. Bob Jaeger, Executive Director of Partners for Sacred Places estimated in 2011 that there were 150 such structures on the endangered list in Philadelphia.

The Church of St. Edward the Confessor was also closed in 1993 and sold to the Highway Temple of Deliverance, one of the many congregations that have taken over the sacred places built by other communities of faith. This African American congregation has maintained the structure and it continues to serve another generation of worshippers.

The Polish church, St. Ladislaus, was still standing when I began this study but was closed in 2003 as the membership declined. The congregation of Triumph Baptist Church, which had already outgrown the building they had

FIGURE 7.1 Highway Temple of Deliverance, formerly a Catholic church.

built in 1981, bought the structure for $1.3 million. Rather than restore the old stone cathedral, they razed the sanctuary in order to build a more modern and versatile facility, and moved into it in 2007. Still, former members of the old St. Ladislaus become nostalgic about the destruction of the building that was so central to the identity of the Polish community in Philadelphia. The last priest to serve there, the Reverend John Wendrychowicz, was more circumspect. " 'Our people had become scattered around the area. Every church is special and sacred, but you can't declare everything historic. Otherwise, you couldn't live. You couldn't touch anything."[1]

As European immigrants were moving into, and eventually through, the city in the 19th and 20th centuries, the Great Migration of African Americans from the South began. The overlap of migrant groups was not always smooth.

FIGURE 7.2 St. Ladislaus Catholic Church served the Polish community.

FIGURE 7.3 Triumph Baptist Church, one of the three mega-churches on the Avenue, now stands at the corner of Germantown and Hunting Park.

The Great Migration North occurred in two major stages. Although there were some African Americans who came north through the Underground Railroad and after the Emancipation Proclamation (Du Bois, 1899), a bigger wave of 1.6 million people made their way to cities in the North between the world wars. The migration slowed during the Depression but picked up again between 1940 and 1970, with as many as 5 million African Americans leaving the South. This huge internal migration resulted in an inversion of the distribution of black Americans: in 1910, 9 out of 10 African Americans lived in the rural South. By the 1960s, that had reversed, and 90% were living in urban areas almost entirely outside the South. In one decade alone—1950–1960— 1.5 million people moved out of the South, which was equivalent to one tenth of the entire American black population (Price-Spratlen, 2008). Those from the coastal states of the Carolinas down to Florida followed routes north to Washington, Baltimore, Philadelphia, and New York. Those from the Gulf states went to cities in the Midwest or to California (Wilkerson, 2010). Historians have tended to focus on the "push factors" that drove African Americans out from the South—the mechanization of cotton picking and the intolerability of Jim Crow laws. Correlated with the waves of migration were spikes in lynchings in the South. Racial injustice in the South and the fear it engendered made northern cities look like the "Promised Land" indeed.

But there were also significant "pull factors" at work. African Americans chose particular urban destinations, not as isolated individual choices but based on the social processes at work that created hospitable communities for them. These processes, known together as *ethnogenesis*, are the ways that immigrants build communities and institutions that result in a coherent urban space with a cultural identity. In other words, African Americans in the South were not just "running from" a negative context but "running to" a positive one. Scholars looking at the cultural capital at work in creating an appealing destination have identified four basic elements at work: the presence of community newspapers that facilitate communication within a racial group; mechanisms to help with job placement; the presence of vibrant churches; and an "ethnogenic richness" of voluntary organizations, particularly the NAACP. The presence of African American newspapers, advocacy groups, and churches provided cultural identity and economic support. Churches in particular played a critical role in the choice of destination during the 1950s wave of the Great Migration (Price-Spratlen, 2008).

The Development of African American Religion in Philadelphia

Churches have consistently been important to the construction of African American neighborhoods in Philadelphia, in terms of both cultural identity and spatial location (Du Bois, 1899; Nash, 1988). Philadelphia had always had a black population, both slave and free. As the central core of the city developed, it became more solidly a "white reserve" (Nash, 1988), pushing the free black families out, particularly to the southern and northern parts of the city. By the end of the 1700s, in fact, about one third of the city's black families lived in the southwestern section and one third had settled in Northern Liberties, near where Germantown Avenue begins. But by 1820 it was clear that Southwark was the center of the black community, which was then home to 80% of the African American population. Why was this? Historians partially credit early developers who constructed cheaper housing, and the attraction of two new churches which were entirely of, by, and for black Philadelphians—St. Thomas Episcopal Church and Mother Bethel A.M.E. Church. The two churches grew out of the Free Africa Society, a mutual-aid society, that had been organized by Richard Allen and Absolom Jones. When they were famously removed from the communion rail at St. George's Methodist Church, where blacks were relegated to worship in the balcony, they walked out and went on to found the churches. St. Thomas became affiliated with the Episcopal Church and the Reverend Jones became the first black rector in that tradition. It has since moved to the Overbrook neighborhood of the city but continues to have a strong African American congregation. Mother Bethel, which had been founded in 1794 by Bishop Richard Allen, is so named because it is the mother church of the African Methodist Episcopal denomination. It continues to do ministry and serve as a cultural center in its original location.

Housing, commerce, and other churches developed around Mother Bethel and St. Thomas, and built up a cultural life in the black community. The Seventh Ward represented a safe space for those of African descent, a resource and a refuge in the hard-knocks life of most African Americans in the City of Brotherly Love. These two congregations and the others that developed close by were very much part of creating the social glue of the community. Du Bois (1899) observed, "Without wholly conscious effort the Negro church has become a centre of social intercourse to a degree unknown in white churches even in the country."[2] Churches became the center of social life, including entertainment and the reinforcement of a class structure. They were community centers and provided a host of social services, including job support, unavailable to the black population elsewhere. Du Bois concluded, "It must not be inferred from all this that the Negro is hypocritical or irreligious. His church is, to be sure, a social institution first, and religious afterwards, but nevertheless, its religious activity is wide and sincere."[3] While members surely valued the social role of the church as well as its spiritual service, they might not have prioritized them in the same way as the eminent sociologist.

African Americans slowly began to move to other parts of the city, including the northwest spur that has Germantown Avenue as its backbone. Two early congregations served the small black populations just north of Center City—Mother Africa Zoar Methodist Church (built in 1796 for the small black community in Northern Liberties) and Union A.M.E. Church (1816). Philadelphia began to grow rapidly at the end of the 19th century and the beginning of the 20th, as boatloads of European immigrants were arriving. The black community also continued to grow, but there was still a smaller proportion of African Americans in the city than was reflected in the national census. As Du Bois carefully chronicled in *The Philadelphia Negro* (1899), there were 22,185 black residents in 1860, compared with a white population of 543,344. By 1890 there was a substantial increase in both groups, with almost 40,000 blacks but over 1 million whites. So even after the Underground Railroad and the end of slavery had brought African Americans north, the influx of other immigrants kept the black population relatively low in Philadelphia: just 3.76% in 1890, compared to 11.93% of the national population. Du Bois reported that there were 55 Negro churches by 1897, with the Baptists showing the most gains.[4]

As ethnic and racial diversity grew, William Penn's "Holy Experiment" hit the rocks. As soon as 1805, a group of whites attacked free blacks at a 4th of July celebration (Nash, 1988). As the century unfolded ethnic groups competed for land, power, work, and wealth. The city experienced a series of riots and other violence, often directed at houses of worship. As discussed in the previous chapter, that history echoes in the present—one of the targeted Catholic churches of those mid-century riots, St. Michael's, has been especially involved with the physical transformation of Al Aqsa and its ongoing work in interfaith dialogue.

The Great Migration began to be felt in Philadelphia as the century was turning. In 1910, the African American population stood at 84,500—more than double its 1890 level; by 1930 it had almost tripled again to 220,600[5]. By 1920, at the height of the first wave of the Great Migration arriving at Philadelphia's shore, black settlements had spread beyond Southwark, into west and north Philadelphia. The proportion of Philadelphia's African American population living in the northern part of the city was now 40%, rivaling the 43% in south Philadelphia (Gregg, 1993). The Great War had cut off the flow of immigrants from Europe, reducing competition for jobs. However, housing could not keep up with the growth of the African American population and in north Philadelphia overcrowding exacerbated social problems. Still, in this period before the Depression, the African American professional class experienced a tremendous increase. There was exponential growth in the number of doctors and lawyers during this time and the number of clergy grew by an astounding 342% (Gregg, 1993).

There was concern in black churches about how to respond to the needs of the growing numbers of migrants from the South. In 1917, the Interdenominational Ministerial Alliance was organized—a predecessor to the current Black Clergy of Philadelphia and Vicinity. They met to discuss how to address the problems created by the swell of newcomers from the South. They worked their networks with southern religious bodies to provide information about jobs and housing to potential migrants. They also encouraged local congregations to take in the new arrivals as lodgers as well as new members for their congregations (Gregg, 1993). The migrants were from rural areas and were overwhelmed by the city. Congregations were their lifelines, helping them find housing and jobs, learn the ways of their new urban home, and meet their basic needs for food and clothing. This was not always an easy sell for the Interdenominational Ministerial Alliance, which encountered some resistance from the established African American community.

Three churches on the Avenue were active in the northwest during this first wave of the Great Migration, all of which continue to have stable worshipping congregations and contribute to the durability of neighborhood identities. The Second Baptist Church purchased a building from Mt. Carmel Methodist Episcopal Church in 1913. One of its pastors, George L. Davis, left to attend law school in Ohio but was called back by the Nazarene Baptist Church where he served for 33 years, until 1954. During his tenure, the church greatly expanded its programming, especially in education and the arts. The

Bethel A.M.E. Church had worshipped in an old theater building since 1914 and eventually moved into their current site up in the Germantown section years later, in 1959. These congregations benefited from the many newcomers from the South in terms of growing their memberships, since most of those coming were from their traditions. Along with other congregations cropping up in North Philadelphia off the Avenue, they contributed to the ethnogenesis of the African American community that was beginning to move into north Philadelphia, and up Germantown Avenue. Through their networks across regions as well as within the city, and through the rich cultural life they provided, they helped to make the Germantown Avenue corridor a destination for migrants.

The Depression slowed black mobility from the South. There was just one Christian church planted on the Avenue during the 1930s and 1940s, Abyssinian Baptist (1932), which remains a vital congregation. Economic hardship created a niche for newer religions as people went looking for new answers and support. It was during this period that Father Divine, Daddy Grace, the Black Jews, and the spiritualist groups began to attract followers. Historian Matthew Hopper (1998) concluded, "the new alternative bodies that typified post-1929 Philadelphia placed more emphasis on the immediate realities of poverty and racial inequality than earlier varieties."[6] The establishment of the Universal Hagar Church in 1935 did just that. The followers of Father Hurley received a message of black exceptionalism, a scathing critique of racism (and of churches as originators of Jim Crow), and an elevation of its followers to a higher spiritual plane (Baer, 1984). The Universal Hagar Church found its way onto the Avenue and continues to hold worship services on the corner of 11th and Germantown in Fairhill.

As the Depression abated and the country was drawn into World War II, the North beckoned again with the possibilities of employment, an escape from Jim Crow, and the welcoming communities that had been established in urban neighborhoods. The larger second wave of the Great Migration brought another 5 million African Americans north between 1940 and 1970. During this period the African American share of the population in the northeastern United States increased from 3.8% to 12.2%. Philadelphia's African American population saw even more dramatic increases, from 10.6% in 1930 to 44.2% by 2010. During the 1950s and 1960s, African Americans from the southern coastal states were joining their friends, relatives, and co-religionists in Philadelphia. Philadelphia County had the third largest African American

FIGURE 7.4 Universal Hagar Church, a Hurleyite congregation, is located across the street from Fair Hill Burial Ground.

population in the country by 1950. The political and cultural scenes were booming, with such prominent artists as Marian Anderson, Paul Robeson, and John Coltrane. Religious institutions were in the thick of the civil rights movement (Gracie, 1994). The Reverend Leon Sullivan, the pastor of Zion Baptist Church, was organizing economic development efforts both locally and nationally. The Church of the Advocate (Episcopal), led by Father Paul Washington, hosted the convention of the Black Panthers in 1968. During these heady years of Black Consciousness and the War on Poverty, churches played a leading role in the cultural, economic, and political emergence of the black community in Philadelphia. The policy of inclusion of local leadership in War on Poverty policies brought urban clergy directly into federally funded housing and economic development projects.

During the postwar years, suburbs were burgeoning, facilitated by the G.I. Bill, the accessibility of mortgages through the Federal Housing Act, and the building of roadways through the National Interstate and Defense Highway Act. As the American Dream of a college education and home ownership became accessible for the first time to veterans, white people fled to the suburbs, vacating neighborhoods and houses of worship. The second wave of African Americans in the Great Migration, who were excluded from the suburbs by racism and unscrupulous real estate and banking practices, moved into the now-available properties.

On the Avenue, a number of congregations were established during this time: Taylor Memorial Baptist Church (1950), King Solomon Baptist Church (1950), Evangel Chapel and Children's Mission (1952), New Bethany Holiness Church (1954), and New Jerusalem Church of God in Christ (1955). The 1960s saw other churches move onto the Avenue: Universal Missionary Baptist (1960), New St. James Baptist Church (1963), St. Luke Second Born Early Apostle Church of God (1966), and Holsey Temple C.M.E. Church (1969). All but one of these congregations acquired religious or commercial buildings that had become available as white flight continued. (The congregation of Holsey Temple, organized in 1905, had worshipped at another location in the area before the construction of their Germantown Avenue structure in 1969.) These congregations provided institutional anchors that stabilized their neighborhoods.

Congregations attracted migrants from particular locations in the South, resulting in a diversity of religious communities from which to choose "just the right spiritual home." Just as a single Catholic identity could not be created out of the differentiated immigrant groups in an earlier era, so too was it impossible to have a monolithic black religious culture (Gregg, 1993). The particularities of place of origin enabled the new arrivals to find a familiar sense of home. A large number of African Americans who migrated north came from Virginia and the Carolinas—including some of the clergy and their congregations we have met, such as Father's House of Prayer, New Bethany Holiness, and Triumph Baptist, all relative newcomers to the Avenue.[7] It is not unusual for congregations to make annual pilgrimages to their pastor's home town in the South. Pastor Hall's extended family from South Carolina was brought to Philadelphia for his birthday, and members were individually introduced at the service at Triumph Baptist Church. The congregation had brought a soloist in from his home church, where he had grown up more than 60 years earlier. Pastor Melanie DeBouse stays in close contact with her family in North Carolina, and keeps the North Carolina area code on her cell phone. Certainly such close ties have contributed to what has been called the "New Great Migration" of African Americans back to the South (Frey, 2004, 2013). Although there was a slight decline in Philadelphia's African American population between 2000 and 2010 (1,836 people), this change is credited mostly to the migration to the suburbs, where the black population grew at a faster pace than other groups. The connection to southern origins continues to be strong among Philadelphians, but for churches on the Avenue it does not appear to be calling them to move back.

Research on ethnogenesis shows gender differences at work in the Great Migration north during the 1950s. Price-Spratlen found that women's migration, more than men's, was driven by the appeal of church participation.[8] He further found that for the women at this time, networking for employment was a stronger incentive than for men.[9] Women came into congregations and participated at higher levels than did the men, even though the church cultures and leadership structures were dominated by men, with a few outstanding exceptions (such as the Hurleyites). Besides the more relational orientation of women, which no doubt accounts for some of this, those coming north needed jobs and the congregations provided the best networking opportunities. As women were supported in their personal ambitions by their congregations (as at New Bethany Holiness) and learned important leadership skills, they eventually rose in the power structures of the churches.

Today the number of women leading congregations on the Avenue dramatically exceeds the national average. Although there is some variation in different studies, the most generous estimates of women leading congregations is 10% to 20%[10]. On the Avenue, 44% of congregations are headed by women. Clearly, women do not head the mosques (although women's leadership is certainly evident at Al Aqsa). Women cannot hold clerical leadership in the Catholic churches, and there are no Catholic churches on the Avenue, although there are many other congregations that have theological reasons for not ordaining women. Yet women are in leadership across the spectrum of traditions here: Baptist, Peace, independent, syncretist, Pentecostal, and half of the Mainline Protestant congregations. There is no indication that their ministry is radically distinctive—the number and types of outreach ministries in female-headed congregations is not statistically different from those in male-headed congregations, for example.

What can account for this phenomenon? There are several possibilities, the first of which is the legacy of the Great Migration and the cultural capital women took away from their participation in urban congregations. A second explanation could be that these might be less prestigious congregations, not the sought-after pulpits in larger congregations that are filled by men. National data show that only 3% of Mainline Protestant congregations of 350 or more members have women as senior pastors (Carroll, 2006). However on the Avenue, clergywomen occupy quite prestigious pastorates: the Presbyterian Church in Chestnut Hill, First United Methodist Church of Germantown, Germantown Mennonite Church, and Seventh-day Adventist of Chestnut Hill, for example. All three of the mega-churches have women in prominent leadership roles: New Covenant and Impacting Your World are led by husband and wife teams; Triumph's highly visible assistant pastor, the Reverend Cathy Johnson, is the daughter of the pastor and presumed heir-apparent. (Since she is not the senior pastor, she was not counted in the female-headed congregations.)

A third possible explanation might be the echo of history, a social process that is difficult to isolate and quantify. Philadelphia has had a rich history of women's ordination, particularly for women of color—it is an enduring narrative. The compelling story of Jarena Lee is an integral part of black history in Philadelphia. After hearing Richard Allen preach in the early 19th century, Lee went through a religious conversion and soon felt called by God to "preach the Gospel." She asked for Allen's permission and he finally authorized her to preach in 1819. Sent out as an evangelist, she later wrote that she had, "traveled two thousand three hundred and twenty-five miles, and preached one hundred and seventy-eight sermons" to racially mixed audiences.[11] Further, she believed slavery was a sin for which there would be divine punishment. Jerena Lee was not formally ordained but, years later, in Philadelphia in 1898, Mary J. Small was ordained as an elder in the African Methodist Episcopal Zion denomination—the first female elder in the Methodist Episcopal denominations. Fast forward to 1974. Eleven women were "irregularly ordained" at the largely African American Episcopal Church of the Advocate in North Philadelphia, creating a crisis, and finally an affirmation by that denomination. A daughter of that church, Barbara Harris, went on to become the first female bishop in the Episcopal church in 1988. Could these women, and others, have created a cultural context in which women feel validated in their impulses to leadership?

For Pastor Jackie Morrow the call to preach was met with a major obstacle: her denomination (the Church of God in Christ) did not believe in the ordination of women. She decided that starting her own church was easier than taking on the power structure of her tradition. Her entrepreneurial spirit led her to purchase the building that now houses Jesus Is the Way—where she leads a congregation, a school, and a summer camp for children. She has a theory about why there are more women in leadership on the Avenue: "I just wanted to be on a busy street in a place that would be easy for people to get to....I think it's safer on a street like this too. Maybe that's why women want to be here."

Whatever dynamic is at work, it certainly poses a question that deserves more research.

The Mobility of People and Religious Groups

The number of new congregations on the Avenue did not grow as rapidly after 1970 as they had during the Great Migration. Those that did arrive have been largely independent Baptist or Pentecostal, including the newest arrivals, Latino storefront churches. The two mosques and three of the Afro-centric syncretistic groups are also relative newcomers. The mean age of congregations in the lower three sections of the Avenue (Kensington, Fairhill, and Hunting Park) is significantly lower than in Germantown, Mt. Airy, and Chestnut Hill. Fairhill has the youngest congregations (at 21.2 years) and Germantown the oldest (163.4 years).[12] There has also been more mobility of congregations lower on the avenue, with new congregations opening and others closing. It should be kept in mind that the last 10 years have also been years of change for congregations across the country for all traditions and contexts. As discussed in the first chapter, the most recent data confirm what religious leaders have noticed in the first decade of the millenium—there are fewer people in the pews. This is true for white "old line protestants" as well as white evangelical groups; it has also been documented in congregations comprising people of color and languages other than English but not nearly to the same degree (Roozen, 2011). There has also been a notable increase in the number of independent Protestant groups and, if considered together, they would now constitute "the third largest cluster of religious adherents in the country, following the Roman Catholic Church and the Southern Baptist Convention"(Thumma, 2011). In that larger context, it is not surprising to see some change in the census of congregations on the Avenue, with some forming and others closing. During the course of the study, the total number of congregations fluctuated.

In 2003 we counted 77 congregations; by 2008 there were 85; in 2009 it jumped to 93 and in 2011 there were 83. The maps in Figures 7.5 and 7.6

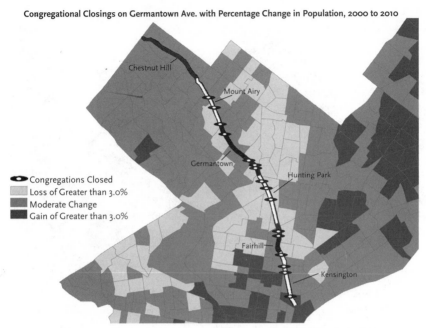

Congregational Closings on Germantown Ave. with Percentage Change in Population, 2000 to 2010

Sources: U.S. Census Bureau, Decennial Census, 2000 and 2010; Metropolitan Philadelphia Indicators Project, 2012

FIGURE 7.5 Congregational closings 2000–2012.

indicate the locations of the new congregations and those that closed in the context of population shifts.

Philadelphia may have been growing, but population and the numbers of congregations do not move together. During the years that Philadelphia was losing population, the numbers of congregations were increasing. Now that it is gaining in population, the religious census, at least on the Avenue, is falling. As can be seen on the maps, the neighborhoods in Philadelphia that were growing in population were not along Germantown Avenue. There does not seem to be a link between population and congregational growth. But by considering all the census tracts along the Avenue together for each section in the study a different picture emerges. As can be seen (Figure 7.7), every section except for Chestnut Hill, saw *more congregations closing than opening between 2000 and 2010*, usually by two times or more. During this time, Philadelphia was experiencing a slight bump up in population (+.56%) although there was a small decline in the numbers of families in the city. All of these sections diverged from the citywide norm: Fairhill, Hunting Park,

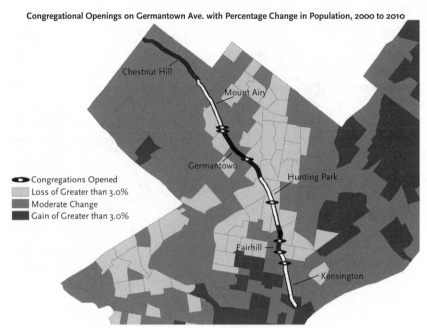

Congregational Openings on Germantown Ave. with Percentage Change in Population, 2000 to 2010

Chestnut Hill

Mount Airy

Germantown

Hunting Park

● Congregations Opened
  Loss of Greater than 3.0%
  Moderate Change
  Gain of Greater than 3.0%

Fairhill

Kensington

Sources: U.S. Census Bureau, Decennial Census, 2000 and 2010; Metropolitan Philadelphia Indicators Project, 2012

FIGURE 7.6 Congregational openings 2000–2012.

Germantown, and Mt. Airy which saw *declines* in their populations, generally. The bigger demographic change was in the proportion of families in each of these neighborhoods. All of the sections running through these older neighborhoods lost families at a rate that greatly outpaced the small decline in families in the city. While plenty of singles can be found in church, most congregations consider families to be their stock in trade. The growing families of the Baby Boom had fueled the growth of religious institutions in the 1950s and 1960s. Congregations direct programs to attracting parents who want religious training for their children. A loss of families is not good news for communities of faith who want to increase their memberships, or just survive.

A further finding with implications for attracting families is that during the first decade of the century, the number of Philadelphians who *did not* own a car fell by 25%, which was reflected, for the most part, along the Germantown corridor. (In Kensington and Fairhill, those without cars also fell, but not so precipitously.) With more mobility, individuals and families have more options—to seek out a house of worship in another neighborhood, or perhaps to go to the shore instead of church on Sunday!

Figure 7.7 Congregations opening and closing in relation to population

Section	Opened	Closed	%Pop Change	%Families
Kensingtn	2	4	9.65	−22.48
Fairhill	1	2	−7.15	−20.16
HtgPark	1	3	−12.19	−18.75
Germantn	2	5	−5.86	−20.14
Mt.Airy	1	2	−6.83	−19.65
ChesHill	0	0	1.2	−13.86
Phila			0.56	−3.4

Kensington has a particular set of dynamics: two congregations were opened, but four have closed, even as they were experiencing a growth in their population which was 10 times higher than that of the city. Germantown Avenue moves through some blighted areas in Kensington before coming to the visually stunning Al Aqsa Islamic Center. However, visible just a few blocks farther south are the modern apartments and renovated shells in Northern Liberties. Years ago it was home to a small African American community and then to European immigrants who would probably not be able to afford to live there now. The median housing value jumped 237% between 2009 and 2010, from $48,053 to $161,751. The number of people in poverty also dropped 45%. There are still more than 650 families living in poverty

Figure 7.8 Families in Poverty for Census Tracts along Germantown Avenue, 2000-2010

Section	% Families in Poverty	
	2000	2010
Kensington	42.4%	30.1%
Fairhill	50%	53.6%
Hunting Park	29.2%	30.9%
Germantown	20.3%	24.3%
Mt. Airy	7.4%	8.5%
Chestnut Hill	2.4%	1.3%

along that corridor, but if trends continue, they will probably be pushed out in the next decade as young, urban professionals will move into the neighborhood now seen as edgy and urbane.

To summarize, population growth in itself did not predict an increase in the numbers of congregations. Only recently have declining populations accompanied declining numbers of congregations in four of the six districts. Looking more closely, as fewer households are composed of traditional families, and if families are increasingly facing poverty, it is less likely that new congregations will be formed. Still, some have opened on the Avenue.

Why Open a Congregation if People Are Leaving?

People seeking to explain religion's role in society often turn to Marx. His familiar argument is that religion serves the purposes of injustice by providing a rationale for the maldistribution of resources (e.g., "This is God's will") and a coping mechanism for the poor, who can find a cathartic experience as well as solace that they will be rewarded for their suffering in heaven. Certainly, as has been seen, many struggling with poverty do find some real comfort in their communities of faith. However, from a Marxist perspective, religious groups should be proliferating in the poorest neighborhoods. Along Germantown Avenue, this has not been the case. Poverty has remained at 25% for the city going into the new century (Pew, 2012). Kensington and Chestnut Hill saw a decrease in poverty—the former a more dramatic drop than the latter (which fell from 2.4% of families living in poverty to 1.3%). However, in the other four sections, there was an increase in poverty. If religion was merely a response to coping with economic hardship, one would predict an increase in the number of congregations in the sections hardest hit by poverty, but that did not occur—more congregations were closing.

One explanation for the opening of new congregations in urban neighborhoods is that affordable real estate becomes available on commercial strips hard-hit by economic downturns. Given the economic hard times after 2008, a boom in congregational openings might have been expected. Certainly for many smaller congregations that opened during this time, affordable space did attract them to properties. However, median house values increased throughout the city and in each of the sections—although not as dramatically as in Kensington. So perhaps rising rents discouraged some religious groups from acquiring space on the Avenue, thereby depressing the census of religious groups on that street. Certainly, some congregational closings, or relocations, can be attributed to the increase in rents, although most congregations owned their buildings. Survey findings suggest that other dynamics were at work when congregations were shuttered, including the death of the pastor and the redevelopment of the parcel where a congregation was located, in the case of closures, or outgrowing the space in relocations.

As members were hit hard by the recession, the offering plates were lighter and it became a challenge for churches to pay their bills. In one historic church in Germantown, Trinity Lutheran, there is a cheerful tree in the space where the congregation gathers for coffee hour, laden with leaves cut out from construction paper and hung with yarn. It looks like the giving trees that many congregations have at Christmas. However, rather than choosing a leaf with a gift idea for a child, on these leaves are written unpaid bills and the amount owed. Members are encouraged to adopt a bill. This grand old church building is badly in need of repair and the small congregation struggles to maintain it.

But congregations open on the Avenue as well, if not at the same rate that they are closing. There is a certain entrepreneurial spirit that is evident in those who organize these new communities of faith. Pastors Jomo Johnson and Curtis Saxton are two young men, fresh from seminary, who started a congregation on the Avenue in Fairhill. On Sunday mornings the grate is raised, exposing the name of the church, "Philly Open Air," which is painted on the plate glass along with a welcoming sign, "We're open!" Jomo and Curtis, at 32, are probably the oldest people in the room and are dressed in sneakers and jeans. They are particularly interested in reaching out to the young African American men in the neighborhood who are challenged with few prospects and lured into the street life. One program, which meets on Saturdays, is called "Man Up!" The energy level in the small but neat worship space is raised when Jomo starts rapping along with a recorded beat, and everyone joins in, including two 10-year-old boys who have been squirming in their metal folding chairs. The sermon is informal yet well prepared, chock-full of illustrations. Curtis interacts with the young flock who feel free to ask questions during the sermon as he exhorts them to keep the sabbath holy. The pastors, who both have undergraduate degrees from Princeton, bring an abundance of skills and experience to this ministry. Jomo is also an author as well as musician and preacher. Curtis has a full-time job in a technology firm. Both of them exude an optimism and enthusiasm that are the very rocket fuel of any successful entrepreneurial endeavor. This spirit continues to inspire faith leaders to see the possibilities for change in the toughest of neighborhoods in the toughest of times.

Why are people attracted to new congregations? There is no one motivation, of course: people come looking for peace, community, healing, opportunity. They might be drawn by a charismatic leader or a desire to return to the tradition of their youth. City dwellers of all races, languages, traditions, and social classes find in communities of faith a sense of place. With migrants to the city coming from the American South or Latin America, newcomers are drawn to a sacred space that is reminiscent of their place of origin. A welcoming community can help them get established and work out a cultural or gendered identity in the destination site. For those overwhelmed by the challenges and complexity of the urban environment, new congregations can attract them by providing a social location, a niche, where "everybody knows your name." Mega-churches do not appeal to everyone. Smaller congregations will continue to provide a diversity of options for those seeking a spiritual community. Despite the larger economic and demographic trends that would predict otherwise, new congregations have continued to form on the Avenue, a phenomenon that is an expression of both entrepreneurship and hope.

Where Do Congregations Go?

To most outsiders, the openings and closings of small churches are frequent and defy explanation. Elijah Anderson, who was clearly focused on social dynamics on the street quite apart from those of religious congregations, wrote, "Along this part of Germantown Avenue, some of the churches are large and well known with a rich history and architecturally resembling those in Chestnut Hill and Mt. Airy, but others are store front churches that tend to come and go with the founding pastor."[13] His fellow University of Pennsylvania professor of an earlier era, W.E.B. Du Bois, was much more dismissive of small, independent churches: "There are…continually springing up and dying a host of little noisy missions which represent the older and more demonstrative worship."[14] He goes on to present what is perhaps the earliest ethnographic description of a storefront congregation by a Reverend Charles Daniel. In it, Daniel describes "a discourse by a very illiterate preacher," and hymns which were "many repetitions of senseless sentiment and exciting cadences." He says that worship is "excitable" with lots of clapping hands;

"This continued for hours, until all were completely exhausted, and some had fainted." Finally, when the congregation closed, "they did so stealthily, under cover of darkness, removed furniture not their own, including the pulpit and left bills unpaid." Du Bois added a footnote to the account, "The writer hardly does justice to the weird witchery of those hymns sung thus rudely."[15] Storefront churches are appreciated, it seems, only by those who are in them. Policymakers, developers, and even sociologists consider them to be a trace element hardly worth any attention beyond recognizing that they exist. They are, in Du Bois's words, no more than "little noisy missions" that can disappear overnight.

Certainly there were congregations that disappeared during the study and, yes, most were storefront churches. (Two were congregations in temporary housing on the Avenue until more permanent worship space could be developed—a mosque and an independent Evangelical church.) Of those that did close, some were impossible to follow. Yet others relocated because they had outgrown their limited space. Mizpah Seventh-day Adventist could no longer accommodate their feeding program in the former school that had been their Germantown Avenue home. They moved to a larger former church building in Kensington and immediately began serving 70 people per day in the new site. Six other congregations that could be tracked had a similar story of outgrowing their space, including Maranatha (described in Chapter 5). A lay leader at Living Water shared a similar story: "We were severely limited by our space. We definitely outgrew it. Our new space provides us with a dedicated sanctuary, one that we don't have to tear down or set up in order to do other things in the same space. We now are able to have multiple meetings at the same time and our children have a fenced-in yard in which to play." There were other issues for Living Water as well. As one of the few congregations welcoming gay and lesbian people in predominantly African American North Philadelphia, they themselves did not always feel welcomed. The neighbors were appreciative of the food, clothing, and health care that the congregation provided, but the love was not often returned.

For two congregations, in Kensington and Fairhill, the land was taken over and redeveloped for public housing. In one case, the building finally collapsed and was razed by the city. Some houses of worship follow their congregants. With the Latino population, in particular, moving into other parts of the city (as the African American population also expanded its footprint a century ago), congregations can be expected to move as well.

FIGURE 7.9 Living Water United Church of Christ outgrew their original space, shown here, a former liquor store, and in 2012 moved to a church building vacated by a Lutheran congregation.

Most independent congregations are intimate gatherings. They may be primarily an extended family or else provide an extended church family where biological families have disintegrated. Either way, they are important sources of support, nurturance, and meaning for those who are part of them. To consider them all the whims of charlatans is to greatly misread their significance for many people.

Religious Agency in the Urban Ecology

The central argument of this book is that communities of faith are crucial participants in the dynamic urban ecology. They are certainly impacted by

demographic, economic, cultural, and social trends, both national and local. But they are not at the mercy of trends. Certainly congregations have been active in helping their members adapt to changing conditions, such as economic downturns and shifting demographics. As has been seen, religious communities help newcomers to negotiate a new culture and a challenging job market. They help fill in the gaps in health care and access to food. They provide values education and opportunities for involvement in the arts in contexts where those important resources are all too scarce. However, they are more than first-responders in complex urban ecologies; they also have agency, acting on their contexts and helping to shape them.

In Chapter 4, part of the story of the Fairhill neighborhood was presented. It is a story about a poor neighborhood that had devolved into near chaos during the crack epidemic and the violence that accompanied the robust drug trade there. Fairhill is a textbook example of deinstitutionaliza-tion of an urban neighborhood, as even the stalwart Catholics and Quakers had left. The burial ground had become a dump and center for drug dealing, deserving of its designation as "The Badlands." But things began to change. The neighbors decided that they had had enough and courageously started a town watch, getting the attention and assistance of the police. The Quakers bought back the burial ground and over time cleaned it up and transformed it into an appealing greenspace with an active gardening program.

But what about the 14–15 storefront churches, seemingly in their own silos as described earlier? Deacon Maria Santiago is from St. Mark's Outreach, the former meetinghouse facing the burial ground. She did take some leader-ship in the neighborhood effort. She remembers the marches against the drug dealers. Sometimes they just sat out in front of their houses and watched. She says it was boring, but it was worth it. They took some risks, she says, confronting the drug dealers. She remembers one time seeing the police up in the trees in the burial ground, watching the drug dealers, and then suddenly swooping down on them.

Although St. Mark's Outreach had worked with Quaker folks at Fair Hill Burial Ground, the other congregations seemed relatively low profile and dis-engaged. For some of the churches with high proportions of commuters, it took some resolve, and some courage, to come into church every week. The neighborhood's deterioration fed congregants' own sense of righteousness and gratitude that they had escaped the hard life on the street. At St. Luke Second Born Early Apostle Church, Deacon James drives in from the suburbs every week. He grew up in this neighborhood, and wasn't always going down the right path, he explained, but the pastor believed in him and was always there for him. He was almost headed to prison at one point but God gave him another chance. He is very aware of the context of the church. "When you come to church down here, you know, there's a graveyard right outside. There's people selling drugs. And you remember how God saved you. It's not like going to a church on a hill in a gated community." Deacon James does not want to engage the local environment, but it is important for him to be there each week.

Rosie Milton, the leader at Universal Hagar Church, knows that drug dealers use the church's corner as a trading area. A trim woman with a warm smile and clear sense of confidence, she preached about God providing for our needs. She also led the congregation in praying for all those who suffer and asked for God Hurley to be present in prisons and "on the street." After the service Reverend Milton talks about the neighborhood, "We've had two block parties and we are going to have a third. Have you seen our mural? We are all one big happy family here." Although she was not publicly identified as a leader in the community organization, and lived outside of the neighborhood, she identified with, and participated in the transformation effort.

Father's House of Prayer also draws a significant number of its members from outside the neighborhood. They have active relationships with several other independent black congregations nearby but not with their Latino Pentecostal neighbors. Like St. Luke Second Born they did not participate in the neighborhood watch organization and seemed unaware of it. But they were very aware of being in the midst of the Badlands. In 1996 they held prayer vigils and open-air services "to drive out the drug dealers." They too worked with police, and reported suspicious activities. In neighborhoods like this one, ratting on drug dealers can have serious repercussions and takes no small bit of courage.

Holy Redeemed is a tiny church in a former television repair shop. Elder Johnson talks about how they write letters to prisoners and give out food. "It's all about building the Kingdom of God." When her nephew's father was shot, she organized an event in the neighborhood to pray for the victims and their families. People from Greater St. Thomas across the street came. "So did people from one of the Spanish churches."

All of these efforts reflect the agency that communities of faith exercise, sometimes spontaneously, in the urban ecology. Just *being there*, with members going to church, regularly going in and out of the building (for a few of the churches, that is almost every day) has an effect on public safety through *natural surveillance*, a place-based approach to crime prevention. In addition, some congregations were taking action in small ways—organizing prayer vigils at murder sites, having open-air worship, and working with the neighborhood organization. In order for citizens to be involved at any level, from natural surveillance to more aggressive actions, there has to be a sense of *territoriality*, or investment in the urban space as defensible (Schneider and Kitchen, 2002). Levels of territoriality vary, with neighborhood residents (particularly those with children) having the highest investment in public safety. But even the smaller congregations with a large proportion commuting in from outside the neighborhood saw Fairhill as defensible space and felt a sense of responsibility for the spatial ecology.

Churchs
help / Impac
an area's
Sufety
especially
w/ regards
to Gun
violence

FIGURE 7.10 Once the epicenter of the neighborhood known as "The Badlands," the Fair Hill Burial Ground after its restoration became a catalyst in the transformation of the neighborhood.

Altogether, these efforts had an effect. Throughout the 1990s, the census tract surrounding the Burial Ground had an average of 10 gun murders per year.[16] In 1999, things changed dramatically: since then, there has been an average of 2.5 murders per year there. People are safer because of an organic collaboration between grassroots, non-profit, and religious organizations and the police. Social boundaries have been crossed in organizing community fairs, health fairs, and arts and food programs. The neighborhood is still poor, but poverty does not mean that violence of a disproportionate level is inevitable. This resonates with Sampson's findings in Chicago that collective

efficacy and civic engagement are correlated with lower crime.[17] Although his study does not find that religious institutions, and particularly black churches, are likely sources of collective action, our research challenges this conclusion.

Along the Avenue, congregations are exercising their own agency, linking with others and organizing actions to improve the quality of life within their neighborhoods. Health fairs in Germantown, Mt. Airy, and Hunting Park brought together members from a variety of faith communities with health services and civic groups for festive events that made positive contributions to the community. The "Germantown Speaks" Project organized congregations, a public high school, a historic preservation group, and an elder-servicing agency into an unlikely alliance. Al Aqsa, the mosque comprised largely of immigrants, collaborated with people of other faith communities around the city, as well as non-profit arts groups, in transforming their building and their mission into a center for interfaith activity. Even congregation-based arts and food programs in storefront churches forged connections with other non-profit and religious groups for their programs.

The Presbyterian Church of Chestnut Hill (PCCH), at the top of the hill, is impressive in a number of ways. The neighborhood itself is known as "the suburb within the city," and indeed many suburbanites do commute in to attend worship in the elegant, sun-drenched sanctuary. There are almost 1,000 members and the budget hovers around $1,000,000. This allows PCCH to have a staff of 10 overseeing a number of programs for the con-gregation. The church is well known for its music program. Not only is the chancel choir of a professional quality but several noted choral groups are based there. Parents count on a well-run Sunday School program with a solid curriculum and an attractive youth program for teenagers. Adults participate in a variety of classes and forums focused on theological and social issues.

FIGURE 7.11 The sanctuary of the Presbyterian Church of Chestnut Hill.

Senior Pastor Cindy Jarvis has a well-deserved reputation for intellectually engaging sermons for the well-educated congregation. The recession hit this congregation as it did all others, ushering in a season of belt tightening. But they did not cut back on their mission giving: in 2010 they continued to contribute over $40,000 to denominational causes as well as to local projects as diverse as a free clinic on Germantown Avenue, several food pantries, and advocacy groups working on the death penalty and human trafficking. This is a congregation that can afford to do checkbook mission.

By the middle of the decade, Reverend Jarvis was becoming alarmed at the high number of gun homicides in Philadelphia—344 in 2006 and 331 in 2007. Gun violence had not touched the congregation but it had certainly impacted other neighborhoods down the Avenue. She teamed up with Reverend Nancy Muth, pastor of First Presbyterian Church of Germantown.[18] Germantown had certainly had its share of gun violence—there had been 18 murders in a 10-block radius around the church in 2006–2007.[19] The two pastors linked with a faith-based gun violence prevention group that was just getting started in Philadelphia called Heeding God's Call. The group had just been in the news because of their vigils in front of a gun shop in Philadelphia that was notorious for its participation in "straw purchasing." This is a common practice in which someone who can pass a background check is paid by a gun trafficker to buy weapons. If a gun used in a crime is ever tracked to the original purchaser, she or he can simply say that it was lost or stolen and the trail goes cold. Mayor Michael Nutter has stated that almost all of the gun violence in the city involves these illegally acquired guns.

The action by Heeding God's Call had involved civil disobedience. Twelve people had been arrested in the high-profile and unlikely confrontation between people of faith and Colossimo's Gun Shop. Eventually, the gun shop was closed. The action gave the organization visibility in attracting clergy farther up Germantown Avenue to the larger cause.

PCCH and First Presbyterian of Germantown organized congregations in the northwest, forming their own chapter of Heeding, called Neighborhood Partners to End Gun Violence (NPEG). Other churches along the Avenue joined the effort, including Chestnut Hill United Church, Germantown Mennonite, and Mt. Airy Presbyterian Church. Living Water U.C.C., in the impoverished Hunting Park section, had been part of the original effort at Colissimo's. Since organizing in 2009, NPEG has sponsored public rallies, held prayer vigils at murder sites, and faithfully held vigils twice a month in

FIGURE 7.12 Heeding God's Call, a faith-based group that has brought congregations across neighborhood and social boundaries to respond to the high levels of gun violence in Philadelphia.

front of another gun shop in the city. The goal is to pressure the gun shop to adopt voluntary business practices (such as installing video cameras) that would discourage straw purchasing.

This growing organization shows a high sense of agency on the part of the congregations involved. Chestnut Hill Presbyterian has taken a strong leadership role in addressing a citywide issue that is outside the direct experience of their members—no one interviewed from that church had been personally affected by gun violence, unlike other congregations in more distressed neighborhoods. Bishop Dwayne Royster, pastor of Living Water United Church of Christ in North Philadelphia, was an early leader in the organization. He talked about the gun violence that was literally at the doorstep of the church:

> I'll never forget the Sunday I came to church and I couldn't even get on the block because there had been a shoot-out on the street. There were 50 shells around the church.... A few years ago a member of our church lost her son. He was a student at St. Joe's Prep and had a full scholarship to Harvard for pre-med. He was gunned down in front of

a Chinese store. We lost a doctor for our community. Every day I drive into the community and pass another mini-altar because someone was shot. You don't necessarily know how to stop it but you know that somewhere along the line you've got to get engaged in it.

Bob Fles is a retired teacher and administrator from a private boys' school and a lay leader at PCCH. He had never been touched by gun violence and was not involved in the movement to end it, but it felt like a natural fit for him. "It resonated with me. I like the public demonstration, living your faith on your feet." Although civil disobedience has not been a strategy in the repertoire of PCCH, he did not consider it "wildly far out." He is theologically reflective about the need for people of religious faith to be involved in efforts at social, including political, change. Coming from a social location of privilege, he has nonetheless taken leadership in maintaining communication with the owner of the gun shop in the working-class neighborhood where the vigils are held. He and co-chair Susan Windle (from Mishkan Shalom Synagogue) have worked to develop relationships in the neighborhood around the gun shop, a neighborhood which has struggled with several tragic gun deaths that have left them shaken.

The organizing effort against gun violence in Philadelphia represents a social dynamic different from the collective action in Fairhill. First, there is a high level of bridging social capital, or connections outside of the immediate context. These Presbyterians are comfortable organizing with groups in other cities, national gun violence prevention organizations, media, and funders. However, the social connections they have cultivated that are less predictable are those that cross lines of neighborhood, social class, religion, race, and experience. Those from relatively safe and affluent neighborhoods do not normally come into contact with the families of murder victims in economically disadvantaged neighborhoods, much less stand with them in genuine solidarity.

Second, in this effort to address public safety, the boundaries of the defensible space are expanded beyond any one neighborhood. As members of the organization travel from Chestnut Hill to a vigil in Tacony, or from Mt. Airy to stand with neighbors in West Philadelphia, the territory being claimed (or re-claimed) is citywide. In the previous discussion of Al Aqsa Islamic Center, a relationship could be drawn between the practice of bridging diversity among the international membership and the capacity to transcend religious differences in facilitating citywide interfaith dialogue. In the case of Heeding God's Call, the bridging social capital is not located in the diversity of the participating congregations. In fact, most of the active congregations are among the least racially diverse in the study. (For some of the more racially diverse congregations, their own diversity is a goal and end in itself, not necessarily leading to bridging outside the congregation's walls.)

For participants in the faith-based gun violence prevention organization, the impulse to define the whole city, rather than just the immediate neighborhood, as defensible space comes from two sources: the broader regional representation of the membership and a highly articulated sense of responsibility in civil society. In its first three years, the members of Heeding God's Call have shown remarkable resolve in tackling an issue that has city officials frustrated. The pro-gun lobby in the state has so far prevented any significant changes in gun laws, even at the municipal level. Their resolve has not been untested: Presbyterians who have quiet and controlled worship services have been at times heckled during vigils and demonstrations. In contrast to those in the city who are stymied in their attempts to stop gun violence, it makes the sense of agency among the faith-based groups in working for change seem quixotic—or perhaps reflecting the kind of public determination that can bring change, as it has with the drunk driving and tobacco issues. Time will tell.

Conclusion

The urban ecology of Germantown Avenue, like any living system, is changing. Between the bookends of the Presbyterian Church of Chestnut Hill and Al Aqsa Islamic Center, communities of faith are echoing their histories and contributing to the durability of neighborhoods, while encountering change and contributing to transformation. By the time this book is published, perhaps there will be a new congregation or two, or a couple fewer. Most likely, there will be more Latino businesses and congregations, but there might be other ethnic congregations as well. Muslims might continue to invest in the neighborhoods around the mosques and forge new relationships, creating more social trust. There might be fewer sermons about expecting prosperity and more encouragement in starting small businesses. Fairhill could be even safer and there might be fewer guns on the streets. The slow economic recovery might inspire new entrepreneurship. There might be fewer soup kitchens and more urban gardens. Change in the urban ecology is certain and communities of faith will be part of it. What is unknown is what faith on the Avenue will look like in 10, 20, or 100 years. That book will have to be written.

NOTES

CHAPTER 1

1. Robert Ezra Park, "The City: Suggestions for the Investigation of Human Behavior in the City Environment," American Journal of Sociology 20(5) (March 1915): 594.
2. (Chicago: University of Chicago Press, 2012).
3. Alfred Lubrano, "Profile of Hunger," *Philadelphia Inquirer,* <series in 2010: 10/10, 10/31, 11/5, 11/30, 12/12, 12/23, 12/29, 12/31.
4. United Nations Office on Drugs and Crime (http://www.unodc.org/unodc/en/data-and-analysis/homicide.html; UCR Summary Data Reports
5. For a detailed description of Philadelphia trends, see Pew Charitable Trusts, *Philadelphia 2011: The State of the City* (Philadelphia: Philadelphia Research Initiative, 2012). www.pewtrusts.org/philaresearch.
6. Ibid., p. 4.
7. Many of the questions were drawn from Cnaan's earlier survey, although that study had not sampled many congregations on the Avenue, and very few of the smaller ones.
8. The research project complied with the Human Subjects Research policies of the Lutheran Theological Seminary.

CHAPTER 2

1. Physician Benjamin Rush, a signer of the Declaration of Independence and known for his views against slavery, convinced Richard Allen, the founder of Bethel African Methodist Episcopal Church, that those of African descent would not contract the disease. The moving history of the black churches' involvement is documented in many sources.
2. Germantown High School was closed in 2013 due to the budget shortfall of the School District of Philadelphia.

3. Interview, September 2, 2009.

4. http://www.philly.com/philly/news/breaking/95117409.html.

5. Interview, October 16, 2009.

6. Field notes, St. Luke's Second Born, March, 29, 2009, Beth Stroud.

7. Interview, September 30, 2007.

8. "The Good Raised Up," composed by John Blake Jr; performed by Keystone State Boychoir and Pennsylvania State Girlchoir, March 2012.

9. G. Van Der Leeuw, *Religion in Essence and Manifestation* (Princeton, NJ: Princeton University Press, 1986), p. 395.

CHAPTER 3

1. Alfred Lubrano, "Portrait of Hunger," *Philadelphia Inquirer,* October 10, 2010–December 31, 2010.

2. Jonathan Bullington, "Evanston Could Scale Back Church Zoning Ordinance," *Evanston Tribune*, December 7, 2010.

3. Jonathan Bullington, "Evanston Scales Back Church Zoning Ordinance," *Evanston Tribune*, December 14, 2010.

4. Interview, January 20, 2011.

5. City of Evanston, Code #6351.

6. Letter to The Honorable Mayor Elizabeth Tisdahl; City Manager Wally Bobkiewicz; Members of the Evanston City Council; Alderman Ann Rainey; Planning and Development Committee; and Zoning Committee, from Evanston Pastor's Fellowship, Concerned Clergy, Religious and Civic Leaders RE: Proposed City Ordinance 77-O-10: *Specific Concerns as Expressed by Clergy and Religious Leaders.*

7. See works by Robert Orsi (1999), Omar McRoberts (2003), Courtney Bender (2003), Lowell Livezey (2000), and Lorentzen, Gonzalez, Chun, and Do (2009).

8. Cnaan, Ram, *The Invisible Caring Hand: American Congregations and the Provision of Welfare* (New York: New York University Press, 2002).

9. Partners for Sacred Places, "Determining the Halo Effect for Historic Congregations," http://www.sacredplaces.org/wp-content/uploads/2012/02/Halo-Effect-White-Paper-1-18-12.pdf.

10. Cnaan, Ram, "Valuing the Contribution of Urban Religious Congregations," *Public Management Review* 11(5) (2009): 641–662.

11. Ram A. Cnaan, Tuomi Forrest, Joseph Carlsmith, and Kelsey Karsh, "Valuing Urban Congregations: A Pilot Study," in *Partners for Sacred Places* (December, 2010).

12. Robert Putnam, *Bowling Alone: The Collapse and Revival of the American Community* (New York: Simon and Schuster, 2000).

13. Family reunions, conferences, weddings, funerals, baptisms, confirmations, bar/bat mitzvahs, birthday parties, artistic performances, museum exhibits, and festivals.

14. http://www.itreetools.org/about.php.

15. Research by M. A. Cohen (1998, 2004) is cited, which concluded that the annual savings is $40,000 per year for a 50-year life span.

16. The seven Historically Black denominations are the African Methodist Episcopal (AME) Church; the African Methodist Episcopal Zion (AMEZ) Church; the Christian Methodist Episcopal (CME) Church; the National Baptist Convention, USA., Incorporated (NBC); the National Baptist Convention of America, Unincorporated (NBCA); the Progressive National Baptist Convention (PNBC); and the Church of God in Christ (COGIC). The denominations traditionally designated as Mainline Protestant are United Methodist, Evangelical Lutheran Church in America, Presbyterian Church U.S.A., the Episcopal Church, American Baptist Churches, the United Church of Christ, and the Disciples of Christ. Because of their decline in membership and cultural prominence, some researchers refer to the group now as "Old Line Protestants." The peace churches are the Society of Friends (Quaker), the Mennonite Church, and the United Brethren Church. All maintain pacifist positions as core theological commitments. Counted among "other religions" are two mosques (both Sunni), two Hebrew Israelite (African American adaptation of Judaism), and one Hurleyite congregation (African American fusion incorporating nationalist and spiritualist themes). The "other Christians" are the Salvation Army, the Seventh-day Adventists, and additional churches that were independent or in tiny denominations and were not predominantly African American.

17. Scott Thumma, "A Report on the 2010 National Profile of U.S. Nondenominational and Independent Churches," Hartford Institute for Religious Research, http://www.hartfordinstitute.org/cong/nondenominational-churches-national-profile-2010.html.

18. The boundary between Germantown and Mt. Airy is somewhat ambiguous. In this analysis, Mt. Airy extends farther south into Germantown than it is normally considered. This was to attain balance in units of analysis. Chestnut Hill is the exception—there are fewer congregations in this section but because of its distinct identity, it could not be folded into another section.

19. Northwest Interfaith Movement, most familiar as "NIM", declared bankruptcy and closed in November, 2012 after a forty year history of cooperative effort among faith groups, particularly in providing social services. This came as a shock to those in Northwest Philadelphia. As of the publication of this book, the clergy continue to meet monthly to find ways to continue collaboration.

20. Omar McRoberts, *Streets of Glory* (Chicago: University of Chicago Press, 2003).

21. Elfriede Wedam, "The 'Religious District' of Elite Congregations: Reproducing Spatial Centrality and Redefining Mission." *Sociology of Religion* 64(1) (2003): 47–64.

22. P = .008

23. David Roozen, "A Decade of Change in American Congregations 2000–2010," Faith Communities Today (FACT).

24. Rather than asking for a dollar figure, six ranges were offered: < $50,000, $50–100,000, $100–200,000, $200–500,000, $500–1,000,000 and >$1,000,000.

25. "It appears that the nation's new minority population is, by and large, creating its own congregations rather than participating in historically white congregations." FACT, p. 5.

26. Philadelphia Public School children have universal accessibility to free meals during the school year.

27. From 74% to 87%.

28. For example, 63% of African Americans opposed same sex marriage according to a poll taken in 2011 by the Public Religion Research Institute. They were behind white evangelicals and Mormons, 75% of whom oppose it (PRRI, 2012).

29. This is not just a local phenomenon but is practiced elsewhere in African American churches. See a story about another pastor http://www.huffingtonpost.com/2012/07/18/rev-anthony-lee-hiv-testing_n_1682532.html?utm_campaign=071912&utm_medium=email&utm_source=Alert-religion&utm_con.

30. For the sample of larger older churches in the Halo Effect research, there was an even higher number, with three fourths of the congregations reporting that they had been able to avert two suicides (Partners for Sacred Places, 2012).

31. "The Great Recession: What Comes Next for America's Metros?," Bruce Katz Brookings Institution, October 27, 2009 (http://www.brookings.edu/research/speeches/2009/10/27-istanbul-katz).

32. Partners for Sacred Places has an online program through which congregations can calculate the economic value of their in-kind contributions of space and volunteer labor to help them build their case for capital campaigns. http://www.sacredplaces.org/what-we-do/publications/#1. http://www.sacredplaces.org/wp-content/uploads/2011/12/tool_kit.pdf.

33. http://www.thebizctr.com/node/1.

34. Deforest B. Soaries, "Black Churches and the Prosperity Gospel," Wall St. Journal, October 1, 2010.

35. Eddie Glaude Jr., "The Black Church Is Dead," *Huffington Post*, February 24, 2010. http://www.huffingtonpost.com/eddie-glaude-jr-phd/the-black-church-is-dead_b_473815.html.

CHAPTER 4

1. "Standing their ground: the struggle for Fair Hill," fairhillburial.org, 2004.
2. Robert J. Sampson, *Great American City: Chicago and the Enduring Neighborhood Effect* (Chicago: University of Chicago Press, 2012), p. 205.
3. Omar McRoberts, *Streets of Glory* (Chicago: University of Chicago Press, 2003).
4. At Father's House of Prayer, the pastor announced on two subsequent Sundays that the researcher, Beth Stroud, would be collecting members' names and addresses, and encouraged the congregation to see her with their information before they left the building. She followed up later with people I had missed on those two Sundays. The list was constructed and included all the regular attenders who had been observed in church. At New Bethany, the pastor instructed one of the deacons to make up a list for the researcher; the list included all the regular attenders she had met.
5. Jerry L. Buckner, "Concerns about the Teaching of T.D. Jakes," *Christian Research Journal* 22(2) (1999), www.equip.org.
6. As Du Bois famously wrote in 1899, "All movements for social betterment are apt to centre in the churches. Beneficial societies in endless number are formed here; secret societies keep in touch; co-operative and building associations have lately sprung up; the minister often acts as an employment agent; considerable charitable and relief work is done and special meetings held to aid special projects" (W.E.B. Du Bois, *The Philadelphia Negro: A Social Study* [New York: Schocken Books, 1899/1970], p. 207).
7. Exodus 12:2.
8. The poet Christina Rossetti wrote in 1863:
   June, the month of months,
   Flowers and fruitage brings too;
   When green trees spread shadiest boughs,
   When each wild bird sings too.
   ("Summer," *Christina Rossetti: The Complete Poems*, ed. Rebecca W. Crump and Betty S. Flowers [New York: Penguin, 2001], p. 819.)

CHAPTER 5

1. Prayer warriors are so designated because they are considered to have deep spirituality and the ability to discern the Spirit of God.
2. All names used in this chapter are pseudonyms.
3. F. Segovia, "Two Places and No Place on Which to Stand. Mixture and Otherness in Hispanic American Theology," *Listening: Journal of Religion and Culture* 27 (1) (1992): 26–40.

4. The term *one and a half generation* (1.5) has been coined to identify those foreign-born children who were brought to the United States between the age of five and adolescence.

5. This is in reference to Exodus 33:3, "Go up to the land flowing with milk and honey." This land is considered a divine destination for the people of Israel fleeing slavery. It is the "Promised Land," a land of all good things and abundant blessings.

6. C. E. Rodriguez, J. Monserrat, M. Lapp, G. Marzan, and the Portfolio Project, *Puerto Ricans: Immigrants and Migrants, a Historical Perspective* (Washington, DC: Portfolio Project, 1990).

7. S. Sullivan, "Sources of Hispanic/Latino American Theology," in *Hispanic/Latino Theology. Challenge and Promise*, ed. Ada María Isasi-Díaz and Fernando Segovia (Minneapolis, MN: Fortress Press, 1996), pp. 134–148.

8. J. L. González, *Alabadle! Hispanic Christian Worship* (Nashville: Abingdon Press, 1996). See also V. P. Elizondo, *Galilean Journey: The Mexican-American Promise* (Maryknoll, NY: Orbis Books, 2000).

9. Elizondo, *Galilean Journey*, p. 10.

10. Marcela Lagarde, "Claves Éticas para el Tercer Milenio," *(FEMPRES) Creencias y Prejuicios de la Modernidad,* June 2010. http://www.congreso.gob.gt/uploadimg/documentos/n3892.doc. My translation from Spanish.

11. Daisy, Machado, "Christ Outside the Gate: Following Jesus beyond Borders," lecture, Orlando E. Costas Lectures, Palmer Seminary, Philadelphia, October 5, 2010.

12. A pseudonym.

13. *Machismo* is an exaggerated sense of manliness and masculinity. In many instances *machista* attitudes can be identified when men consider themselves authorized to dominate women in private or in public. *Machista* men may be aggressive towards women as they consider themselves more powerful and superior.

14. In ethnographic conversations with the pastor and hearing his biblical interpretations in Bible study and in preaching, the pastor has demonstrated fundamentalist and literal interpretations of the biblical text. Although he is not extreme in his interpretation of women's inability to preach or speak in the congregation (1 Cor. 7 and 1 Tim.2), as a man, he is first and foremost, the authority by which all things concerning this church are mediated. As such, in this particular case, he has demonstrated both his biblical interpretation and machista attitudes.

15. I Cor. 7.

16. Hebrews 13:17.

17. Anna Adams, "Perception Matters: Pentecostal Latinas in Allentown, Pennsylvania," in *A Reader in Latina Feminist Theology*, ed. Maria Pilar Aquino, Daisy L. Machado, and Jeannette Rodriguez (Austin: University of Texas Press, 2002), pp. 98–113. See also Lori Ann Lorentzen and Rosalina Mira, "El Milagro

Esta en Casa: Gender and Private and Public Empowerment in a Migrant Pentecostal Church," in *Religion at the Corner of Bliss and Nirvana: Politics, Identity and Faith in New Migrant Communities*, ed. Lois Ann Lorentzen, Joaquin Jay Gonzalez II, Kevin M. Chun, and Hein Duc Do (Durham, NC: Duke University Press, 2009).

CHAPTER 6

1. There was a Nation of Islam congregation which was temporarily meeting in a Montessori School after a fire in their masjid. They rebuilt and relocated to their permanent home on another street, and are not included in the census of faith communities on the Avenue.
2. Muslims are required to make a pilgrimage to the holy city of Mecca at least once in their lifetime. It is one of the "five pillars of Islam" guiding the religious life of Muslims.
3. The FBI reported a 1600% increase in hate crime incidents against Muslims in 2001 (U.S. Department of Justice, 2011).
4. This phrase is normally repeated after speaking the name of the Prophet. In print, it is indicated by the letters PBUH.
5. Rhys H. Williams, "Review Essay: Religion, Community, and Place: Locating the TranscendentAuthor(s)," *Religion and American Culture: A Journal of Interpretation* 12(2) (Summer, 2002): 259.
6. Elijah Anderson, *Code of the Street: Decency, Violence and the Moral Life of the Inner City* (New York: W.W. Norton, 1999), p. 33.
7. Anderson, *Code of the Street*, p. 33.
8. Robert D. Putnam and David E. Campbell, *American Grace: How Religion Divides and Unites Us* (New York: Simon and Schuster, 2010), p. 523.
9. Putnam and Campbell, *American Grace*, p. 526.
10. All data are taken from the crimebase and neighborhoodbase of the Cartographic Modeling Lab at the University of Pennsylvania.
11. The mosque sits on the border between two census tracts, so the poverty rates were combined and the mean taken. In 2000, the rates were 29.06 and 29.04; by 2009 they were 37.07 and 46.53, according to the U.S. Census and American Communities Survey.
12. Walking the Walk is a program of the Interfaith Center of Greater Philadelphia. It was organized in 2005 and is related to the work of Eboo Patel of the Interfaith Youth Core, a national organization that develops programs to advance interfaith understanding and respect among young people. http://www.interfaithcenterpa.org/si/wwy/.
13. A witness to the faith.

14. http://www.arabamericancdc.org/.

15. Robert D. Putnam, *Bowling Alone: The Collapse and Revival of American Community* (New York: Simon and Schuster, 2000).

16. Putnam, *Bowling Alone.*

17. Al Aqsa Islamic Center website: http://174.136.32.67/~alaqsais/index.php.

18. Pew Charitable Trusts, *Philadelphia 2011: The State of the City* (Philadelphia: Philadelphia Research Initiative, 2012).<yes, this is a publication published in 2012 about Philadelphia in 2011

19. Real estate sales went from 29 in 1999 to 66 in 2006, lien sales from 243 in 1999 to 76 in 2006.

20. CML (Cartographic Modeling Lab, University of Pennsylvania), nbase data.

21. Aminah Beverly McCloud, *African American Islam* (New York: Routledge, 1995), p. 4.

22. Ihsan Bagby, "The American Mosque 2011, Reports 1 and 2," Report 1, p. 23, Council on American-Islamic Relations (CAIR), http://faithcommunitiestoday.org/2011-mosque-report-ihsan-bagby.

23. McCloud, *African American Islam.*

24. Hans A. Baer, *The Black Spiritual Movement: A Religious Response to Racism* (2nd ed.) (Knoxville: University of Tennessee Press, 2001).

25. From *Aquarian Age*, June 1942, as quoted in Baer, *The Black Spiritual Movement*, p. 96.

26. This is theologically close to the "Black Hebrews" sect, founded by William S. Crowdy in 1896. In the early 20th century his congregation in Philadelphia had 3,000 members and still survives today on Broad St. There does not seem to be an institutional relationship with the Islamic Hebrews, however.

27. For a history and explanation of beliefs, see the website, http://africanhebrewisraelitesofjerusalem.com/.

28. Baer, *The Black Spiritual Movement.*

29. http://www.zimbio.com/War+on+Terrorism/articles/1390132/Philadelphia+Mosque+Refuses+Bury+Bank+Robber.

CHAPTER 7

1. Jim Remson, "St. Ladislaus Will Fall so that Triumph Baptist May Rise on the Site in Nicetown," *Philadelphia Inquirer*, Sunday, March 14, 2004, Section C, p. 4 (accessed September 3, 2009.

2. W.E.B. Du Bois, *The Philadelphia Negro: A Social Study* (New York: Schocken Books, 1899/1970), p. 203.

3. Du Bois, *The Philadelphia Negro*, p. 206.
4. Only three black Baptist churches were identified in 1857, but by 1896, there were 17 in the city, according to Du Bois (1899).
5. http://www.pbs.org/jazz/places/faces_migration.htm.
6. Matthew S. Hopper, *From Refuge to Strength: The Rise of the African American Church in Philadelphia, 1787–1949* (Philadelphia: Preservation Alliance for Greater Philadelphia, 1998), p. 38.
7. Triumph was founded in 1963 but moved into its new building at the corner of Germantown and Hunting Park in 2007. New Bethany Holiness was organized in 1954 and moved to its current location in 1974. Father's House of Prayer was founded at its current address in 1984.
8. Townsand Price-Spratlen, "Urban Destination Selection among African Americans during the 1950's Great Migration," *Social Science History* 32(3) (Fall 2008): 441.
9. Price-Spratlen, "Urban Destination," p. 456.
10. http://www.nytimes.com/2006/08/26/us/26clergy.html?pagewanted=all&_r=0
11. From the PBS series, "God in America," http://www.pbs.org/godinamerica/people/jarena-lee.html.
12. Kensington congregations have a mean age of 21.4 years, and Hunting Park's congregations are 59.2 years old, on average. Mt. Airy's congregations are 136.4 years and Chestnut Hill's are 142.8 years. The difference is significant (Anova F = 3.7, P = .008).
13. Elijah Anderson, *Code of the Street: Decency, Violence and the Moral Life of the Inner City* (New York: W.W. Norton, 1999), p. 25.
14. Du Bois, *The Philadelphia Negro*, p. 220.
15. Du Bois, *The Philadelphia Negro*, pp. 220–221
16. *Philadelphia Inquirer*, http://www.philly.com/philly/news/special_packages/inquirer/136746563.html.
17. Robert J. Sampson, *Great American City: Chicago and the Enduring Neighborhood Effect* (Chicago: University of Chicago Press, 2012), chapter 7.
18. First Presbyterian of Germantown is just off the Avenue and so was not included in the sample for this study.
19. "Philadelphia Homicides 1988–2011," *Philadelphia Inquirer,* (http://www.philly.com/philly/news/special_packages/inquirer/136746563.html).

BIBLIOGRAPHY

Adams, Anna. "Perception Matters: Pentecostal Latinas in Allentown, Pennsylvania." In *A Reader in Latina Feminist Theology*, ed. Maria Pilar Aquino, Daisy L. Machado and Jeannette Rodriguez. Austin: University of Texas Press, 2002.

Alexander, Michelle. *The New Jim Crow: Mass Incarceration in the Age of Colorblindness.* New York: New Press, 2010.

Ammerman, Nancy, Jackson Carroll, Carl Dudley, and William McKinney. *Studying Congregations.* Nashville, TN: Abingdon, 1998.

Ammerman, Nancy T. *Everyday Religion.* New York: Oxford University Press, 2007.

Ammerman, Nancy Tatom. *Pillars of Faith.* Berkeley: University of California Press, 2005.

Ammerman, Nancy Tatom. *Congregation and Community.* New Brunswick, NJ: Rutgers, 1997.

Anderson, Elijah. *Code of the Street: Decency, Violence and the Moral Life of the Inner City.* New York: W.W. Norton, 1999.

Baer, Hans A. *The Black Spiritual Movement: A Religious Response to Racism* (2nd ed.). Knoxville: University of Tennessee Press, 2001.

Becker, Penny Edgell. *Congregations in Conflict: Cultural Models of Local Religious Life.* New York: Cambridge University Press, 1999.

Bender, Courtney. *Heaven's Kitchen: Living Religion at God's Love We Deliver.* Chicago: University of Chicago Press, 2003.

Berger, Peter. *The Desecularization of the World: Resurgent Religion and World Politics.* Grand Rapids, MI: Eerdmans, 1999.

Best, Wallace D. *Passionately Human, No Less Divine: Religion and Culture in Black Chicago, 1915–1952.* Princeton, NJ: Princeton University Press, 2005.

Bourdieu, Pierre. *Outline of a Theory of Practice.* New York: Cambridge University Press, 1977.

Carroll, Jackson. *God's Potters: Pastoral Leadership and the Shaping of Congregations.* (Grand Rapids, MI: Eerdman's Publishing), 2006.

Chaves, Mark. *Congregations in America*. Cambridge, MA: Harvard University Press, 2004.

Chidester, David, and Edward T. Linenthal, eds. *American Sacred Space*. Bloomington: Indiana University Press, 1995.

Cimino, Richard, Nadia A. Mian, and Weishan Huang, eds. *Ecologies of Faith in New York City: The Evolution of Religious Institutions*. Bloomington: University of Indiana Press, 2013.

Cnaan, Ram A. *The Invisible Caring Hand: American Congregations and the Provision of Welfare*. New York: New York University Press, 2002.

Cnaan, Ram A., Stephanie C. Boddie, Charlene C. McGrew, and Jennifer Kang. *The Other Philadelphia Story: How Local Congregations Support Quality of Life in Urban America*. Philadelphia: University of Pennsylvania Press, 2006.

Du Bois, W.E.B. *The Philadelphia Negro: A Social Study*. New York: Schocken Books, 1899/ 1970.

Durkheim Emile. *The Elementary Forms of the Religious Life* (1912; English translation by Joseph Swain, 1915). New York: Free Press, 1965.

Eliade, Mircea. *The Sacred and the Profane: The Nature of Religion* (translated from French by Willard R. Trask). New York: Harvest/HBJ Publishers, 1957.

Elizondo, Virgilio. *Galilean Journey: The Mexican-American Promise*. Maryknoll, NY: Orbis Books, 2000.

Emerson, Michael O., and Christian Smith. *Divided by Faith: Evangelical Religion and the Problem of Race in America*. New York: Oxford University Press, 2000.

Frey, William H. *Diversity Explosion: How New Racial Demographics Are Remaking America*. Washington, DC: Brookings Institution, 2013.

Gregg, Robert. *Sparks from the Anvil of Oppression: Philadelphia's African Methodists and Southern Migrants, 1890–1940*. Philadelphia: Temple University Press, 1993.

González, Justo. *¡Alabadle! Hispanic Christian Worship*. Nashville: Abingdon Press, 1996.

Hammonds, Kenneth A. *Historical Directory of Presbyterian Churches and Presbyteries of Greater Philadelphia Related to the Presbyterian Church (U.S.A.) and Its Antecedents 1690–1990*. Philadelphia: Presbyterian Historical Society, 1993.

Hopper, Matthew S. *From Refuge to Strength: The Rise of the African American Church in Philadelphia, 1787–1949*. Philadelphia: Preservation Alliance for Greater Philadelphia, 1998.

Kostarelos, Frances. *Feeling the Spirit: Faith and Hope in an Evangelical Black Storefront Church*. Columbia: University of South Carolina Press, 1995.

Lagarde, Marcela. "Claves Éticas para el Tercer Milenio" (FEMPRES) Creencias y Prejuicios de la Modernidad. June 2010. htttp://www.congreso.gob.gt/uploadimg/documentos/n3892.doc.

Livezey, Lowell W. *Public Religion and Urban Transformation: Faith in the City.* New York: New York University Press, 2000.

Lorentzen, Lois Ann, Joaquin Jan Gonzalez III, Kevin M. Chun, and Hien Duc Do, eds. *Religion at the Corner of Bliss and Nirvana: Politics, Identity, and Faith in the New Migrant Communities.* Durham, NC: Duke University Press, 2009.

McCloud, Beverly Aminah. *African American Islam.* New York: Routledge, 1995.

McGuire, Meredith. *Lived Religion: Faith and Practice in Everyday Life.* New York: Oxford University Press, 2008.

McRoberts, Omar. *Streets of Glory.* Chicago: University of Chicago Press, 2003.

Nash, Gary B. *Forging Freedom: The Formation of Philadelphia's Black Community 1720–1840.* Cambridge, MA: Harvard University Press, 1988.

Nelson, Louis P., ed. *American Sanctuary: Understanding Sacred Places.* Bloomington: Indiana University Press, 2006.

Nelson, Timothy. *Every Time I Feel the Spirit: Religious Experience and Ritual in an African American Church.* New York: New York University Press, 2005.

Orsi, Robert, ed. *Gods of the City: Religion and the American Urban Landscape.* Bloomington: Indiana University Press, 1999.

Park, Robert Ezra. *Human Community, the City and Human Ecology.* Glencoe, IL: Free Press, 1952.

Park, Robert E., Ernest Watson Burgess, and Roderick D. McKenzie. *The City.* Chicago: University of Chicago Press, 1967.

Putnam, Robert D. *Bowling Alone: The Collapse and Revival of American Community.* New York: Simon and Schuster, 2000.

Putnam, Robert D., and David E. Campbell. *American Grace: How Religion Divides and Unites Us.* New York: Simon and Schuster, 2010.

Rodriguez, Clara. *Puerto Ricans: Immigrants and Migrants, a Historical Perspective.* Washington, DC: Portfolio Project, 1990.

Rouse, Carolyn Moxley. *Engaged Surrender: African American Women and Islam.* Berkeley: University of California Press, 2004.

Sampson, Robert J. *Great American City: Chicago and the Enduring Neighborhood Effect.* Chicago: University of Chicago Press, 2012.

Schneider, Richard H., and Ted Kitchen. *Planning for Crime Prevention: A TransAtlantic Perspective.* London: Routledge, 2002.

Schreiter, Robert J. *Constructing Local Theologies.* Maryknoll, NY: Orbis Books, 1985.

Shaull, Richard and Cesar, Waldo. *Pentecostalism and the Future of Christian Churches: Promises, Limitations, Challenges.* (Grand Rapids, MI: Eerdman's Publishing), 2000.

Sullivan, Samuel. "Sources of Hispanic/Latino American Theology." In *Hispanic/ Latino Theology. Challenge and Promise,* ed. Ada María Isasi-Díaz and Fernando Segovia. Minneapolis, MN: Fortress Press, 1996.

Van Der Leeuw, G. *Religion in Essence and Manifestation*. Princeton, NJ: Princeton University Press, 1986.

Walton, Jonathan L. *Watch This! The Ethics and Aesthetics of Black Televangelism*. New York: New York University Press, 2009.

Washington, Paul, with David McI. Gracie. *Other Sheep I Have: The Autobiography of Paul M. Washington*. Philadelphia: Temple University Press, 1994.

Weber, Max. *The Protestant Ethic and the Spirit of Capitalism* (translated by Talcott Parsons). New York: Routledge, 2001.

Wilkerson, Isabel. *The Warmth of Other Suns: The Epic Story of America's Great Migration*. New York: Random House, 2010.

Wilson, William Julius. *The Truly Disadvantaged*. Chicago: University of Chicago Press, 1987.

Woolever, Cynthia and Bruce, Deborah. *A Field Guide to U.S. Congregations: Who's Going Where and Why*. (Louisville, KY: Westminster John Knox Press), First edition,2002; Second edition, 2010.

Wuthnow, Robert. *Producing the Sacred: An Essay on Public Religion*. Champaign, IL: University of Illinois, 1994.

ARTICLES CITED

Bagby, Ihsan. "The American Mosque 2011, Reports 1 and 2," Council on American-Islamic Relations (CAIR), http://faithcommunitiestoday.org/2 011-mosque-report-ihsan-bagby.

Banerjee, Neela. "Clergywomen find hard path to bigger pulpit," *New York Times*, August 26, 2006.

Buckner, Jerry L. "Concerns about the Teaching of T. D. Jakes." *Christian Research Journal* 22(2) (1999), www.equip.org.

Cnaan, Ram A. "Valuing the Contribution of Urban Religious Congregations." *Public Management Review* 11(5) (2009): 641–662.

Cnaan, Ram A., Tuomi Forrest, Joseph Carlsmith, and Kelsey Karsh. "Valuing Urban Congregations: A Pilot Study." *Partners for Sacred Places* (December 2010)

Crabtree, Steve. "Religiosity Highest in World's Poorest Nations." *Gallup Global Reports* (August 31, 2010), http://www.gallup.com/poll/142727/religiosity-highest-wo rld-poorest-nations.aspx.

Frey, William. "The New Great Migration: Black Americans' Return to the South, 1965–2000." Brookings Institution, Living Cities Census Series, May 2004, http://www.brookings.edu/urban/pubs/20040524_Frey.pdf.

Gerbner, Katharine. "We Are Against the Traffick of Mens-body: The Germantown Quaker Protest of 1688 and the Origins of American Abolitionism." *Pennsylvania History: A Journal of Mid-Atlantic Studies* (Spring 2007).

Kinney, Nancy T., William E. Winter. "Places of Worship and Neighborhood Stability." Journal of Urban Affairs 28(4) (2006): 335–352.

Lubrano, Alfred. "Portrait of Hunger." *Philadelphia Inquirer*, October 10, 2010; October 31, 2010; November 5, 2010; November 30, 2010; December 12, 2010; December 23, 2010; December 29, 2010; December 31, 2010.

Machado, Daisy. "Christ Outside the Gate: Following Jesus beyond Borders." Lecture. Orlando E. Costas Lectures. Palmer Seminary, Philadelphia, October 5, 2010.

Newport, Frank. "Despite Recession, No Uptick in Americans' Religiosity." Gallup, March 23, 2009, http://www.gallup.com/poll/117040/Despite-Recession-No-Uptick-Americans-Religiosity.aspx.

Park, Robert E. "The City: Suggestions for the Investigation of Human Behavior in the City Environment." *American Journal of Sociology* 20(5) (March 1915): 577–612.

Pew Charitable Trusts. "Philadelphia 2011: The State of the City." Philadelphia Research Initiative, 2012.

Philadelphia Citizens for Children and Youth. "Strengthening the Arts by Supporting Arts Teachers." Philadelphia, June 2011.

Price-Spratlen, Townsand. "Urban Destination Selection among African Americans during the 1950's Great Migration." *Social Science History* 32(3) (Fall 2008).

Reilly, David. "A Study Asks: What's a Church's Economic Worth?" *Philadelphia Inquirer*, February 1, 2011, http://articles.philly.com/2011-02-01/news/27092987_1_partners-for-sacred-places-congregations-churches.

Roozen, David. "A Decade of Change in American Congregations 2000-2010," Faith Communities Today (2011) http://faithcommunitiestoday.org/sites/faithcommunitiestoday.org/files/Decade%20of%20Change%20Final_0.pdf

——"Holy Toll: The Impact of the 2008 Recession on American Congregations," Faith Communities Today (2010) http://faithcommunitiestoday.org/sites/faithcommunitiestoday.org/files/HolyTollReport.pdf

Rosin, Hanna. "Did Christianity Cause the Crash?" *Atlantic Monthly,* December 2009.

Segovia, Fernando. "Two Places and No Place on Which to Stand. Mixture and Otherness in Hispanic American Theology." *Listening: Journal of Religion and Culture* 27(1) (1992): 26–40.

Sinha, Jill Witmer, Amy Hillier, Ram A. Cnaan, and Charlene C. McGrew. "Proximity Matters: Exploring Relationships among Neighborhoods, Congregations, and the Residential Patterns of Members." *Journal for the Scientific Study of Religion* 46(2) (2007): 245–260.

Slobodzian, Joseph. "Philadelphia Advocates Clash with the City over New Rules on Feeding the Homeless." *Philadelphia Inquirer,* July 10, 2012.

Sutton, Constance R. "Celebrating Ourselves: The Family Reunion Rituals of African-Caribbean Transnational Families." *Global Networks* 4(3) (July 2004): 243–257.

Thumma, Scott. "A Report on the 2010 National Profile of U.S. Nondenominational and Independent Churches." Hartford Institute for Religious Research, Http://www.hartfordinstitute.org/cong/.

US Department of Justice. "Confronting Discrimination in the Post-9/11 Era: Challenges and Opportunities Ten Years Later." (2011), http://www.justice._gov/crt/publications/post911/post911summit_report_2012-04.pdf.

Wedam, Elfriede. "The 'Religious District' of Elite Congregations: Reproducing Spatial Centrality and Redefining Mission." *Sociology of Religion* 64(1) (Spring 2003): 47–64.

Williams, Rhys H. "Review Essay: Religion, Community, and Place: Locating the Transcendent Author(s)." *Religion and American Culture: A Journal of Interpretation* 12(2) (Summer 2002): 249–263.

WEBSITES

Al Aqsa Islamic Center, http://174.136.32.67/~alaqsais/index.php.

Association of Religious Data Archives (ARDA), http://www.thearda.com/.

Athenaeum of Philadelphia, Greater Philadelphia Geo History: philageohistory.org

Cartographic Modeling Lab, University of Pennsylvania, crimebase, cml.upenn.edu/crimebase, and neighborhood base, cml.upenn.edu/nbase)

Citysoup of Philadelphia, http://www.citysoupphilly.org/FactsOnHunger/index.html.

Faith Communities Today (FACT) (faithcommunitiestoday.org)

Historic Fair Hill, "Standing Their Ground: The Struggle for Fair Hill," 2004, http://www.fairhillburial.org/.

Interfaith Center of Greater Philadelphia, http://www.interfaithcenterpa.org/.

Partners for Sacred Places, "Determining the Halo Effect for Historic Congregations," http://www.sacredplaces.org/wp-content/uploads/2012/02/Halo-Effect-White-Paper-1-18-12.pdf.

"Philadelphia County Census Data," http://census- statistics.findthedata.org/l/2334/Philadelphia-County-Pa.

Preservation Alliance for Greater Philadelphia preservationalliance.com/programs/religious/index.php/inventory/searchReligious/original_architect.

Public Religion Research Institute, "Beyond Secular vs. Religious: Religious Divides in Support for Same Sex Marriage," http://publicreligion.org/research/2012/01/research-note-beyond-secular-vs-religious-religious-divides-in-support-fo r-same-sex-marriage/.

US Census Bureau, American Fact Finder, http://factfinder2.census.gov/faces/nav/jsf/pages/index.xhtml.

INDEX

Windle, Susan, 217
women
   Al Aqsa and, 172, 173
   ethnogenesis and, 198
   Germantown Masjid and, 163–64
   Latino congregations and, 144–158,
     144, *153*, *156*, *157*
   as leaders, 198–200
   Universal Hagar Church and, 182

Wood, Eddie P. Jr., 115
Wood, Helen, 116
World War I, 194
World War II, 195

Yellow Fever Epidemic (1793), 1, 36
Young, David, 35, 39

Zion Baptist Church, 91–92, 196